Frontier Defense in the Civil War

NUMBER FORTY
Centennial Series of the Association of Former Students,
Texas A&M University

Frontier Defense
in the Civil War

TEXAS' RANGERS AND REBELS

David Paul Smith

Texas A&M University Press
COLLEGE STATION

The paper used in this book meets the minimum requirements
of the American National Standard for Permanence
of Paper for Printed Library Materials, Z39.48-1984.
Binding materials have been chosen for durability.

LIBRARY OF CONGRESS CATALOGING-IN-PUBLICATION DATA

Smith, David Paul, 1949–
    Frontier defense in the Civil War : Texas Rangers
and rebels / David Paul Smith. — 1st ed.
        p.   cm. — (Centennial series of the Association
of Former Students, Texas A&M University ; no. 40)
    Includes bibliographical references (p.   ) and index.
    ISBN 0-89096-484-X
    1. Texas—History—Civil War, 1861–1865.   2. Texas
Rangers—History—19th century.   I. Title.   II. Series.
E532.S65   1992
973.7'464—dc20   91-17077
                                                            CIP

Contents

vii

Maps

Introduction

The story of the Texas Rangers who protected the Indian frontier of Texas is well chronicled for the years that preceded and followed the American Civil War. Many years ago, while reading Walter Prescott Webb's outstanding history of the Texas Rangers, I was intrigued to find that he covered the Civil War years in less than one page. For that era, he concluded, "it is practically impossible to follow the activities of the so-called Texas Rangers," and he added that "if the story is ever told, it will be fragmentary."[1] The present work attempts to tell that story.

In many ways the picture of the Rangers for the 1861–65 period is unrecognizable as the rough-hewn and dashing men whom Webb portrayed so vividly. In the last two years of the Civil War Rangers garnered little glory in tracking down those who deserted or evaded conscription or in protecting the frontier against bushwhackers and renegades. Against the Indians Rangers scored no decisive victories such as Plum Creek or "Rip" Ford's success along the Washita; instead, veterans would look back years later and remember the Dove Creek disaster of 1865, or that no captain like Jack Hays made his mark on the land.

Historians have often dismissed as ineffectual the efforts of those men who guarded the Indian frontier of Texas during 1861–65. Little analysis is given to exactly what the government required of the Rangers or to the obstacles they confronted. In 1861 these Texans faced the responsibility of doing what one-fourth of the U.S. Army, combined with Texas Rangers, had failed to do in antebellum days—end the Indian depredations along the Texas frontier counties. By mid-1863 the question of frontier defense for Texas was no longer clearly defined.

Before the war the Indian threat was the Rangers' only responsibility; but the magnitude of Civil War necessarily widened the scope of frontier protection.

From late 1863 until the end of the war frontier defenders served as police, protecting frontier Texans from other foes as deadly as Indians—that is, from each other. On the frontier massed bands of deserters, draft dodgers, and criminals came to dominate the activities of the frontier defense organizations. This added complexity of Civil War soon produced problems that no Rangers, before or after the war, faced—internal turmoil that more often than not placed Indians in the category of "the least talked of, the least thought of, and the least dreaded of all the evils that threatened and afflicted the frontier."[2]

The story that unfolds may be confusing if one searches only for an organized body of men called "Texas Rangers." There was, of course, no such permanent, institutionalized force either before or during the Civil War. The frontier guardians within these pages are called minutemen, state troops, Texas Mounted Rifles, Frontier Regiment, and Border Regiment—names given to those local, state, and Confederate organizations that protected the frontier counties. In every instance, their standards and the instructions they received were identical to those given to Rangers for over twenty-five years, since men first volunteered to "range" the frontier line of Texas.

Other Confederate states faced the dilemma of disaffection, desertion, and draft evasion, but only Texas faced these problems in the presence of unrelenting pressure by Plains Indians.

When European and Plains Indian cultures collided, nowhere was the clash more intense or protracted than along the Texas frontier. Particularly after 1836, American settlers pushed westward from the forests of East Texas and pressed into the domain of the Comanches and Kiowas. Texans, not unlike generations of other American settlers who moved westward, did not try to appreciate the richness of Indian tradition and culture. They saw the Indians as essentially savages or barbarians and made little effort to understand their humanity. Instead, they confronted the Comanches with a ruthless determination unlike anything the Plains Indians had yet seen. The Comanches and Kiowas, so accustomed to long raids into Mexico, began in the late 1830s and 1840s to strike the settlers who moved relentlessly into lands where they had long held sway. Texans could not understand a warfare of revenge by Comanches and Kiowas that ravaged and mutilated women and children, and they matched atrocities with their foes. This warfare, which brutalized the natures of those on both sides, continued into the post–Civil War years. The conflict in cultures, perhaps an unavoidable one, darkened Texans' views of all Indians along the frontier. The violence that marked contact between the races left ingrained hatred on both sides; in fact, Comanches came to see Texans as different from other Americans.

As the Plains Indians fought aggressively to defend their lands and way of life in the only way they knew how, frontier Texans intensified their efforts to protect the men, women, and children who advanced westward. Only what Texans perceived as the savage and inhuman warfare of their foes can explain the monumental effort by Texans to defend their frontier in the manner they did. Loss of life alone cannot explain their insistence on removing the Indian threat completely or explain their unique evolution of frontier defense; only the nature of the warfare they experienced can account for that.

The Confederate government, responsible for guarding the Indian frontier, preferred instead to use its military strength to face threatened Union invasions from the east and the coast. The combination of these internal and external factors was unique to Texas. The following story attempts to trace frontier society's response to such a crisis and to examine Texans' continuing search, in the face of manpower and financial shortages, for a system that could hold together the social fabric of the frontier.

The manner of frontier defense continued to evolve throughout the war until it culminated in the Frontier Organization provided by the Texas Legislature in December of 1863. This organization, drawn from a Texas tradition of minutemen companies of Rangers, evolved in response to an increased need for frontier protection, a need forged out of the crucible of Civil War and a state's-rights conflict between Texas and the Confederate government. This Frontier Organization, whose story has never before been fully told, became the primary means of defending the limits of the Indian frontier from January, 1864, until the surrender of the Trans-Mississippi Confederacy in May, 1865. Its remnants in the summer of 1865 formed the backbone of the protection offered to a Texas frontier denuded of state or national troops.

One last word concerns the scope of this work. In 1861, Texans spoke of the state's three frontiers: that along the Red River from Preston Bend eastward to Arkansas, facing the Civilized Tribes in Indian Territory; the Rio Grande frontier, broadly extending from Brownsville to El Paso; and the Indian frontier, running from the vicinity of Eagle Pass, on the Rio Grande, northward to the confluence of the Wichita and Red rivers, then eastward along the Red River to Preston Bend. This narrative examines the Indian frontier, over four hundred miles in length. The complex story of the Rio Grande line, involving coastal defense, relations with Mexican authorities, and the trans-Pecos region, is outside the scope of this work and could constitute a separate volume of its own. When Texans of the 1860s spoke of frontier defense, they referred to the Indian frontier here defined.

Frontier Defense in the Civil War

1

Prelude to Civil War

During the years of the Republic of Texas, 1836–45, no issue touching upon frontier defense so polarized Texans as the contrasting views taken by the nation's first two presidents, Sam Houston and Mirabeau B. Lamar. Houston came to office in 1836 faced with a treasury that was nearly bare and with a policy of moderation toward the Indians. Along the frontier, settlers who lived in constant danger of Comanche attack were never satisfied by Houston's policy, which they saw as unrealistically charitable. They welcomed Houston's successor, Lamar, who vowed an increased military presence and aggressive action against incursions by the Plains Indians.

The two presidents took opposite approaches to the three major problems of frontier defense. Their solutions for using regular troops and Rangers to combat the Indian and Mexican threats, for easing strained finances, and for answering the constant demand for protection of the frontier counties mirrored the situation that faced Texas leaders during the Civil War. Then the challenge would be to provide protection against both Indians and a hostile United States. The old problems remained, in the forms of inadequate funds and controversy over whether regular troops or Rangers should be used. A new problem emerged, one that no antebellum leader ever faced—one of disaffection and desertion among the populace and troops in the frontier counties. The Texans' response to these problems of frontier defense in antebellum years forged the policies that would be used from 1861 to 1865.

As early as 1823 the term "Ranger" had been applied to those who volunteered to help defend the Indian frontier of Texas. The force did not receive legal status until 1835 when a "permanent council" of Texans met in consultation at San Felipe de Austin to direct the affairs

3

of the Mexican-Texas conflict. On November 1, 1835, the Permanent Council authorized a body of Rangers to protect the Indian frontier and eight days later commissioned the raising of twenty men for this new service. During the period of the Republic the Rangers, in the absence of a permanent army, became the best solution to defend the Indian frontier and to oppose Mexican incursions.[1]

At the end of the Mexican War the federal government assumed the responsibility of protecting the Texas frontier. Presumably, this put the Texas Rangers out of business. The relatively peaceful frontier during the years 1846 to 1848 changed dramatically in the latter year when Indian raids increased on a large scale. For the next decade the Rangers would be called upon to varying extents by the governors of Texas in times of emergency or when dissatisfied settlers no longer believed the U.S. Army could offer effective protection. During this ten-year period, until their decisive use in 1858, the Rangers conducted no extensive military campaigns, yet state authorities called them out with increasing frequency over the decade to meet a growing Indian threat.[2]

A description of the interaction between the Texas Rangers and the U.S. Army explains and clarifies the manner in which Texans evolved their system of frontier protection in the period 1861 to 1865. The Civil War experience drew upon the tradition of both the army and the Rangers in an attempt to achieve the proper tactics and strategy necessary to protect the frontier. The mistakes and successes of the 1860s, in the face of the added complexity of Civil War, had roots in the means by which both Rangers and army went about their business during the 1848–60 period.

In 1848 the U.S. War Department established the Eighth Military Department, later renamed the Department of Texas. Maj. Gen. George Mercer Brooke assumed command in 1849 and proceeded to establish a chain of forts slightly in advance of the frontier. Included were Fort Worth, on the Trinity River; Fort Graham, on the Brazos River fourteen miles west of present Hillsboro; Fort Gates, on the Leon River a few miles east of present Gatesville; Fort Croghan, on Hamilton Creek in Burnet County at the present town of Burnet; Fort Bliss, just outside El Paso; and Fort Martin Scott, on the Guadalupe River northwest of San Antonio at Fredericksburg. Between 1848 and 1854, under the provisions of the Treaty of Guadalupe Hidalgo, the United States was bound to keep Indian raiders out of Mexico. The presence of twenty-two companies of the U.S. Army, assigned to prevent raids against the

Mexican nation and Texas settlers, failed to stem the rising tide of Indian raiding parties, largely because sixteen of the companies consisted of infantrymen who lacked knowledge about tracking Indians or about the terrain.[3]

Widespread public dissatisfaction with the army's efforts still did nothing to discourage an increasing wave of new settlers to the Texas frontier. In 1850 just over four thousand people lived along the frontier line; for the next decade the yearly advance of the frontier averaged ten miles, and the population increased nearly five thousand per year. A revision of the entire system of defense began in 1851 upon the death of General Brooke. His successor, Maj. Gen. Persifor F. Smith, began the process by extending a line of forts about 150 miles in advance of the old one. The northern anchor of this second or outer chain of forts began with Fort Belknap, located about 2 miles from the Salt Fork of the Brazos, in present Young County. From Fort Belknap the line of forts curved westward to Fort Phantom Hill, on the Clear Fork of the Brazos just north of present Abilene; to Fort Chadbourne, on Oak Creek just north of its junction with the Colorado River; to Fort McKavett, on the San Saba River in western Menard County; to Fort Terrett, on the North Llano River between the present towns of Junction and Sonora; to Fort Mason, between the San Saba and the Llano at present Mason; and to the southern anchor, Fort Clark, on Las Moras Creek just opposite the town of Bracketville.[4]

With two lines of forts completed by the end of 1852 and available to protect the frontier settlements, General Smith set out to increase the force to occupy them. The plan of defense called for manning the outer forts with infantry and the inner ones with cavalry. The infantry was somehow to alert the cavalry to the presence of Indian raiding parties so that the cavalry could pursue, while the infantry cut off the escape routes of the invaders. The important point missed, which did not escape the attention of Ranger veterans and frontier settlers, was that only the mobility of cavalry could detect and stop the Indians before they reached the settlements.[5]

During this three-year period, 1849–52, the U.S. Army attempted to supplement its lack of numbers by using Ranger companies. In the summer of 1849 General Brooke called upon Gov. George Wood for three companies of Rangers to patrol the area between Goliad and the Rio Grande for a six-month period. The brief episode of Texas Rangers in federal service ended in 1851 by order of General Brooke, with the

Ranger companies still subject to call in time of emergency upon responsibility of the governor. From 1852 through 1855 petitions to the
governor increased as angry settlers agitated for better protection. To
guard an Indian frontier extending more than five hundred miles from
the Red River to the Rio Grande and an international boundary extending more than one thousand miles from El Paso to the Gulf of
Mexico, the Army deployed approximately sixteen hundred officers and
soldiers within the Department of Texas.[6]

In the face of perceived Army deficiencies, Texans continued their
own efforts to provide for frontier defense. In 1855 Gov. Elisha Pease
called out a company of Rangers commanded by James Hughes Callahan; the state treasury depleted, the men took to the field with the
understanding that future legislation would provide for their pay. The
Callahan expedition ended in disgrace when it crossed the Rio Grande
in pursuit of Indians, only to end up fighting Mexicans as well as Indians and burning the Mexican town of Piedras Negras in the process.

A bill for frontier protection that would provide funding for Rangers in the field failed to pass the state legislature in December. State
senator Henry Eustace McCulloch, a former Ranger captain, introduced
the bill with a passionate speech that vividly depicted Indian depredations in the country west of the Guadalupe River. The bill called for
funding and equipping a Ranger force of one thousand men, but it
failed to pass the legislature because many legislators feared that such
a force was destined for a filibustering expedition rather than for service on the Indian frontier.[7] The problem of financing Ranger companies always plagued the Texas government; the decade of the 1850s
saw constant disenchantment by state authorities who tried to acquire
federal appropriations, or at least receive reimbursement, for the service of Ranger companies. The financial question itself, which led to
a search for expediency and efficiency in the frontier forces, served
naturally to delay implementation of any proposed system of frontier
defense.

While Texas governors continued to call upon Rangers, or minutemen companies as they were often known, in time of emergency, the
national government in conjunction with the state turned to a reservation system to help combat the Indian threat. A number of people
came to believe that the clash between cultures could be lessened if
the tribes had a permanent location in Texas. As early as 1847 Gov.
James Pinckney Henderson proposed that Texas sell to the national

government part of its public lands to be used for the settlement of various tribes, in hopes that this would enable the United States to better control the situation. Nothing came of the proposal at the time, but five years later the Texas legislature took the first step in setting aside land. A resolution authorized the governor to negotiate with the federal government to establish an Indian territory along the northern frontier of the state. Finally, in 1854 the state legislature authorized the federal government to select from Texas's vacant public lands a maximum of twelve leagues for the exclusive use of the Texas tribes.[8] Even before the Texas land grant, a number of tribes began gathering in semipermanent locations. Scourged with poverty and near starvation, or simply weary of conflict, hundreds of Indians, representing dozens of tribes, requested areas of settlement.

On May 9, 1853, Robert Simpson Neighbors, state legislator and member of the Committee on Indian Affairs, was appointed supervising agent of the Indian service in Texas. In 1854 Neighbors and U.S. Army captain Randolph B. Marcy proceeded to locate and survey land suitable for the proposed reservations. After an extensive reconnaissance the men selected two tracts that came to be known as the Brazos Reservation (or the lower reserve) and the Comanche Indian Reservation (also known as the Clear Fork Reservation or the upper reserve). The Brazos agency comprised approximately 37,000 acres on the upper Brazos in present Young County; it was intended for various scattered tribes of East and Central Texas—Anadarko, Caddo, Waco, and Tonkawa. The Comanches settled on the upper reserve of approximately 18,500 acres located forty miles from Fort Belknap, in present Throckmorton County. By late summer of 1856 Major Neighbors reported a total of 948 Indians at the Brazos agency and 557 Comanches at the Comanche reserve, with a total of 740 acres under cultivation at the two locations.[9]

The reservation system, intended to lessen conflict between Indians and Texans, actually aggravated an already complex military situation. Raids from Indian Territory, north of the Red River, increased in frequency in the late 1850s, and both the army and the Ranger companies were hard-pressed to meet the threat. This was coupled with a growing dissatisfaction by Texas settlers who refused to trust in the docility of the reservation Indians.

Indian raids increased dramatically in 1854, requiring General Smith to ask Governor Pease to augment the federal forces with six companies of Rangers. This combination provided only temporary relief, as the Rangers served for just three months. Furthermore, problems in "Bleeding Kansas" in mid-1855 required that some of the federal mounted troops in Texas be reassigned. To provide relief from the resurgence of Indian depredations that followed this action, in late 1855 the newly formed Second United States Cavalry Regiment arrived on the Texas frontier. An elite organization, the Second Cavalry came to be involved directly not only with frontier protection but with the Texas Indian Reservation.[10]

Upon the arrival of the regiment in Texas in December of 1855, Col. Albert Sidney Johnston assigned five companies to occupy Fort Mason, regimental headquarters, while four companies under Maj. William J. Hardee left to establish a new post, Camp Cooper, on the Clear Fork of the Brazos. In addition to Camp Cooper the army established six more posts during the next three years: Camp Colorado, in Coleman County about six miles north of the Colorado River; Camp Verde, three miles outside Bandera Pass in southern Kerr County; Camp Hudson, on San Pedro Creek near Devil's River in Val Verde County; Camp Wood, in Real County; Fort Quitman, on the Rio Grande in south-central Hudspeth County; Fort Lancaster, at the junction of Live Oak Creek and the Pecos River; and Fort Stockton, near Comanche Springs in Pecos County.[11]

With the presence of the Second United States Cavalry in Texas, the army no longer maintained merely a passive patrol system as practiced since the Mexican War. Company commanders now kept as many patrols in the field as possible, in order to discover any sign of Indians and then to trail them relentlessly to bring them to battle. The Second Cavalry took to the field just as the frequency of raids by northern Comanches and Kiowas increased. The state-federal response brought another company of Rangers into service, confined the settled Indians to the reservations, declared all Indians outside the reservations hostile, and unleashed the Second Cavalry in offensive action against the raiders. For several months afterward, in the spring of 1856, the frontier was as peaceful as it had been at any time since the Texas Revolution, a condition attributed by at least one Texan, Indian agent Robert S. Neighbors, to the presence of the Second United States Cavalry.[12]

The peace would be short-lived. In the winter of 1856–57 the frontier once again ignited in warfare as war parties of northern Comanches went from their lands in Kansas to raid in Mexico and back again.

The marked increase in Indian attacks occurred mostly north and east of the site of raids in previous years. With the line of the Rio Grande better protected, the Indians in many instances curtailed their raids into Mexico and attacked the more settled districts of the Texas frontier, particularly the area near the two Indian reservations. The frontier Texans' general feelings of hostility toward Indians led, invariably, to suspicions by many settlers that the reservation Indians were responsible. One of Major Neighbors's agents, John Robert Baylor, not only stated that the reservation Indians were not responsible for the attacks, but that they inquired of him why other Indians were allowed to roam at will seemingly without being punished.[13] The evidence reveals that raiding Indians often made clear false trails leading to the reservations and even suggests that upon occasion Texan thieves camouflaged their operations to shift blame to the reservation Indians.[14]

As conditions grew worse in 1857, Governor Pease again called on minutemen companies, that is, Ranger companies, to augment the army troops in Texas. Many of these were local contingents, consisting of only twenty men who served in the vicinity of their home counties. The following is an example of the governor's instructions to such a company raised in Coryell and Comanche counties:

> Each man will furnish himself with a good rifle or double barrel shot gun, and one or more pistols, with a sufficient quantity of ammunition, a good horse, saddle and bridle. The Officers and men respectively, will be paid by the State, while in actual service, at the same rate, as mounted volunteers were paid by the United States during the Mexican War.[15]

Clamoring settlers insisted that the army no longer provided the necessary protection; they demanded better. By autumn of that year the governor of Texas agreed that the U.S. Army forces assigned to the frontier were no longer adequate, necessitating the calling up of not just local minutemen companies of Rangers, but an entire volunteer Ranger regiment. Governor Pease believed that the new commander of the Military Department of Texas, Maj. Gen. David Twiggs, had done everything possible for the frontier but that his force was simply inadequate in numbers to deal with the crisis. Yet the thirty-six hundred soldiers in Texas represented over one-fourth of the entire U.S. Army.[16]

A new governor took office in January of 1858. Hardin Richard Runnels, who defeated Sam Houston in the 1857 campaign, entered office determined to give better protection to the frontier. By so doing he would give the Texas Rangers their most decisive service on the Texas frontier.[17] In the Texas legislature, a select Senate committee reviewed the situation regarding the reservation policy and the failure of federal authorities to prevent the incursion of Indians from Indian Territory and Kansas. The committee made the wry observation that the Indians roaming the borders of Texas "were not friendly disposed."[18]

The committee agreed with former governor Pease that the United States should declare war against all Indians found outside the reservations and employ and fund a regiment of Texas Rangers to help protect the frontier.[19] Such a suggestion had been put to General Twiggs some months before when, in addition to complaints from frontier settlers, Governor Pease learned that the Second United States Cavalry, the only effective army unit (in the eyes of Texans) would soon be transferred from the state. Pease pleaded that only a mobile force should replace the Second Cavalry, and that such a force of Ranger veterans, under Twiggs's direction, could soon put an end to the Indian depredations. Sam Houston agreed with this proposal and remarked that setting up one regiment of well-supplied and well-armed Rangers would allow Texas to dispense with every regular soldier within the state, or at any rate, "she would not require more than fifty men at each post which the Government has established there."[20]

By the third week of January, 1858, four companies of Rangers served on the frontier. Three numbered twenty men each and one numbered thirty, with one stationed at the headwaters of the Guadalupe River, one on the Colorado, and two on the Brazos. Runnels considered this force inadequate to meet the pressing need of the frontier. Because General Twiggs sent word that even his capacity as military department commander would not allow him to call civilians into service, the governor urged the legislature to provide for the force. Texas lawmakers responded promptly by passing "An Act for the better protection of the Frontier," which Governor Runnels approved on January 27, 1858. It authorized the governor to call into service one hundred mounted volunteers (Rangers), in addition to the force already in service on the frontier, for a six-month period. The proposed regiment was to be discharged "whenever an efficient force shall be placed on the frontier by the Government of the United States." Significantly, if the Indian attacks increased, or if the U.S. Army could no longer protect the frontier, the legislature authorized the governor to "call out any number of men" to carry out "active and offensive operations" against the hostile Indians.[21]

On the following day Governor Runnels commissioned John Salmon "Rip" Ford with the rank of senior captain to command all state forces. The forty-two-year-old Ford had experienced a varied and illustrious career in Texas. In addition to practicing medicine, editing a newspaper, and serving as state senator, Fort had been a Texas Ranger captain in 1849. He would now prove to be an excellent choice to lead the present contingent of Rangers.[22] Ford quickly recruited volunteers to join those companies already in service and in just a few weeks left for the frontier to direct operations against the Indian raiding parties.

Before detailing the extraordinary campaigns of the Texas Rangers and the U.S. Army in 1858, it would serve to examine not only how their strategy of Indian warfare altered in the upcoming campaigns, but also to take a closer look at the men who made up these elements of frontier defense in Texas. Before the Civil War there was no organization by the official title of Texas Rangers. Between the Mexican War and the Civil War they were called out in emergencies, sometimes for periods up to six months, but never became a permanent institution until 1874. The tendency has been to picture them as an elite fighting body, when actually they consisted of citizens who lived in the frontier counties, men who by necessity learned the art of plains warfare from their enemies.[23]

A Ranger was only as good as his horse; the men were all mounted, not only to traverse the great distances of Texas, but to match the mounted Indians and Mexicans they continually fought. With the acquisition of Colt revolvers by 1839, Texans finally could match the firepower of their Indian opponents without dismounting. For the most part, they were an undisciplined group of civilian volunteers who would follow only men they trusted and who had proved themselves in battle.

As these Rangers, or minutemen companies, were usually called out only in an emergency, the Indian raid normally had already taken place; the Rangers' job was then to pursue and, if possible, destroy the retreating enemy. Until 1858 punitive expeditions were rare, as normally the companies were composed of citizen soldiers who took the field for only a short period of time. After the Mexican War, the Texas government requested on numerous occasions that the United States pay for the expense of maintaining Rangers in the field, and this the federal government usually refused to do. The army was not about to admit that Texan civilian soldiers, no matter how experienced in Indian fighting, were superior to federal troops stationed in Texas with the responsibility of guarding the frontier.[24]

In those instances when the governor called out the Rangers for several months, patrols usually served as the manner of defense. A good example of this system of defense, one which Texans later used throughout the Civil War, occurred in 1850 and 1851. General Brooke called upon the governor of Texas for three mounted companies, later expanded to five, for service upon the southwest frontier of the state. Henry McCulloch, younger brother of former Ranger captain Ben McCulloch, commanded one of these companies. The younger McCulloch first engaged Plains Indians in combat in 1838, participated in the famous Battle of Plum Creek against the Comanches two years later, and spent much of the 1840s in Ranger service. In 1850 Governor Bell recommended the thirty-four-year-old McCulloch to General Brooke and described him as "a well tried frontier officer, a bold and energetic man."[25]

McCulloch posted his company in a manner consistent with his past experience. He sent regular patrols in intervals from the various camps, thus covering the entire perimeter of the assigned area at least once each week. Vigilantly, his men searched for Indian signs, especially near the hill passes and fords of surrounding streams and rivers. The company quartermaster, John R. King, distributed supplies to the scattered camps of the company and coordinated all scouting pursuits when his men discovered Indian signs.

On Christmas Eve, 1850, McCulloch returned to his headquarters from a scout to discover five parties of his men in pursuit of Indians after finding their trail the day before. It was Lieutenant King who led the force that came upon the encamped Indians between the Medio Creek and the Aransas River. Two Indians of the Lipan tribe died in the ensuing fight, while King took an arrow in the chest, an injury from which he later recovered. Word passed immediately to nearby scouts on patrol duty to cover the line between the Papalote Creek and the Nueces River to block the Indians' retreat. Then, after pursuing the Lipans for over twenty-five miles, finding blankets, saddles, bridles, and lariats discarded by the Indians to lighten their load, McCulloch and his men abandoned the chase.[26] For most of the time, however, on these three-month or six-month periods of duty, there was only the monotony of patrol, broken occasionally by Indian signs and a short, sharp fight. This was the system, then, that Henry McCulloch knew best, the system that he installed as standard operating procedure when he assumed command of the Indian frontier in 1861.

If patrol duty was a dreary monotony to Rangers, it was a way of life to the regulars of the U.S. Army on the Texas frontier. For these men, living conditions and food were usually abominable, the sickness rate high, the discipline harsh and exacting, and the hard work often done with a shovel and ax rather than with a gun. For the officers, low pay and slow promotion with no adequate retirement system led to the burdening of the top ranks of the army with worn-out or incapable men in positions of responsibility. For men on the frontier, garrison duty rather than the pursuit of Indians occupied most of their time. Of the approximately two hundred engagements recorded between regulars and Indians along the entire U.S. frontier from 1848 to 1861, it has been estimated that an enlisted man might participate in one Indian fight for each five years of service.[27] But if he served in Texas, at least the chance for action was greater than anywhere else.

In spite of the army's heavy commitment, Texans continued to criticize or discredit its attempts to offer protection to frontier settlers. To guard effectively a thousand-mile international boundary as well as an extensive frontier line within the state would have taxed double the approximately thirty-five hundred men who actually served; but more directly, Texans complained about the strategy used to do so. For the army to make up over two-thirds of its force with infantry stationed at the frontier forts seemed ludicrous to Texans. Lack of strength and the high costs of maintaining cavalry regiments may have been the official reasons why offensive operations were not the norm until the coming of the Second United States Cavalry, or attempted en masse until 1858; but the army seems to have learned too slowly an old military lesson, that a cordon defense is inherently weak when penetrated by highly mobile attackers. As traveler Frederick Law Olmstead put it: "Keeping a bulldog to chase mosquitoes would be no greater nonsense than the stationing of six-pounders, bayonets, and dragoons for the pursuit of these red wolves."[28]

Texans who witnessed Rangers pursue and dispatch Indian raiders could not understand the army's failure to do so on any regular basis. The army's solution might have been to erect a line of forts closer to the settlements and reinforce the installations with additional troops; but once again, the expense of such expansion was prohibitive. Failing this, the army needed a preponderance of highly skilled, mobile troops. This goal military officials obtained, partially, with the coming of the Second United States Cavalry, the only army unit on the frontier to have its praises sung by Texans. But even this regiment was only 750 strong, too weak to protect the entire line from the Red River to the Rio Grande. A change of strategy was needed, a change to be implemented in 1858 by both the army and the Texas Rangers.[29]

By February of 1858 "Rip" Ford and his Rangers were on the move to carry out a campaign north of the Red River against the Comanches and Kiowas. By early March Ford arrived on the upper Brazos, having directed his troops to that vicinity by four main groups, sweeping the terrain in between for Indian signs. Before the final push to the Comanche hunting grounds, Ford's men delayed while waiting for reinforcements, including some from units recruited on the march. On April 22 Ford set out with just over one hundred Rangers, more than one hundred and ten Indian volunteers from the reservations, two wagons, an ambulance, and more than a dozen pack mules.

Just a week later the strike force crossed the Red River, journeyed through the valley of the Washita, and found a large body of Comanches on May 11, 1858. The Rangers and their Indian allies, mostly Tonkawas, attacked the Comanche camp early the next morning. For seven hours the fight raged, with charge after counter-charge until the Ranger force finally prevailed over the Comanches, led by Iron Jacket. A reported force of Comanches under Buffalo Hump, said to be only twelve miles away, was not pursued because of the utter exhaustion of the victors. Ford estimated that he engaged over three hundred warriors, killed seventy-six, and captured eighteen women and children. On the debit side, the Texans lost but two killed and two wounded.[30] This engagement, needless to say, did not stop Indian raids on the Texas frontier, but it did demonstrate, in conjunction with the army campaign that followed, that whites would pursue their Indian attackers beyond the borders of the state to destroy them. Extermination was the solution according to Texans; the army hoped that such campaigns would convince the hostiles to come to the reservations in peace.

The army would have been the first to point out that such an extensive campaign by the Texans beyond the boundary of the state did not exactly leave the frontier unprotected in their absence. Army units still maintained their patrols along the frontier while the Rangers undertook their punitive expedition. Texans and General Twiggs expressed concern, however, in April, when Army authorities informed Twiggs that the Second Cavalry had been relieved from duty in the state.[31] While the Second Cavalry concentrated near Fort Belknap prior to leaving the state, Governor Runnels authorized Ford to call even more men into service, as little faith remained that the few remaining federals, mostly infantry, could effect anything against further Indian attacks.[32]

When General Twiggs learned that army authorities had revoked the order for the Second Cavalry to leave the state, he informed Governor Runnels that he wished to modify army policy on the Texas frontier. The army would also take the war to the enemy and strike the marauding bands in Indian Territory. The expedition consisted of four companies of the Second Cavalry, a detachment of the First Infantry, and about sixty Indians, under the overall command of Capt. Earl Van Dorn. The force left Fort Belknap in mid-September, crossed the Red River, and learned from scouts about a large party of Comanches found near Wichita Village in the Choctaw Nation.

Van Dorn's exhausted command reached a point near the Indian encampment on the last day of September and at daybreak the next morning charged the camp, which consisted of about five hundred Indians. The main battle lasted about thirty minutes, the pursuit of fleeing Comanches another two hours. The army force captured over three hundred horses and killed fifty-six warriors at a cost of five soldiers killed and ten wounded. While it was the most complete victory the army ever achieved against the Comanches, their chief, Buffalo Hump, escaped with approximately two-thirds of his warriors to fight again.[33]

It seemed as if the Plains Indians surely could not recover from such a combined onslaught from the Ranger and army expeditions of 1858. Nonetheless, the settlers who lived along the northwestern frontier of Texas experienced little relief. As one historian observed, such offensive operations would certainly drive old men, women and children to the reservations, but many young warriors would not go; rather they would seek out bands like themselves. They would thus be far from the restraints of organized society and, eager for revenge, would be more than ready to carry the war to the Texas settlements. There were increased reports of attacks all along the frontier in late 1858 and throughout 1859, although the size of the raiding parties had diminished.[34] While Rangers and the army attempted a military solution to the question of frontier defense, a number of citizens in north Texas believed part of the problem stemmed from the large number of Indians living on the two Brazos River reservations. Scattered complaints about these Indians began surfacing in 1857, and by 1858 a campaign began shaping to force their removal.

John R. Baylor, a former agent to the Comanches, led the move to rid Texas of the reservations. Baylor kept the public mind agitated against the reservation Indians and Supervising Agent Neighbors in particular, even though some prominent Texans, including Sam Houston, constantly praised the various tribes and the work done by the agent. After his dismissal as agent in May, 1857, Baylor's consuming desire to arouse settlers against the Indians led to his appellation as "the man that made the Indians move out of Texas," while his newspaper, *The White Man*, kept the public mind inflamed against the tribes.[35]

Matters came to a head in December, 1858, when a party of whites murdered seven blameless reservation Indians. With difficulty, Neighbors restrained the Indians from retaliating, and he obtained a judge's order to arrest the whites. No one did. "Rip" Ford never tried, and Governor Runnels's proclamation calling for their arrest was simply ignored. Instead, many settlers in the vicinity of the Brazos reservations, spurred on by Baylor and others, began to assemble groups of minutemen intent on using force to remove the eleven hundred reservation Indians from their midst. By March over one hundred whites from Jack, Palo Pinto, and Wise counties had gathered on Rock Creek, near the Brazos Agency, but speeches by levelheaded frontier citizens defused the situation.[36]

Not all the men dispersed; some drifted to the fringes of the reservations and began to kill Indians who left its bounds. Others remained with Baylor and waited for a chance to move against the reservations, or at least against Neighbors. When a party of reservation Indians, accompanied by an army officer, went in search of the murderer of one of the Indians, Baylor sent a force of 250 men to the Comanche Reservation and led a group of the same size against the Brazos Agency in a desperate attempt to force the tribes from Texas. Disgruntled frontiersmen under Baylor had no desire to attack the U.S. Army units posted to protect the reserves, but as Baylor's assemblage left the Brazos reserve, they murdered two elderly Indians. The Indians on the reservation could stand no more. Some fifty warriors, many of whom previously fought alongside Ford and Van Dorn, attacked Baylor's party, drove them back eight miles, and killed seven whites in the process.

To prevent an anticipated onslaught against the reservations, Neighbors repeated his recommendation to federal authorities to remove the Texas Indians, for their own safety, to Indian Territory.[37]

The order to move the Indians north of the Red River came on June 11, 1859. The Indians loaded up their personal property on wagons and began their journey by the first of August. Most of their livestock remained behind when the Rangers, sent by Governor Runnels to help the army supervise the exodus, would not allow the Indians to go out on their own to gather their stock.[38] The reservation experiment in Texas ended on a shabby note that brought no credit to the settlers who rode with Baylor. On a more pragmatic note, although a grim one, the end of the reservation system meant that if any Indian now appeared on the Texas frontier "it was at his own peril, and it was the duty of any Texan to kill him and *then* inquire as to his intentions."[39] What of the Indians who fought so bravely alongside the Texans and the army in the 1858 campaigns, the enemies of the Comanches and Kiowas? For one tribe, the Tonkawas, the last years of the Civil War would once more see them trying to fight against the Comanches for white Texans, who once more would rarely trust them.

Not surprisingly, the Indian removal brought little change to conditions along the settlement line of Texas. Shortly after the Indian exodus Rip Ford discharged his command upon the expiration of their time of service and left frontier protection to the army and local minutemen companies of Rangers. It soon fell to another administration in Austin to try and turn the tide of Indian depredations. The old Hero of San Jacinto, sixty-six-year-old Sam Houston, just completing his term of office as U.S. Senator, defeated Hardin R. Runnels in the 1859 gubernatorial contest. His inauguration took place in December, and during the following months the frontier of the state became the scene of hostility as settlers and soldiers reported raids from the Red River to the San Saba.

The legislature responded immediately, voicing disgust that "the Federal Government, whose duty it is primarily to protect the State from such hostilities, has not efficiently afforded such protection." Legislators quickly passed a new frontier protection act authorizing the governor to raise a regiment of mounted men, comprising up to ten companies. This force was to be placed on the frontier for a period of twelve months, with an option to reenlist for an additional twelve months. Each company was to consist of eighty-three men. The act charged the regiment with patroling from the Red River to the Rio Grande. Foreshadowing a later conflict with the government of the Confederacy, the lawmakers added, somewhat optimistically, that the entire force could be turned over to the United States, with the implication that Texans could best defend their own frontier if funded and provisioned by the federal government.[40]

Immediately, the governor took personal charge of raising the companies stipulated by the legislature, taking care to specify their exact station and duties.[41] Indicative of the service expected by Houston were the orders he sent to company commanders Edward Burleson, Jr., and William Cornelius Dalrymple. Their commands were to be divided into as many as three camps, each covering the greatest extent of territory possible. In the tradition of past Ranger patrols, Houston directed them to scout diligently from camp to camp across the company line. The governor also strictly prohibited horse racing, gambling, or intoxicating liquors—three favorite diversions of the Regular Army in Texas—within the company camps.[42]

The legislature, in its parsimonious zeal, allocated only enough money to sustain some of the companies for a short period of time. This compelled the governor to cut the company sizes down to 60 men each and to suspend raising the full complement of ten companies until the lawmakers made adequate appropriations. When pleas for help continued to pour in from the frontier, some from counties where citizens were forming their own Ranger companies, Houston made an executive proclamation to the chief justices of twenty-three frontier counties and instructed them to organize a "Minute detachment" of 15 men in each county. In the Ranger tradition, these companies were directed to scout their county lines for Indian signs and pursue all fresh trails. By the middle of March Houston had a state force of 730 men in service on the Indian frontier. This number was few enough, in his thinking, considering the havoc wrought by Indian raids since he took office at the end of 1859. In that short period, Houston reported, Indians had killed at least 51 citizens, wounded many, and stolen more than eighteen hundred horses.[43]

The governor disbanded the county minutemen companies on May 18, 1860, subject to recall by the chief justices of the respective counties. He now had two other plans at hand to provide for frontier defense, neither of which was new. Earlier in the year Houston made two appeals to Washington, to Pres. James Buchanan and to Sec. of

War John B. Floyd, calling for the U.S. government to enter into a treaty with the "wild Indians," to save the government millions in defense and bring peace to the frontier of Texas. To Houston the answer was either extermination of these hostile tribes or peace with them — the present state of affairs was simply intolerable.[44]

While the governor talked of peace treaties, he prepared with the sword. In a move reminiscent of the punitive, or search and destroy, expeditions of 1858, Houston assigned Col. Middleton Tate Johnson to take seven companies into Indian Territory to recover stolen horses and punish Indians who were ravaging the northwest frontier of the state. The force of more than four hundred Rangers left Fort Belknap on May 23, 1860, crossed the Red River, traveled as far as the Kansas border, and then returned with little to show for a lofty effort.[45]

Despite disparagement by Texas lawmakers and the governor, the regulars of the U.S. Army were still seen by Washington as the backbone of frontier defense in Texas. At San Antonio, headquarters of the army in Texas, a temporary change in command took place. Lt. Col. Robert E. Lee assumed command of the Department, and General Twiggs went on sick leave to his home in Georgia. But repercussions of Juan Cortina's 1859 invasion of Brownsville drew Lee's attention to the Rio Grande during his first months in command. With four companies of the Second Cavalry then stationed along the Rio Grande for much of the year, companies that remained on the Indian frontier were stretched to the limit, while the infantry regulars there provided little protection. The year ended with Twiggs's return in December, whereupon Lee took command of the Second Cavalry. Six days later, after five years of almost constant warfare against the Plains Indians, the Second United States Cavalry fought its last engagement in Texas, this time along the Pease River.[46]

Although the U.S. Army had devoted a dozen years to frontier duty in Texas, the Plains Indians, particularly Comanches and Kiowas, devastated the Texas settlements more in 1859 and 1860 than in the first years after the Mexican War. Long-suffering frontier citizens by 1860 believed that the federal government had "displayed a cold blooded indifference to our condition"; they had lost almost all hope that the federal government could protect them.[47] The government's failure to protect its citizens on the frontier was a theme often repeated in the secessionist rhetoric of 1860–61. It was one of several factors that moved the frontier counties to endorse secession.[48] But it is perhaps understandable that neither Texans nor the U.S. Army in the state concentrated entirely on frontier problems in those last days of 1860. With the election of Abraham Lincoln as president, army units soon realized that the state of Texas might conceivably announce its withdrawal from the Union. Some of the Rangers, who so often fought alongside the army, now had to contemplate the possibility of fighting against former friends and allies.

2

Federals, Indians, and the Frontier

1861

From year's end in 1860 to the first weeks of February, 1861, minute-men companies of Rangers, some called up by the governor and some by local communities, guarded the Indian frontier of Texas. Gov. Sam Houston authorized E. W. Rogers to raise a Ranger company of sixty enlisted men to proceed to Fort Belknap and cooperate with Capt. Sul Ross in patrolling the northwestern frontier. They were to regard "every Indian caught this side of Red River as an enemy to Texas."[1] By the end of December Col. William C. Dalrymple, former aide-de-camp to Governor Houston, assumed command of all Ranger forces on the northwestern Indian frontier and established the headquarters of his six companies at the old Comanche Reservation on the Clear Fork of the Brazos near Camp Cooper.

In January Dalrymple began organizing his forces to cover the northwestern frontier. He implemented Houston's orders of the year before that prohibited horse racing, gambling, or liquor within the Ranger camps and instituted the familiar service of constant scouts and patrols. By mid-February Dalrymple located his own company in the vicinity of his new headquarters near the junction of Hubbard's Creek and the Clear Fork of the Brazos, in Stephens County, about midway between the Comanche and Brazos Indian agencies. He established the companies of his battalion on a general north-south line extending from his headquarters: Captain Burleson's company on the upper San Saba River, in two camps twenty-five miles apart; Capt. Curtis Mays near the mouth of the San Saba, covering the ground between that point and Pecan Bayou; Capt. Thomas Harrison's company reinforcing Dalrymple's force at Hubbard's Creek; Capt. David L. Sublett's company on Elm Creek; and E. W. Rogers's company along Lost Valley

Creek in Jack County, patrolling from that point to the Red River. Attached to this force was an "Indian Spy Company" led by Capt. Peter Fulkerson Ross, older brother of Sul Ross. This company, organized on July 1, 1860, consisted of thirty-five "spies" and ten "guides," mostly Tonkawas, who remained in Texas in service to the state.[2]

A period of transition in frontier defense, began amidst confusion in early 1861, as southern states followed South Carolina's lead and passed ordinances of secession. After Lincoln's election groups of secessionists held rallies across the state, condemned Lincoln's coming "abolitionist" government, and broke up meetings of Unionist sympathizers. As advocates of secession clamored for a secession convention, many of them began to organize military units in towns across Texas. Rumors abounded that John R. Baylor was in the process of organizing one thousand men for a "buffalo hunt," believed to be a pretense to seize U.S. Army headquarters at San Antonio, should Texas leave the Union.[3]

Governor Houston responded to the excitement by calling for a special session of the state legislature to meet on January 21, 1861. Houston held off the call for a secession convention; he instead endorsed sending Texas delegates to a convention of southern states to consider future action. But a group of secessionists in the state then issued their own call for a People's Convention to meet at Austin on January 28, 1861, with delegates to be chosen by election on January 8. On February 1, 1861, the Secession Convention of Texas adopted an ordinance of secession which declared Texas a separate sovereign state absolved from all allegiances to the United States. They also voted to submit the ordinance to a vote of the people of Texas on February 23; if approved, the measure would take effect on March 2, 1861. Houston announced the legislature's approval of the ordinance on February 4, and five days later he proclaimed officially that the ordinance would be submitted to the people for ratification.[4]

On February 6 Houston reminded the legislature of a detail almost overlooked by state politicians in the crisis-filled days of January and February—the necessity to provide for an adequate force on the frontier if the nearly three thousand federal troops in the state were withdrawn. The lawmakers immediately made temporary provisions; they directed all counties on the frontier to organize minutemen companies of Rangers of twenty to forty men each, and appropriated an additional twenty-five thousand dollars to supply the companies already in the field under Colonel Dalrymple. The question of frontier defense from February to April, however, came under the direction, so to speak, of a Committee of Public Safety appointed by the Secession Convention to secure the public property in U.S. Army posts across Texas and to remove the federal troops.[5] The context of frontier defense thus altered. During the next two months Texans removed one threat, the U.S. Army, and attempted to hold at bay another menace, the Comanches and Kiowas on the northwestern limits of settled Texas.[6]

The troubled army commander of the Department of Texas, Gen. David Twiggs, twisted and turned to fend off the responsibility of his office as secession approached. The seventy-year-old veteran of the War of 1812, Georgia-born, with a wife from New Orleans, had strong southern sympathies. Not long after his return to Texas from sick leave in December, 1860, Twiggs appealed repeatedly to army authorities for instructions regarding U.S. property in the event Texas seceded. As senior officer in the army next to Gen. Winfield Scott, Twiggs received word that he was to have sole administration of his command, since Scott could not or would not give special advice. A melancholy Twiggs in mid-January asked to be relieved as commander of the department, adding that "as soon as I know Georgia has separated from the Union I must, of course, follow her."[7] The high command in Washington received Twiggs's request on January 28, approved it at once, and sent the desired transfer by mail; Twiggs did not receive the response until February 15.[8]

When the Secession Convention passed its Ordinance of Secession, Twiggs inquired of his government what was to be done with the troops in Texas. Meanwhile he began making plans for provisions and transportation for their removal from the frontier. On February 5, 1861, the day after Twiggs posted his inquiry, the Committee of Public Safety initiated action to deal with federal troops in the state. On this date the Committee divided the frontier line of defense into three districts and commissioned three men with the rank of colonel to take possession of the military posts from the army and to provide for frontier protection. John S. "Rip" Ford, a member of the Committee, received command of the Rio Grande line from Brownsville to a point midway between Fort McIntosh and Fort Duncan. Ben McCulloch assumed command of the middle district from the point midway between Fort McIntosh and Fort Duncan extending to Fort Chadbourne; McCulloch's immediate task concerned General Twiggs and the surrender of the entire department. McCulloch's brother, Henry, then took charge of the extensive line of posts on the northwestern frontier from Fort Chadbourne to the Red River.[9]

The key to a peaceful seizure of the army posts rested with General Twiggs in San Antonio, and it was there that commissioners appointed by the Committee hastened. Negotiations were under way between Twiggs and the commissioners when Twiggs received word on February 15 of his removal from command; his successor, Colonel Waite, was some sixty miles away at Camp Verde. Rumors abounded that the Texans assembled under Ben McCulloch would soon move against the army depots and arsenal located near the Alamo. Twiggs issued orders to officers of the Eighth United States Infantry in the city that no resistance was to be displayed if a force of Texans demanded access to Army headquarters.

Just after 4:00 A.M. on the morning of February 16 a large force under Ben McCulloch, carrying the Lone Star flag before them, swarmed across the downtown plaza and without resistance began to occupy all the U.S. Army buildings. Within a few hours Twiggs basically agreed to the demands already put to him by the commissioners: All U.S. property, excepting the soldiers' arms, would be turned over to Texas, and army units across the state would be granted transit to the coast for transportation back east.[10] The Northern public later reviled Twiggs for his part in the drama acted out in Texas. On March 1, 1861, three days before the inauguration of Abraham Lincoln, the army, at the direction of Pres. James Buchanan, dismissed Twiggs from the service "for his treachery to the flag of his country."[11] Eulogized by the Texas legislature for his patriotism, Twiggs was appointed major general in the Confederate Army in command of the District of Louisiana. Poor health kept him from the active command of his district, and he died on July 15, 1862.[12]

Word of the surrender by Twiggs made its way slowly to the army commands around the state, then being pressed by Rip Ford and Henry McCulloch. McCulloch's activities on the northwestern frontier of Texas require detailed attention. He proceeded to demand the surrender of the forts before Twiggs's orders to do so arrived. Had his action led to an armed conflict, the war's first shots might have been fired in Texas, rather than at Fort Sumter a month later. Here, too, was the most threatened section of the Indian frontier, a sector to be protected by Rangers under McCulloch's command after hostilities with the United States began in South Carolina.

Henry McCulloch began organizing his troops on February 5 and set out for Camp Colorado from Austin six days later. His initial call for companies of one hundred men went to Thomas C. Frost of Comanche County, B. B. Holley of Coryell, James Buckner Barry of Bosque, and D. C. Cowan of San Saba, all of whom were lieutenants in local minutemen companies. McCulloch's first destination was Camp Colorado, in Coleman County, where Capt. Edmund Kirby Smith commanded Company B of the Second United States Cavalry. McCulloch arrived near Brownwood after a trip of six days and 165 miles; but with only two hundred men under his command McCulloch determined to keep a constant watch on the activities of the troops in nearby Camp Colorado while he awaited reinforcements.[13]

On February 22, McCulloch, accompanied by some two hundred men including citizen volunteers from Brownwood, made his way to the post to demand its surrender. About 4:00 P.M. McCulloch entered into negotiations with Captain Smith and, as instructed by the Committee, called upon him to surrender all the arms, horses, ordnance, quartermaster's property, commissary's stores, medical, and hospital stores at the post. At the same time he offered the promise of Confederate service to any who wished to remain in Texas. The captain replied negatively, stating that he could never negotiate terms that would dishonor the troops under his command and, if offered no alternative, would mount his command and try to cut his way through any force which opposed him.[14]

Negotiations continued into the night until McCulloch finally left and agreed to return the next morning. On the next day he dutifully instructed his company commanders to conduct an election among the troops; this was the date set aside for voters of the state to ratify or reject the ordinance of secession passed earlier by the Secession Convention. When negotiations with Smith continued, the captain still insisted that he could not turn over his arms and horses. However, he seemed willing to come to terms about the fort itself, whereupon McCulloch agreed that the federal troops should keep their mounts, arms, transportation, and necessary subsistence stores for a ten-day supply, on condition that everything except rations would be surrendered to an agent of Texas when the troops arrived on the coast.[15]

Just before the two men signed an agreement to that effect, a messenger rode in bearing orders from General Twiggs as well as a circular from the commissioners relating the agreement signed in San Antonio a week earlier. The agreement stated that all soldiers of the U.S. Army should leave the state by way of the coast; they could take their arms with them and carry all medical and quartermaster stores deemed necessary for the journey to the Gulf. McCulloch thought these terms too generous, as did a number of Texans. In fact, Ranger captain Aaron Burleson called the commissioners in San Antonio "a set of jackasses in allowing the regular troops in leaving Texas with their arms." But with tension growing between McCulloch's troops and the federals, Captain Smith made his final arrangements as quickly as possible and departed with his force from Camp Colorado on the morning of February 26.[16]

After he initiated an inventory of stores and provisions at the camp, McCulloch headed for Fort Chadbourne on February 27. He left Lieutenant Frost's undersized company to man Camp Colorado and complete the inventory. Before leaving, however, McCulloch appointed James B. "Buck" Barry and Thomas C. Frost as his senior captains, thus commencing the organization that eventually evolved into regiment strength. To aid Frost's company in shouldering the departed Company B's duties of protecting the frontier, McCulloch placed Captain Burleson's small company on patrol from Camp Colorado to a midway point from Fort Chadbourne. On reconnaissance during the previous week, McCulloch had surveyed the condition of the land, appalled as he viewed the number of deserted and destroyed farms and ranches which resulted from constant Indian raids throughout the area. He lamented that in such a country few recruits and even fewer horses could be found to fill up his ranks, and he determined not to rest until the people of this part of state received adequate protection.[17]

A day's journey brought his force to Fort Chadbourne, on Oak Creek about thirty miles above its junction with the Colorado River. An unusual situation confronted McCulloch upon his arrival at the fort, for part of the detachment of First United States Infantry soldiers there had already surrendered to a body of Texans unauthorized by the Committee of Public Safety. Col. William C. Dalrymple still held his commission from Sam Houston as commander of state forces on the northwest frontier. He had received no information at all from the Committee of Public Safety, so on learning of the passage of the Ordinance of Secession, he took it upon himself to clear all federal troops from his section of the country.

Leading nearly two hundred men, Dalrymple reached the vicinity

of Camp Cooper on February 16 and two days later demanded its surrender by its commander, Capt. Stephen D. Carpenter, Company H,
First United States Infantry. In fact, Dalrymple arrived to find a large
posse of citizens under H. A. Hamner, former editor of *The White Man*,
already keeping close watch on the activities of the soldiers in the fort.
Over two weeks earlier, even before he learned of the secession vote,
Hamner and his friends had determined to move upon Camp Cooper.

Carpenter acknowledged Dalrymple's commission from Governor
Houston and viewed the demand as one authorized by the State of
Texas. Having no orders to the contrary, and believing that his government wished no resistance that would lead to a greater conflict,
Carpenter turned over Camp Cooper to Dalrymple's men. Carpenter's
command pulled out on February 21, made their way to Fort Chadbourne, and arrived there before McCulloch's state force. When Mc-
Culloch negotiated the transfer of Fort Chadbourne with its commander,
Lt. Col. Governeur Morris, First United States Infantry, McCulloch
insisted that Carpenter's men surrender again, this time to him. The
bewildered federals had no choice but to comply. Noting the unauthorized seizure by Dalrymple's force, McCulloch explained that his action required putting all federals on the northwestern frontier "under
the agreement made by General Twiggs and the commissioners at San
Antonio."[18]

Morris indicated that he lacked sufficient transportation to carry
needed equipment and supplies for his men on their journey to the
coast, and McCulloch barely had enough for his own force. Furthermore, the agreement signed by General Twiggs did not specify whether
the state or the army should supply such necessities. McCulloch and
Colonel Morris finally agreed that the federal troops would remain at
Fort Chadbourne with a company of Texans under Captain Holley
stationed nearby. Holley prepared to scout for Indian signs, while
presumably keeping an eye on Fort Chadbourne. By their presence
at the fort Morris's men, under honor to leave as soon as transportation arrived, at least represented in an unusual manner some security
for the region.[19]

Accompanied by Capt. "Buck" Barry's company, McCulloch reached
Camp Cooper late on the night of March 6 and entered the post early
the next morning. Capt. E. W. Rogers commanded the garrison left
there by Colonel Dalrymple. McCulloch, directed by the Committee
to "demand, receive and take charge" of the federal property even if

in the possession of someone other than U.S. soldiers, promptly demanded that his fellow Texans turn over the camp and all its military stores. If there was cause for concern on McCulloch's part over a possible conflict of authority, he was soon put at ease. Rogers was glad to turn over Camp Cooper to someone delegated by the Secession Convention; in fact, his men preferred Indian scouting to the monotony of post duty. McCulloch then ordered Captain Barry's command of forty troopers to take charge of the camp and instructed officers to complete inventory procedures involved in the transfer of property and stores.[20]

Shortly after the affair at Camp Cooper McCulloch ensured that his men would continue to safeguard this threatened part of the Indian frontier. For the next month McCulloch's troopers set up patrols along the line from Fort Chadbourne to Camp Cooper. The move came just in time to replace a worn-out company of Rangers under John Baylor, whose scouting farther west indicated signs of Indian encampments along the headwaters of the Brazos and the Colorado. Because McCulloch's men were too few in number to cover the line from Camp Cooper to the Red River, Dalrymple's companies cooperated and agreed to hold that sector. Meanwhile, McCulloch made an urgent request that the Committee sustain Dalrymple's contingent in the field until a coordinated and reinforced effort could be made for frontier protection. Prior to the Sumter crisis, McCulloch had accompanied several members of the Committee of Public Safety on an inspection tour of the northwestern frontier of the state. He returned to Austin and reported to the committee the findings and opinions of those comprising the tour; as a result of his report, the reassembled Secession Convention adopted a resolution for the defense of the Texas frontier.[21]

In March state and Confederate authorities began that effort. About the same time that Henry McCulloch urged the Convention to organize a system of defense for the Indian frontier, his brother Ben received a request from Leroy Pope Walker, Confederate Secretary of War, to raise a regiment to secure the defenses of the Texas frontier. Ben McCulloch's regiment was to consist of ten companies of sixty to eighty men each; if he declined to accept charge of this force, Walker authorized him to "designate some suitable person for that duty."[22]

Later that month William Simpson Oldham and John Hemphill, two Texas delegates to the Confederate Provisional Congress, informed Secretary Walker of their own views on frontier defense. They outlined three principal sections of the Texas frontier: the length of the Rio Grande from the Gulf to the New Mexico border, the frontier settlements from the Rio Grande to Preston Bend on the Red River, and the stretch from Preston Bend eastward to the Arkansas border. They briefly described the Rio Grande section and expressed the belief that troops of the regular army could hold it by garrisoning fortified points. For the northern section they believed, mistakenly, that no defenses were required, because of the friendly Choctows and Chickasaws who lived north of the Red River.

Their chief concern was with the devastated condition of the line of frontier settlements from the Red River to the Rio Grande. They pointed out to Walker the particular character of troops required for service on this line: "They must be brave, good horsemen, acquainted with the country, and able to perform the most fatiguing service. They must be acquainted with the character and habits of the Indians, and always ready to mount the saddle and start in the pursuit the moment the trail of the enemy is discovered. The volunteer rangers of Texas possess all these requisites." They then recited the well-known litany of the inadequate defense provided by the federal government in years past and outlined the Texas legislature's intentions for providing immediate protection for the frontier. That body provided for the raising of a regiment of one thousand mounted riflemen, enrolled for one year, to be placed on the frontier at once. The state was to arm and equip the regiment initially, but the Texas delegates prevailed upon Walker to accept the regiment into Confederate service, along with the regiment already assigned to Ben McCulloch.[23]

During the last week of March Henry McCulloch informed the secretary of war that his brother had transferred to him the responsibility for raising the volunteer regiment for service on the frontier. By this time Henry McCulloch's men were strung out on patrol against Indian raiders from the Colorado to the Red River. The specific duty of his proposed regiment was to guard against Indian depredations along the frontier. McCulloch requested that he be assigned only the territory then occupied by his companies, from just north of the Rio Grande to the Red River; he argued that even a full regiment would be hard-pressed to guard so extensive an area as the whole expanse of the Texas frontier. In addition, he recommended that Rip Ford remain in command of the Rio Grande line. McCulloch then had in service five under-strength companies, including the company authorized specifically by the Committee of Public Safety; the other four companies he called his "heelfly" force.[24]

A few days later Gov. Edward Clark, in an appeal to Pres. Jefferson Davis, insisted that the Confederate government must assume responsibility for frontier defense in Texas. This must commence with acceptance into Confederate service of the regiment of Rangers recently created by the Texas legislature. Now began the first salvo in a war of conflicting views between Confederate authorities and the Texas government on the issue of frontier defense. The problem centered on the question of money, on who was to bear the expense of frontier protection; within a year, however, it evolved into a state's-rights debate over control of the troops that would serve on the frontier. Conscription and its effect on the Texas frontier counties later compounded the problem.

Secretary of War Walker concluded that the vast expense of maintaining cavalry regiments would likely prevent the Confederate government from receiving into the service both the unit being raised by Henry McCulloch and the force called into being by the Texas legislature. Downplaying the seriousness of the Indian threat, Walker labeled the frontier conflict there "merely predatory and incursional, and carried on only by roving tribes of Indians." He believed one regiment should suffice, while a second regiment of infantry could be sent to the Rio Grande.[25]

Meanwhile, throughout the end of March and early April Henry McCulloch continued to organize the regiment authorized by the Confederacy, while Rip Ford took command of the regiment called forth by the state. Ford's regiment of state troops, eventually strung out along the thousand-mile-line of the Rio Grande, consisted partially of infantry and artillery as well as cavalry. As hoped by Texans, it entered Confederate service as the Second Regiment, Texas Mounted Rifles.[26] The duty for McCulloch's lone regiment then was to guard the Indian frontier of Texas from the Red River to the Rio Grande, a task which in the 1850s had strained both Rangers and one-fourth of the entire United States Army. Such an ambitious assignment would only be as successful as the soldiers who held it. Henry McCulloch set out to find the best.

Designated a colonel by the Provisional Confederate Congress dating from March 4, McCulloch accepted his brother's commission and began recruiting three weeks later. He soon turned over command of the existing troops at Camp Colorado to Capt. Thomas C. Frost and headed for Austin in order to look for new men to bring his regiment up to strength. On March 26 McCulloch ordered his officers to proceed to enroll companies of mounted volunteers for service in the Confederate Provisional Army. For the men he sought, McCulloch set a standard familiar to those who had served as Texas Rangers in years past. A recruit must be over eighteen but under forty-five years of age, a good rider and marksman, a person of good moral character, and not a "professional gambler or habitual drunkard." Each man was to provide his own horse, saddle, blankets, canteen, "six shooting pistol," and, if possible, a shotgun or rifle.[27]

By the early part of April McCulloch had organized his regiment. Ten companies existed, as indicated in the following list of elected captains and counties of organization: William G. Tobin, Bexar County; Governeur Nelson, Bexar County; William A. Pitts, Travis County; Travis H. Ashby, Gonzales County; Green Davidson, Bell County; Thomas C. Frost, Comanche County; James "Buck" Barry, Bosque County; Milton M. Bogges, Rusk County; James H. Fry, Burleson County; and Milton Webb, Lamar County.[28] Six of the companies were ordered to report to San Antonio by April 15, while the other four companies were to remain stationed at either Camp Colorado, Fort Chadbourne, or Camp Cooper. The men already on the frontier who wished to join the new regiment had to be mustered out of state service and into Confederate service; the government sent an officer to Texas to do just that.

By mid-April, then, McCulloch's new regiment entered Confederate service as the First Regiment, Texas Mounted Riflemen, usually referred to by its officers as the First Texas Mounted Rifles. Not only was this the state's first regiment organized for Confederate service, but the original commission to Ben McCulloch was one of the first in the Confederacy. In the months to come most public attention focused on Texas units that headed east to confront Union armies; but within Texas those in the western counties put their faith and lives in the hands of the one thousand men who rode with Henry McCulloch.[29]

On April 21 the dashing Col. Earl Van Dorn, formerly of the Second United States Cavalry, assumed command of the newly created Department of Texas and set about organizing its defense. The day before Van Dorn took charge, a veteran of the U.S. Army in Texas, Edmund Kirby Smith, recommended that two defense lines be established:

one regiment of infantry to occupy the Rio Grande line, with particular attention to the lower Rio Grande from Fort Duncan (Eagle Pass) to Brownsville; and five companies of infantry posted at Fort Inge, Camp Verde, Fort Mason, Camp Colorado, and the vicinity of Fort Belknap to cover the settlement line. To this second line, he said, should be added two regiments of mounted troops concentrated in just a few points, to enable them to converge with force on invaders.[30] Smith's entire plan called for five regiments to be deployed along the two lines of defense. Van Dorn's task, then, was to create similar defensive lines with only the two regiments he had available.

The department commander's proposed system of defense also called for an extensive line of posts to be held along the length of the Rio Grande; the occupying forces would be composed of Ford's Mounted Rifles, one company of infantry, and two artillery batteries. Henry McCulloch's regiment and one artillery battery were to hold a line from a point on the Red River southwestward to Camp Cooper, Fort Chadbourne, Camp Colorado, a point at the junction of the North Concho and Main Concho rivers (present San Angelo), and Fort Mason. The heaviest concentration, four companies and the artillery, was to be on the Red River, with two companies at Camp Cooper, two companies at Fort Chadbourne, and two companies at the North and Main Concho. Only a lieutenant and twenty men were posted at Camp Colorado and Fort Mason.[31]

Barry's and Frost's companies were already at their frontier posts, filling their ranks and electing officers on April 17, when word came of the surrender of Fort Sumter to the Confederate troops at Charleston, South Carolina, just three days earlier. McCulloch still had six of his companies at San Antonio in preparation for a movement to the frontier, but now he chose to meet another threat, the presence of a large contingent of federal soldiers moving to the coast under the agreement signed by General Twiggs and the commissioners. McCulloch was unaware that just the week before Van Dorn had received instructions to hasten to Texas and prepare to seize any federal troops as prisoners of war, upon the condition of hostilities existing between the Confederate States and the United States. McCulloch then wrote to the secretary of war that, unless he received word to the contrary, he would immediately move to force the federals' surrender. Leaving San Antonio with five companies of his regiment, McCulloch headed for Indianola, the embarkation point for the federals. He was too late, however, as word came that the recently arrived Van Dorn had taken charge of the operation and arrested several hundred Union troops waiting to leave.[32]

Before they left for the frontier, however, the First Texas Mounted Rifles had a brief moment of action against the only Union soldiers the regiment would see during its twelve-month enlistment. Van Dorn ordered McCulloch and six of his companies to San Lucas Springs, some thirteen miles west of San Antonio, to arrest nearly three hundred men of the Eighth United States Infantry then on the march to Indianola. The Confederates, including a detachment of cavalry and artillery from Rip Ford's command, totaled approximately thirteen hundred men under Henry McCulloch's direction. On May 9 the last federals left in Texas surrendered to the overwhelming force facing them. Thus ended the relatively smooth transfer of posts, supplies, and responsibility from the United States regulars to the Texas Confederates that had begun with Twiggs's surrender on February 16. Not only did this transfer clear the state of an early military threat, but it also obtained an extensive chain of military posts for Confederate use and secured military stores worth over $1.5 million that would supply the early Confederate war effort in Texas.[33]

The First Regiment, Texas Mounted Riflemen, left San Antonio on May 29 to join the companies already on the frontier. McCulloch prepared to organize and post the defensive line assigned him by Van Dorn. Then, in an order that could have delayed his defensive preparations for some time, the department commander instructed McCulloch to take the bulk of his regiment to the Red River, leaving only detachments at posts along the way. There he was to take command of the state troops organized in north Texas by William Cocke Young, a native of Red River County. This force was then to enter the Chickasaw Nation, in Indian Territory, to capture federal-held Fort Cobb and Fort Arbuckle. Fortunately for the settlers of frontier Texas, McCulloch's regiment never completed this additional assignment outside Texas; word reached Van Dorn that Confederates had already occupied the forts after a federal retreat.[34]

Upon reaching the Red River, McCulloch and Ed Burleson, major of the regiment, left Texas on June 29 and journeyed through Indian Territory to the Wichita-Caddo Reservation. Here the two tribes were in negotiation with Colonel Young for a treaty of peace. McCulloch wished to explain to the assembly of two thousand or more that he planned to pursue the trails of any who raided into Texas, even if the pursuit came to their reserve. He said he would extend them friendship and protection so long as they committed no depredations upon Texas.[35]

McCulloch then turned westward to the domain of the Comanches to see if he could come to some agreement with them. As one did not go deep into Comanche country unprepared, McCulloch and Burleson, along with five companies of the regiment and Tonkawa guides as scouts, traveled to the vicinity of Antelope Hills, north of the Red River. Guided by Charles Goodnight and accompanied by a small escort of about a dozen men, McCulloch met not only with Red Bear and Eagle Chief, of the Comanches, but with Lone Wolf, Satank, and Satanta, of the Kiowas. Thanks to the nearby location of half a regiment of Rangers, McCulloch's party at least left in safety. Nonetheless, the Indian leaders refused to come to terms with the Confederacy because, they said, they preferred to fight the Texans and steal from them.

This expedition also had the dubious distinction of angering the recently appointed Confederate Commissioner to the Indian Nations, Albert Pike. On August 9 Pike had concluded a peace treaty with four bands of Comanches, including some of the very Indians with whom McCulloch just treated. Pike earnestly believed that if Texans would only have patience, all the Comanches could be brought in to reservations. He therefore urged Texas authorities to prohibit any force of Texans from crossing the Red River between the ninety-eighth and one-hundredth meridians of longitude.[36]

When the expedition returned, McCulloch ordered Major Burleson to take charge of the line from Fort Phantom Hill to the Red River, with headquarters at newly created Camp Jackson, located on the southwest bank of the junction of the Big Wichita and Red rivers. He told Burleson to take every precaution to prevent a conflict between his troops and the friendly residents of Indian Territory. McCulloch refused, however, to permit any of these Indians to cross the Red River and hunt on the Texas side or to cross into Texas for any reason unless by permission of an Indian agent and with a white man as escort. Any Indians found south of the river under any other conditions were to be "considered as enemies and treated as such."[37]

Shortly after sending these instructions to Major Burleson, McCulloch received a letter from his brother Ben, then in Indian Territory, relating the Confederate government's desire to make peace with the "wild tribes." McCulloch again cautioned Burleson to be prudent in his dealings with any Indians who indicated a desire to go to a reservation. They were to be given rations and sent on their way to Fort Cobb, in Indian Territory, until a permanent treaty could be made. As word then arrived of increased raids in the Red River counties, McCulloch prepared for aggressive scouting expeditions just the same. He told Burleson "it would be worse than madness to sit still and see them rob and kill our people and not chastise them if within our power."[38]

By mid-summer McCulloch's regiment occupied the intended line; fortunately, until then the Indian raids had been minimal. In addition to the problem of trying to cover the four-hundred-mile line of sparsely settled country with a single regiment, there remained the logistical question of keeping men and horses supplied. Distribution of provisions to the First Texas Mounted Rifles was a problem largely because of the distance between the widely separated posts and lack of transportation facilities. McCulloch partially relieved the problems when he added to his defensive line two abandoned Army outposts, Fort Phantom Hill and Fort McKavett. Supplies shipped northward from San Antonio went to Camp Colorado, which served as the sub-depot for the four posts to the north, Fort Phantom Hill, Camp Cooper, Fort Belknap, and Camp Jackson.[39]

McCulloch placed his old friend from Ranger service, John R. King, as assistant commissary in San Antonio to forward supplies to the regiment as quickly as possible. Even so, the Texans had no regular system for transporting supplies throughout the summer of 1861 because of the scarcity of wagons. To help relieve the situation, McCulloch allowed sutlers to sell supplies and forage at the forts in his command, but he still had to go as far away as Paris, Texas, to find citizens willing to contract with the army. For flour and beef supplies the regiment usually relied upon donations from grateful citizens or purchases by agents who obtained goods "upon the faith of the Confederate States."[40] Lack of ammunition and ordnance stores also created difficulties and led McCulloch to issue a strict caution against wasting ammunition. On at least one occasion soldiers in the command broke off a running battle with Comanches because ammunition nearly ran out.[41]

The regiment settled into the routine of its duties, which consisted chiefly of the patrol operations so familiar to anyone ever associated with the Ranger service. The system devised by McCulloch reflected the manner in which he had established patrols over a decade earlier.

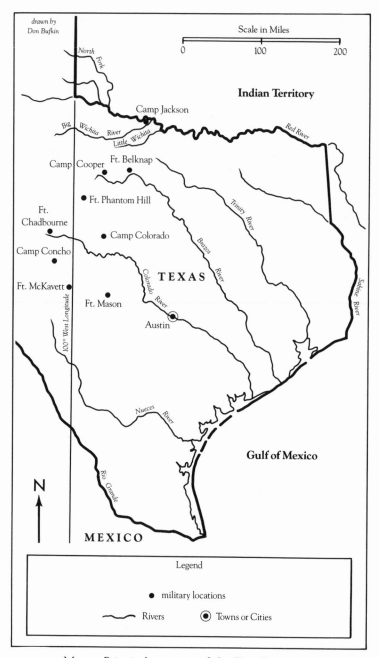

MAP 1. Principal outposts of the First Regiment,
Texas Mounted Riflemen, 1861–62

For example, the instructions given to Captain Barry in June at Camp Cooper are representative of the pattern employed along the entire four-hundred mile line:

> This company will cover the country from its Post at the Willow Springs, on the road to . . . [Camp Jackson], and will keep a detachment of 20 men under a Lieut. on a branch at or near the road, two or three miles beyond the Brazos, to be relieved by similar attachments every two weeks . . . and will keep up weekly scouts, in small parties, from the Post to that detachment, by starting the scouts on each Friday morning, directing them to meet the detachment on the next day. The detachment will send a scout on to the Willow Springs on Sunday, so as to meet and spend each Sunday night at that place, with the scouts from the Red river command.[42]

In this manner the regiment covered every mile at regular intervals, with men from one company able to relay any word of Indians to neighboring commands. The lack of regimental strength necessitated this type of patrol as an alternative to large punitive expeditions.

Expeditions of the size and scope of those of 1858 now had two disadvantages. Obviously, if such a large operation were undertaken, there would be practically no protection left for the settlers along the frontier, as Indian raids occurred more frequently beginning in mid-summer. There was no longer a large force of the U.S. Army to back them up as before, nor anyone else, for that matter. When federal troops threatened an invasion of the coast later in the year, and companies organized for Confederate service outside Texas, the thin line of Rangers on the frontier stood alone against their old foes. Second, Confederate officials insisted that Indian Territory not be violated by Texans chasing fleeing hostiles; this kept the homelands of many of the Comanche and Kiowa raiders off limits to the Texans.

Reluctantly, in September McCulloch withdrew his three companies from Camp Jackson on the Red River because Pike protested their proximity to Indian Territory. This wish to placate the Indian allies of the Five Civilized Tribes in Indian Territory was almost more than Henry McCulloch could bear. He sent word to Major Burleson that "General Pike has blocked the game on us as far as Indian operations are concerned" but admonished him to pursue any Indians who committed depredations in Texas and "follow them no odds where they go, and if you can come up with them whip them."[43]

The regiment whipped few Indians throughout that long summer. Large scouts went out periodically to sweep suspected haunts of hostiles and could be gone for up to three or four weeks at a time. Such operations broke the patrol pattern that sometimes became too familiar to Indians seeking to slip through to the settlements. One such large scout set out in late July to the area between the Pease River and the Prairie Dog Town Fork of the Red River but resulted only in fatigued horses and men. During the first week of August a large band of raiders engaged a detachment under the lieutenant colonel of the regiment, Thomas C. Frost. In a running fight the Texans killed two Indians but suffered the loss of Capt. Green Davidson and a private, both killed. The Indians, on superb mounts, noticed the jaded condition of Frost's horses, then turned and offered battle in the open to their outnumbered pursuers. Frost declined, and his troopers returned to camp. It is not difficult to imagine McCulloch's feelings when he wrote of the episode that "this cannot be regarded as one of those brilliant achievements which so often mark the conflicts between our rangers and the Indians."[44]

McCulloch could understand that lack of forage and hard riding had weakened the horses, but rarely before had a force of Rangers ever failed to attack their Indian opponents, even when outnumbered. Just a week earlier a fight had taken place near the road between Camp Cooper and Camp Jackson; this time, a band of some forty Indians attacked ten men of Captain Barry's Company C and surrounded them on the prairie. With little cover, Barry's men held them off for five hours; five horses and one soldier were killed and six soldiers wounded, while the Indians suffered two killed and an undetermined number wounded.[45] While McCulloch praised the courage of his men, the fact remains that from the time the regiment entered Confederate service in mid-April, over six months passed before it achieved any type of outstanding victory over the Indians, who continued to ravage the frontier.

That first major victory for the regiment came on November 1 when Captain Barry, on an extended scout, defeated a party of Indians, probably Comanches, along the Pease River. For some time McCulloch had planned for an aggressive scouting expedition to sweep through the land north of the headwaters of the Colorado River. On July 17 he left Camp Jackson to journey to Camp Colorado to make final arrangements for the expedition. An enlisted man under McCulloch described the plans in colorful terms: "And should old 'Abe' not send us 'work' from Kansas it is intended to make a Grand Campaign of the entire Regiment against the Red Rascals in the Autumn."[46] Detachments of thirty-five men each from Fort Chadbourne, Camp Cooper, Fort Phantom Hill, and Camp Colorado rendezvoused at the latter post on September 15.

No Indians were spotted until the first of November when, in a running battle, six of Barry's men caught up with a group of Indians who fell behind their comrades. The six soldiers held them at bay until the rest of the detachment came up. They then killed ten of these Indians and wounded two others, while the main body escaped.[47] Few though the victories were, it should be noted that no major incursions by hostile Indians took place on the north-central Texas frontier from mid-October, 1861, to mid-January, 1862. To this it should also be added, as pointed out earlier, that the Indian raids of 1861 did not match the size or intensity of previous years.

Regimental headquarters remained at Camp Colorado through the summer and into the fall, but McCulloch did not remain there in charge. Van Dorn's reassignment east of the Mississippi brought McCulloch to San Antonio on September 4 to become temporary department commander until the arrival of the new commander, Gen. Paul Octave Hebert. McCulloch remained in San Antonio to await Hebert, but upon the general's arrival in Texas on September 18 he relieved McCulloch by dispatch and proceeded to make his headquarters first at Galveston, then permanently at Houston.[48] McCulloch commanded the First Texas Mounted Rifles for a time through his adjutant, William O. Yager, then later through Lieutenant Colonel Frost and Major Burleson.

McCulloch never returned to immediate command of his regiment on the Texas frontier. In late October regimental headquarters moved to Fort Mason, and until the following spring the regiment continued to be run by his subordinates. McCulloch remained in San Antonio and in December assumed command of the new Western Military District of Texas, which embraced not only the military posts northwest, west, and south of San Antonio, but also the posts at Victoria and Saluria. Technically still in command of the First Regiment, Texas Mounted Riflemen, McCulloch shifted his attention to the Rio Grande and Texas coast, just as Hebert and the two department commanders who succeeded him focused on threats to Texas from all sides but minimized the dangers on the Indian frontier.[49]

The people who lived on that frontier never relented in their appeals to the state government for better protection. In this instance, at least, the state's-rights conflict with the Confederate government later in the war perhaps helped retain for the frontier a measure of protection it would never have received from the Confederacy. When Gov. Edward Clark heard rumors in October of 1861 that General Hebert planned to remove McCulloch's regiment from the frontier when its term of enlistment ran out in early spring, he immediately began working toward a plan to provide the best, permanent protection to the Indian frontier. It fell to the newly elected governor, Francis Richard Lubbock, to complete the plan. As he received an increasing number of complaints from the frontier counties in November and December, Lubbock confessed that the force then on the frontier simply did not offer adequate protection. With McCulloch's regiment to reach the end of its enlistment in early spring and devastating Indian raids sure to follow its removal, Governor Lubbock and the Texas legislature prepared to prevent such a crisis.[50]

3

The Frontier Regiment

1862–63

When the Texas legislature met in November of 1861, its members made quite clear the urgent necessity that required them to answer the clamor for frontier defense. The companies of the First Regiment, Texas Mounted Riflemen, were under strength, its commander now had responsibilities that called his attention to South Texas, and the few minutemen companies formed under the law of the previous February were largely ineffectual. The greatest concern, perhaps, lay in the knowledge that the Confederacy, with all its other problems, might not be able after all to maintain an effective military presence on the Indian frontier of Texas.

Gov. Francis Richard Lubbock pointed out to the legislature that the frontier would never be defended properly until the Indians were made to suffer for their raids. Although Lubbock spoke highly of Henry McCulloch's "fine regiment," only infrequently did it mete out punishment to raiders. Realizing that any Confederate force on the frontier was subject only to Confederate command and control, Lubbock anticipated a plan of protection drawn up by Texans knowledgeable of frontier conditions, a plan to be adopted and funded by the Confederate government.[1] As the legislature considered these matters, the Committee on Indian Affairs concluded that the present troops on the frontier were stationed not only too far apart but too far from the line of settlements. These Confederate troops, furthermore, had little assistance from local minutemen units, largely because of lack of cooperation between officers and men and poor communication between these volunteers and the companies of regulars stationed on the frontier.[2]

The debate over frontier defense continued in the state legislature for the first few weeks in December. By this time Henry McCulloch was anxious to withdraw his regiment from the frontier in order to meet Union military threats along the Texas coast. He requested at least six companies of eighty men each, recruited from the frontier counties to replace his forces from Fort McKavett to the Red River. The sooner this could be done, the better, noted McCulloch, as "the Indians follow the buffalo down in the winter and get much nearer our border than in summer and must be closely watched or they will make heavy inroads upon the settlements this winter or towards spring."[3] He believed that few men in his regiment would choose to serve on the frontier after their present term of service. Their reasons were much like those of McCulloch, who wished only that he be sent where he could "at least see the flag of the enemy and hear the roar of their cannon."[4]

McCulloch's companies then serving on the frontier consisted of only about forty men each, with their time of enlistment nearly up. In light of this reality, the legislature took the initiative and acted promptly by passing "An Act to provide for the protection of the Frontier of the State of Texas," approved on December 21, 1861. The body of Rangers established by this bill became known as the Frontier Regiment, formed by a law that called for a twelve-month enlistment of ten companies, with the men furnishing their own weapons, horses, and accoutrements. It called for nine companies to be raised in counties along the frontier, with one company each from the following groups of counties: Clay, Montague, Cooke, and Wise; Young, Jack, Palo Pinto, and Parker; Stephens, Eastland, Erath, and Bosque; Coryell, Hamilton, Lampasas, Comanche, and Brown; San Saba, Mason, Llano, and Burnet; Gillespie, Hays, and Kerr; Blanco, Bandera, Medina, and Uvalde; Frio, Atascosa, Live Oak, Karnes, and Bee; El Paso and Presidio. The tenth company was to be raised by the governor from any section of the state.[5]

The new law even touched upon the tactics to be used by the regiment. It directed that the companies were to be divided into detachments of at least twenty-five men, stationed just beyond the line of settlements from some point on the Red River to the Rio Grande. The posts of the regiment were to be about twenty-five miles apart and, in a system reminiscent of McCulloch's Texas Mounted Rifles, scouts from each post were to journey to adjacent posts once a day. Of primary importance, according to Governor Lubbock, was the stationing of the recruits in the vicinity of their home counties. Often fearful of leaving for Confederate service because of dangers to their families left behind, these men would leave "others free to give their services against our Abolition Enemies."[6]

The law specified that the troops raised under the act should be subject to the rules and regulations of the Confederate States Army, adding emphatically that the regiment "shall always be subject to the authorities of the State of Texas for frontier service, and shall not be removed beyond the limits of the State of Texas." The legislature then urged that the newly formed regiment should be accepted into the Confederate States Army in lieu of the First Regiment, Texas Mounted Riflemen. Lawmakers and the governor saw this plan as "the most effective and economical mode of frontier protection."[7]

Texas congressmen in Richmond, along with the secretary of war, received copies of the bill, and it quickly came up for debate before the Confederate Congress. On January 17, 1862, that body enacted a law authorizing the secretary of war to receive the proposed Frontier Regiment into the service of the Confederacy for the protection of the Indian frontier of Texas. Congress also concurred with the law as passed, including the stipulation that the regiment should not be removed from Texas during its term of service. This would have been the culmination of what Texans had wanted from a national government since the early years of statehood—a force of Rangers on the frontier paid for and provisioned by the government but under the direction of Texans. It was not to be; five days later Pres. Jefferson Davis vetoed the act. He explained that the measure withheld the control of the executive of the Confederate States over such troops and necessarily complicated the Confederacy's system of military administration. The primary clash came over the Texas legislature's wish to keep the regiment under state control; for two years the state and national governments debated the point while, as one historian put it, the regiment's "orphan troopers stayed alive by hunting buffalo."[8]

While Austin and Richmond debated, the unglamorous life of those Rangers on frontier patrol continued as before, with some men no doubt marking time until their enlistment ran out. Constant drilling of the men continued, and while such exercises right out of Hardee's *Light Infantry Tactics* were of dubious use in a running Indian fight, some of the officers hoped that close attention to army procedure would bring them promotion and transfer to another theater of war. Colonel McCulloch continued to require strict obedience to regimental orders that

prohibited horse racing, card playing, or gambling of any form, orders
similar to the standards laid down by Sam Houston when he commissioned minutemen companies of Rangers for frontier service. Special
attention prohibiting the possession of alcohol among his troops extended to preventing sutlers from selling whiskey to anyone in the regiment, "except for medical purposes." Ironically, the ban against horse
racing, in the orders above, emanated from Fort Mason, site of numerous runs of "the Fort Mason Derby" by men of the Second United
States Cavalry during the summer of 1856.[9]

On February 1, 1862, the men of the Texas Mounted Rifles elected
James "Buck" Barry as major to replace Ed Burleson, Jr., who had resigned in December. Barry then took direction of the northern portion of the defensive line, from Camp Cooper to the Red River, while
Lieutenant Colonel Frost handled affairs south of Camp Cooper. Orders
came to the captains of the regiment to begin assembling the companies of the First Regiment, Texas Mounted Riflemen, for discharge in
April at Fort Mason. While on the way to the fort, the regiment waged
its last Indian fight. Buck Barry's old company encountered a sizable
Indian party along the San Saba on April 9, 1862. The raiders wounded
four of Barry's men, but they suffered three killed and one wounded
themselves and soon retreated.

Most of the companies reported to Fort Mason by mid- to late April
to discover disconcerting news, for on April 16 the Confederate Congress passed the country's first military draft law. This act of conscription specified that men between the ages of eighteen and thirty-five
already in service were to continue serving for three years from the
date of their enlistment. A few of the men went back to frontier service, but most of them enlisted in the Eighth Texas Cavalry Battalion,
a unit that later merged into what became the First Texas Cavalry
Regiment.[10]

At the expense of the State of Texas, while McCulloch's men went
about their duties on the Indian frontier, the Frontier Regiment began
organizing in January of 1862. In the first week of the year Governor
Lubbock appointed enrolling officers who had little time to recruit the
required one hundred men per company (with no fewer than sixty-
four privates in each). The enrolling officers were to place a priority
on men who presented themselves for service with good horses and
proper arms; they were to emphasize finding those who were "Indian
fighters." On January 29, 1862, Lubbock appointed the ranking officers

of the regiment: Col. James M. Norris, Lt. Col. Alfred J. Obenchain, and Maj. James Ebenezer McCord.[11]

In the midst of these preparations, a new militia law also went into effect. Passed by the legislature, as proposed earlier by Governor Lubbock, the law of December 25, 1861, provided for the enrollment (with numerous exemptions) of free white males in Texas between the ages of eighteen and fifty. The bill created thirty-three brigade districts in Texas, including the counties along the frontier line, with the militia in each liable to take the field upon the judgment of the governor in time of "invasion, insurrection or rebellion."[12] In 1862 and 1863 the militia in the districts adjoining the frontier gave only occasional aid against the Indian threat, although the Twenty-First Brigade District often rendered extensive service. This district contained the counties of the northwestern frontier of the state, the sector hardest hit by Indian raids.

Meanwhile, the Frontier Regiment continued to organize. On the day of their appointment, the new officers received orders to journey immediately to the frontier. They were to inspect the frontier line for the best location of the proposed outposts of the regiment, making arrangements for their men to occupy the line by mid-March. Between March 17 and April 7 Colonel Norris posted his troopers along the new defensive line.

Eighteen camps were occupied for use of the regiment. Part of A. Brunson's Company A deployed in northeastern Wichita County, not far from the Big Wichita, with the rest probably at the old Texas Mounted Rifles camp at the junction of Beaver Creek and the Big Wichita River, in southwestern Wichita County. This company soon shifted eastward to Red River Station, in Montague County. Part of Capt. Jack Cureton's Company B was posted at Camp Cureton, where the Gainesville–Fort Belknap road crossed the West Fork of the Trinity River, in Archer County, with the rest of the company at Camp Belknap near Fort Belknap. Half of Capt. John Salmon's Company C was stationed at Camp Breckenridge, in Stephens County; the other half at Camp Salmon near Sloan's Ranch on the East Fork of Hubbard's Creek, in northeastern Callahan County. Half of Capt. T. N. Collier's Company D was posted at Camp Pecan, where the Camp Cooper–Camp Colorado Road crossed Pecan Bayou, in Callahan County; the other half at Camp Collier at Vaughn's Springs on Clear Creek, in Brown County. Half of Capt. N. D. McMillan's Company E was stationed at Camp McMillan near Hall's Spring at the headwaters of Richland Creek, in San Saba County; the other half at Camp San Saba, where the Camp Colorado–Fort Mason Road crossed the San Saba River.

Other companies were similarly deployed. Half of Capt. H. T. Davis's Company F located at Camp Llano near the mouth of Rock Creek on the Llano River, in Mason County; the other half at Camp Davis on Whitlock Creek about four miles from its junction with the Pedernales River. Half of Capt. Charles De Montel's Company G deployed at Camp Verde, two miles below old Camp Verde, in Kerr County; the other half at Camp Montel on the head of Seco Creek, in Bandera County. Half of Capt. J. J. Dix's Company K was posted at Camp Dix where the Sabinal–Uvalde road crossed the Rio Frio, in Uvalde County; the other half at Camp Nueces where the San Antonio–Eagle Pass Road crossed the Nueces River. Half of Capt. Thomas Robb's Company H was stationed at Camp Robb where the San Antonio–Eagle Pass Road crossed Elm Creek, with the other half at Rio Grande Station and old Fort Duncan.[13]

Eventually, only nine companies of the regiment entered the service because John S. "Rip" Ford's regiment occupied the line from Fort Brown to Fort Bliss. Ford's assignment served to make up for the failure of citizens in Presidio and El Paso counties to raise their quota of soldiers for the Frontier Regiment. The patrols set up by these companies, or outposts of about fifty men each, differed little from the system used by the Texas Mounted Rifles. Units patrolled from their camp to the adjacent camp to the south at two-day intervals, and each patrol usually consisted of five privates and one officer.

Plotting the Frontier Regiment's line of outposts on a map reveals that the defensive line was not as far westward as the one drawn the year before by Earl Van Dorn, although there were twice as many camps. The sector on the exposed northern portion of the line remained about the same; it ran from the vicinity of Fort Belknap to Red River Station on the Red River, rather than to Camp Jackson on that same river. It was this section of the line, so vulnerable to raids of Comanche and Kiowa tribesmen coming from Indian Territory and the Texas Panhandle, that saw the greatest concentration of strength throughout the Frontier Regiment's length of service.[14]

The regiment got off to an inauspicious start in the spring of 1862.

MAP 2. Posts of the Frontier Regiment, 1862–63

On April 9 a party of about twelve Indians killed a small boy, wounded another, and severely wounded a man some twelve miles west of Lampasas. The raiders escaped with only one casualty. Not long afterwards, some enlisted men of the Frontier Regiment "behaved most cowardly and disgracefully"; they refused to obey orders and then ran away when approached by a small group of Indians. Thus began a series of courts-martial that continued throughout the spring and summer.

Colonel Norris, the forty-two-year-old commander of the regiment, failed to command the respect of his men, unlike his predecessor on the frontier, Henry McCulloch. Norris, a former lawyer and merchant, simply did not have the experience of serving on the Indian frontier that warranted his position. The colonel resorted to courts-martial in an effort to establish discipline; predictably, the situation grew worse, and Norris became even more unpopular. The discipline problem extended even to the officers. During the summer of 1862 Captain Cureton became involved in a quarrel with Lieutenant Colonel Obenchain, and as a result Obenchain brought charges against Cureton. Two of Cureton's friends murdered Obenchain but escaped and were never brought to justice. This debacle brought Major McCord to the position of lieutenant colonel of the regiment, and Buck Barry took McCord's place as major.[15]

To add to these woes, the problem of logistics that plagued so many Texas commands during the war surfaced almost immediately. Shipments of ammunition and percussion caps rarely met a regular schedule during the years that the state handled the provisioning of the regiment, and powder remained in short supply. In June of 1862 Norris complained that the poor quality of the powder made it unreliable. As he put it, "a great part of the powder sent us would not kill a man ten steps from the muzzle . . . loaded with all the powder that could be forced into the cylinder."

This shortage of powder and shot continued throughout the following year. In April the regiment requested that the Texas State Military Board supply five thousand pounds of powder to cover the period from May 1 to October 31. Even though the state's Chief of Ordnance ordered one thousand pounds to be shipped right away, the powder still had not reached the regiment a month later. The regiment relied for supplies on what they could procure themselves or obtain through channels in Austin by contracts with civilians. The regiment apparently had no commissary officer the caliber of John King, of the Texas

Mounted Rifles, and a lack of forage, pack saddles, and camp equipage remained a problem.[16]

The adjutant and inspector general of Texas, Jeremiah Yellott Dashiell, evidently concluded otherwise. In October of 1862 he reported that the regiment was efficiently armed and "has been most bountifully supplied with camp and garrison equipage." Dashiell's report indicated that the nine companies of the regiment averaged an effective strength of 115 men, with the total force at 1,050. By contrast, in late Spring, 1862, Major Barry estimated the regimental strength at over 1,200, while Colonel Norris's official report for the last six months of 1862 gave the strength as 1,153 officers and enlisted men. Dashiell's report not only enumerated the commissary and quartermaster stores available but also cited the effectiveness of the force in its assigned duties on the frontier. The operations of the first six months resulted in 21 Indians killed and two hundred horses captured. Taking into account Dashiell's exaggeration, and noting that there had been fewer Indian raids than in the period immediately prior to the Civil War, the Frontier Regiment's performance in 1862 may be judged adequate. Nonetheless, it was not what many Texans expected of a Ranger regiment on the frontier. The Indians, too, quickly discovered the weakness of a patrol system so familiar in routine and during the winter of 1862–63 began making more numerous and bolder raids.[17]

Dashiell's embellishment of the Frontier Regiment's prowess is explained by noting the actual purpose of his report to Gen. Paul Hebert. With the original financial appropriation for the regiment nearly exhausted, the state government once more called upon the Confederacy to receive the unit into the army. In the name of Governor Lubbock, Dashiell offered the regiment to the commander of the District of Texas, General Hebert, with the proviso that it be used to protect the Indian frontier. A month later Governor Lubbock received a reply from Assistant Adjutant-General Samuel Boyer Davis. The offer of a mounted regiment supposedly so well armed and equipped appealed to Hebert, and he accepted the regiment into Confederate service, subject to approval by President Davis. He added the following stipulations: first, another company should be added to the regiment to bring it to a full complement under Confederate Army regulations; second, the regiment should be offered without conditions or restrictions as to service or command; third, the regiment must be mustered into service for three years or the duration of the war; and lastly, the department commander would receive the regiment into service when the state legislature complied with the conditions above.[18]

Texas officials would soon have another department commander to deal with over the transfer of the Frontier Regiment. The theatrical Maj. Gen. John Bankhead Magruder arrived in Texas under a cloud of disfavor because of his conduct during the Seven Days' Campaign in Virginia in June and July of 1862. He would soon somewhat redeem himself by recapturing Galveston from Union troops in January of 1863. For the moment, Magruder was anxious to receive the services of another regiment of cavalry for Confederate service, and he assumed that Richmond would soon approve the transfer of the regiment. With little regard for conditions on the Indian frontier, he then ordered Brig. Gen. Hamilton Prioleau Bee, commander of the Sub-Military District of the Rio Grande, to prepare to take charge of five companies of the Frontier Regiment and to post them at Ringgold Barracks, on the Rio Grande, in anticipation of a supposed federal invasion of the lower Texas coast.

Even though Governor Lubbock proposed originally to transfer the regiment with no restriction on its service, he was frankly alarmed by the prospective Confederate plan for removing over half the regiment from the frontier without plans for replacing them. He therefore issued a call for an extra session of the legislature to convene on February 3, 1863, to consider, among other items of discussion, the dilemma created by the proposed transfer of the Frontier Regiment.[19] Lubbock once more stated his views before that body. It was the duty of the Confederate government to protect the Texas frontier. He explained, however, that he simply could not approve dividing the regiment, even if it meant that the transfer could not take place. Unless protection be afforded to the frontier counties, he noted, "the frontier must recede . . . for just as soon as you fail to keep up a system of defense in your outer counties, [the Indians will] press forward upon the interior, murdering and robbing."[20]

The financial imperative was always present in Texas officials' desire to have the Confederacy assume responsibility for frontier defense. The cost of sustaining the Frontier Regiment for the first ten months of its existence was $800,000. Yet Lubbock and most of the legislators were unwilling to relieve a financial burden by acquiescing to Confederate control if doing so might strip the frontier of its best means of defense. Lubbock then outlined a new plan of frontier defense, one that had its roots in the minutemen companies of Rangers of years past. He proposed that each of twenty-five frontier counties from the Red River to the Rio Grande organize its own company of one captain and twenty enlisted men to offer protection to the frontier in the vicinity of the county. If the men and home county could provide arms, horses, and subsistence for these companies, the cost to the state could be held to $300,000 per year. The state could then turn over the Frontier Regiment to the Confederacy, and the Confederacy would presumably transfer a unit of regimental strength to the frontier to replace the minutemen companies.[21]

The legislature rejected Lubbock's county plan, in the expectation that an arrangement could still be made with Richmond to transfer the Frontier Regiment to Confederate service. Accordingly, Lubbock set out to reorganize the regiment. To meet the requirements of the Confederate States Army regulations, Lubbock disbanded the regiment and then reorganized it into ten companies mustered into service for a period of three years, with the new title of Mounted Regiment, Texas State Troops. However, Texans continued to call the outfit by its original name, the Frontier Regiment. Colonel Norris tendered his resignation, and James Ebenezer McCord took his place as colonel, elected by the men rather than appointed by Lubbock.[22]

With the reorganization of the regiment completed on February 11, 1863, the legislature enacted a frontier defense bill. The new act authorized the governor to transfer the regiment to Confederate service, with the stipulation that it "shall be retained and remain upon the Indian frontier of the State of Texas, for its protection; in which event said regiment shall be subject solely to the military authorities of the Confederate States."[23] This plan basically called for the same condition rejected by President Davis a year earlier, but now Lubbock prevailed upon him to reconsider.

Lubbock's written statement to President Davis contained a brief summary of the United States' past attempts to protect the settlers of the Texas frontier and emphasized the state's necessary reliance on "the light troops known as the Texas Ranger." The governor pointed out the patriotic zeal of the frontiersmen of Texas who had gone to fight for the Confederacy, "leaving their wives and children on the frontier, subject to be butchered by savages"; these men trusted in Texas to protect their families. This the state had done, argued Lubbock, and its effort deserved the consideration of the Confederate government to remedy the problem of frontier defense and to relieve the Texas treasury of the burden. He once more implored Davis to accept the transfer of the Frontier Regiment with the single stipulation that its service should remain on the Texas frontier.[24]

While waiting for Jefferson Davis to reply, General Magruder, to whom Lubbock tendered the regiment, made plans to include it as part of his order of battle. Just one day after Lubbock wrote his letter to Davis, Magruder, subject to the president's approval of the transfer, turned over defense of the Indian frontier to Brig. Gen. William Read Scurry, commander of the Eastern Sub-District of Texas. Magruder instructed Scurry to form a defensive line from Montague County, adjacent to the Red River, to Fort Clark, near Bracketville. The choice of Scurry for this command was an unusual one, not because of ability, as the forty-two-year-old former lawyer was an adequate commander, but because the sub-district he commanded embodied that portion of Texas east of the Brazos River. Such a command covered only the extreme northern section of the frontier line assigned by Magruder. Most of the four thousand men he commanded were located in the Houston-Galveston vicinity in southeastern Texas. A more logical choice would have been the Western Sub-District commander, General Bee, though he had earlier protested that his headquarters at Goliad and attention to the south Texas coast and Mexico border rendered him unable to take charge of the Indian frontier. General Magruder then ordered Col. William Bradfute to take immediate command of the Indian frontier, subordinated to General Scurry. Bradfute was to be given a regiment of regulars to cover the northern part of the line, while some companies of the Frontier Regiment would cover the southern end.[25]

As plans progressed for Confederate military authorities to assume responsibility for the frontier, word arrived in Austin from President Davis. He still refused to accept the Frontier Regiment if bound by the condition that it remain under the direction of Texas, rather than the Confederacy. It would be imprudent, however, to reason that Confederate control would have ensured better protection for the Texas frontier counties. In planning his frontier defense line, Magruder directed Scurry to require the regimental commanders of the proposed line "to spread out their companies as much as possible, so as to form a secure protection for persons and property."[26] The weakness of such a passive defense readily showed in Colonel Norris's direction of the Frontier Regiment, in which aggressive scouting expeditions, seen previously on occasion by the Texas Mounted Rifles, was absent. Col. James McCord would now have an opportunity to improve the system.

When McCord assumed command in February of 1863, the regiment finally had someone in charge who, unlike Norris, had practical experience on the Indian frontier. Upon arriving in Texas a scant ten years earlier, McCord had sound employment in leading a survey party to locate lines for a new chain of counties along the western edge of the Texas frontier. In this manner he had become familiar with the terrain over which he later led his regiment. In 1860, when Governor Houston ordered out local Ranger companies to help defend the frontier, McCord served a six-month term as first lieutenant in Capt. Ed Burleson's company and then served with William C. Dalrymple's command on the northwestern frontier of Texas in early 1861.[27] His Ranger background prepared him for the task at hand in 1863.

Armed with evidence that the current passive patrol system was breaking down, McCord began plans to institute a series of aggressive actions against the Comanche and Kiowa raiding parties. He called upon his captains to express their views on discontinuing the patrol system, and after he received positive responses, the reorganization began. By that time the patrol system operated from more than just the original camps selected for the regiment. Through the years, detachments had occupied many of the old U.S. Army forts, including Camp Cooper and Forts Phantom Hill, Chadbourne, McKavett, Croghan, and Mason.

McCord now placed Maj. W. J. Alexander in command of four companies of the regiment along the southern sector of the line, from Camp Colorado to the Rio Grande. In the heavily threatened northern sector, six companies were placed under Lt. Col. James "Buck" Barry, who was probably the most experienced Indian fighter in the regiment. Barry's men covered the line from Camp Colorado to Red River Station, in Montague County. The forty-one-year-old Barry, twelve years McCord's senior, combined his vast experience of Indian warfare with McCord's administrative ability and leadership qualities to lead the Frontier Regiment to the days of its greatest effectiveness—the summer and fall of 1863.[28]

From his headquarters at Camp Colorado, on May 26, 1863, McCord ordered the regular patrol system discontinued. The new scouting expeditions used larger, stronger contingents of Rangers to sweep areas to the west and northwest of their camps; this method resembled the extended scouts undertaken from time to time by McCulloch's Texas Mounted Rifles. Often of company strength or greater, these reconnaissances would take about three to four weeks to complete. Even though the official order to change the system came in late May, Barry anticipated the directive; he had previously ordered portions of three companies on a large scout north of the Red River, in the vicinity of the Wichita Mountains. The companies split up on the way back and reached their camps in mid-June. No Indian fights took place, but data collected on the availability of grass and water in the vicinity of the Red River could be used for future forays.[29]

Not all scouts undertaken that summer were large ones, but even smaller ventures were aggressive in nature. An example is a scout undertaken by Capt. M. B. Lloyd, who left from Camp Colorado with seven men on July 19. His patrol traveled up the Clear Fork of the Brazos for five days and, after finding Indian signs, journeyed to Camp Cooper for supplies and reinforcements. Bolstered by the addition of eight men from that post, Lloyd and his men returned to the area and, as expected, came upon a party of Indians equal in number to the Texans. The Rangers surprised their foes, and a sharp fight on horseback ensued, leaving one Texan killed, four wounded, and the Indians in flight. Lloyd cut short the pursuit, sent to Camp Cooper for assistance, and renewed the chase with fresh horses. The Indians had too much of a lead, however, and after tracking them for twenty-five miles, Lloyd's men turned back.

Such fights were typical of those throughout the rest of the year. There were no major battles involving scores of combatants, but dozens of small skirmishes were made possible by the relentless scouts, or sweeps, of the frontier, particularly in that exposed sector protected by Barry's men. Activities now only faintly resembled the regular patrols of Norris's system. The exception was the express system set up by McCord, whereby mail and dispatch runs regularly went from camp to camp. In this way, Indian signs leading to the settlements could often be discovered, and McCord could gather information from the extreme limits of his defense line at least every two weeks.[30]

Although a major offensive operation was planned on the scale of those of 1858, it never took place. In May of 1863 Colonel McCord began preliminary preparations for a proposed three-month expedition

into Indian Territory. Initially, he planned the move to take place between September and December of that year, with Fort Belknap as
a probable site of supply concentration and a jumping-off point for
the campaign. Governor Lubbock never gave his approval for such an
operation, partly because he thought the regiment might be needed
to repel a federal invasion after the fall of Vicksburg and also because
the meager funds appropriated for the regiment ran low by late summer.

Two additional reasons concerned conditions along the northwest
frontier. Captain Rowland, stationed in Montague County, expressed
the view that the citizens along his part of the line feared an onslaught
of Indians if so many of the regiment were sent on an extended expedition. Lastly, confirmation of plans for massive raids into the counties just south of the Red River came to the governor from an unusual
source, General Magruder, headquartered in Houston. Magruder heard
rumors of such plans and requested Governor Lubbock to concentrate
the Frontier Regiment at Fort Belknap where, under Confederate officers and authority, the force could meet the coming threat. Ever mind-
ful of state authority and aware of the logistical nightmare of concen-
trating the regiment for an unspecified length of time for a raid that
might not materialize, Lubbock cautioned McCord not to yield control to Confederate command but to be ready to concentrate at Belknap if the need arose.[31]

McCord's change of policy brought immediate results. Within months
the Frontier Regiment fought more engagements with Indians and captured more horses than at any time previously. Yet in the fall of 1863
the regiment faced another problem never before encountered by Rangers on the frontier, the job of policing the frontier counties for men
who evaded the conscription laws.[32] The duty entailed arresting draft
evaders and deserters and turning them over to the proper authorities.
This seemingly secondary role for the regiment quickly expanded, as
the problem escalated among state and Confederate forces across all
of north Texas and the northwestern Indian frontier. Even the omni-
present Indian menace receded in importance as attention turned to
deserters and concomitant problems.

To better understand how Texas and Confederate authorities cooperated to meet these twin threats in the midst of Civil War, it is necessary to examine the circumstances that led to the creation of the
Northern Sub-District of Texas, the organizational structure designed

to manage these problems. Such a discussion reports not only the manner of protection given this part of Texas, by local militia rather than the Texas Mounted Rifles or the Frontier Regiment, but also reviews the conditions that transformed the Texas frontier into a Trans-Mississippi haven for draft evaders, deserters, and renegades.

4

Creation of the Northern Sub-District

The most active defense of the Indian frontier during the last two years of the war remained, as it had for the first two years, on the northwest line of organized counties. As Lt. Col. James "Buck" Barry noted, "Most of the important operations along the northern part of the Frontier Regiment's line of defense centered around Fort Belknap, which faced the hostile tribes across the Red River."[1] Throughout the term of service of Henry McCulloch's Texas Mounted Rifles and the Frontier Regiment, the frontier was threatened along a general line from Cooke County westward to Clay County, then southward to Eastland County. The protection offered to the counties along this line in 1861–63, like that offered by the U.S. Army and Texas Rangers in the 1850s, was never enough to eliminate the raids of Comanches and Kiowas from north of the Red River or from the Texas Panhandle. Local needs for defense brought forth local responses to supplement the force stationed permanently on the frontier.

Until the passage of the new Militia Law in December of 1861, the counties along the northwest frontier complemented the regular defense force with minutemen companies established by the "Minute Men Law" passed by the Texas legislature the previous February. In counties along and adjacent to the Red River, these companies of fewer than forty men each helped spread the alarm in the event of an Indian attack and then gave chase as far as practicable. Although they were not constantly in the field, these guardians of the frontier maintained, or attempted to maintain, a high state of readiness in order to react at a minute's notice. By law, no more than ten men and one commissioned officer were on patrol at any one time along the county lines. It was not an unfamiliar routine; local groups of citizens, already in the habit of responding to Indian threats, also regularly patrolled county lines in search of runaway slaves.

In addition, the commissioners' court in some communities established patrols for local protection during the summer of 1861, because much of the manpower had left to enroll in state or Confederate units. During the phase of the full moon the minutemen patrols intensified; for this short period more men were called upon to maintain regular patrols across the northern and western boundaries of each county. The frontiersmen believed that a "Comanche moon" gave Indians better light to ride by. The minutemen may also have suspected that the Comanches rarely raided during a crescent moon, as the Indians believed that imminent rain would slow down the riders and leave mud to give away their tracks.[2]

Small parties of raiders continued to slip through the grasp of McCulloch's Texas Mounted Rifles to raid the settlements beyond, and the counties on the northwest frontier cried for more protection from the state. Now, however, an additional factor emerged. Evidence accumulated by Gov. Edward Clark by late spring of 1861 led him to believe that much of the Indian trouble stemmed from provocation by Kansas Jayhawkers.[3] Before the governor could react to this menace from Indian Territory, the citizens of north Texas took it upon themselves to do so. A rumored move by federal troops or Jayhawkers against north Texas led Mexican War veteran William Cocke Young, of Cooke County, to act. He gathered a makeshift regiment of more than five hundred men, crossed the Red River, and seized the federal forts in Indian Territory. This force crossed the river during the first week in May of 1861 and by May 5 proceeded to occupy forts Arbuckle, Cobb, and Washita, all abandoned by retreating federals under Lt. Col. William H. Emory.[4]

To offer more permanent protection against this new threat, Governor Clark mustered into service four regiments. Drawn from the counties between the Red River and Dallas–Fort Worth, these troops were to protect the Red River line from Montague County to the Louisiana border. The governor called out these four regiments for a twelve-month term of service, but he could offer them only a promise of being paid by future legislation. Meanwhile, the men were to furnish their own horses and arms. One of the regiments was already in the field, under Young; the other three, initially known as the First Texas Division, consisted of enthusiastic volunteers mustered during June and July of 1861.

In only a short while it became evident that these four regiments would not be stationed the full twelve months on the Red River line. Had they been, the northern flank of McCulloch's First Texas Mounted Rifles, then covering the Indian frontier, would have been aided immeasurably. At the time, however, McCulloch's force was believed to be sufficient, and the state did not want to bear the burden of maintaining an entire division, now idle, on its northern frontier. Cautioning Governor Clark on the dangers of keeping volunteers inactive for a long period of time, Colonel Young requested that the division be allowed to join Gen. Ben McCulloch's army in Missouri. Clark was unable to authorize such a move unless the Confederate Army accepted the force into its service, or until the governor of Missouri requested aid from Texas. Clark's appeal to General Hebert to accept the division was successful, and the regiments were transferred to Confederate authority in October of 1861; the division soon left Texas for service in Arkansas and Missouri.[5]

In December of 1861 the legislature reorganized the state militia; of the thirty-three brigade districts created, the Twenty-first Brigade, more than any other, actively participated in frontier protection. This district encompassed the northwest frontier of the state and included the counties of Cooke, Denton, Wise, Montague, Jack, Young, Clay, Wichita, Archer, Wilbarger, Baylor, Throckmorton, Hardeman, Knox, Haskell, Stephens, Shackelford, and Jones. Each district was to maintain a brigade strength of at least 400, and as many as 1,200 men. Maintaining these numbers would be difficult for the Twenty-first Brigade, for the eleven counties west of Jack and Clay had a combined population in 1860 of only 720 men, women, and children. Indian raids early in the war soon forced settlers to completely abandon Clay County, leaving a vast part of the district to be protected initially by McCulloch's Texas Mounted Rifles and later by a few companies of the Frontier Regiment and the Twenty-first Brigade militia.[6]

When Governor Lubbock reorganized the militia in 1861–62, his first choice for a brigadier general to command the Twenty-first Brigade District had been James Bourland, of Cooke County. Bourland declined the appointment, but he later figured prominently in frontier defense in another capacity from 1862 until the end of the war. William Hudson accepted the leadership of the Twenty-first and served until the militia was again reorganized two years later. Hudson, like Bourland a native of South Carolina, was also a Cooke County resident. Earlier, in May of 1861 as a member of the Cooke County commissioners' court, he had directed the outfitting and supplying of the first company organized in Gainesville. General Hudson established brigade headquarters at Gainesville and began the slow process of organizing the companies, battalions, and regiments of his brigade. As the law required, justices of the peace of each county acted as enrolling officers, and all white males between the ages of eighteen and fifty were expected to accept service in either the Confederate Army or the militia. In counties with no justice of the peace, Hudson appointed respected men in the community to handle the job. For example, in Wise County he selected thirty-seven-year-old John W. Hale, a former sheriff of Wise County, who continued in the post through all organizations of the militia during the war.[7]

In January of 1862 the First Regiment, Texas Mounted Riflemen, had guarded the western extreme of the Twenty-first Brigade District, but it will be recalled that late in 1861 Henry McCulloch, on the insistence of Indian Commissioner Albert Pike, had pulled his companies away from their Red River camp in northern Clay County. Therefore, the Confederate troops charged specifically with protection of the frontier, nearest to the more populous area of the Twenty-first Brigade District, operated out of Fort Belknap, in Young County, with patrols that extended to the Red River. The Frontier Regiment later established a temporary post on the Red River at Preston Bend, in Grayson County, during the summer of 1862. Nevertheless, counties along and adjacent to the Red River relied heavily upon local militia and volunteer units for protection against Indian raids from the northwest and against the growing threat of Jayhawkers and federal regulars from the northeast.

Volunteers in these counties worked to strengthen the defenses against Indian assaults. One prominent citizen went so far as to plan a citizens' expedition to go into Indian Territory and catch the hostiles by surprise. Oliver Loving believed such a move could not only recover more than two thousand stolen horses but also surmised that "the Indians can be whiped [sic] out." The operation never got started, but the citizens of North Texas continued local attempts at defense. In Cooke County James Bourland supervised the construction of several stockades along the Red River approaches, from Sivells Bend westward to Fish Creek, then southward to the Branch Fork of the Trinity River. The militia in the area also helped settlers build palisades around their cabins for extra protection from an Indian attack.[8]

Throughout the spring and early summer of 1862 the settlers on the northwest frontier still felt the effects of hostile Indians who slipped past the Frontier Regiment and militia patrols. But at least they worried little about a federal advance from Indian Territory. During this time a large number of Confederate soldiers concentrated in northeast Texas in preparation for assignment on the Arkansas front, and their presence at least gave some relief to the Twenty-first Brigade District's eastern flank. By late summer the move to Arkansas ended; no longer did officials mass Confederate troops in northeast Texas to counter a federal threat through Indian Territory. At this time, while the porous patrols of Colonel Norris's Frontier Regiment accomplished little along the western line of counties, word came to North Texas of a planned invasion of Texas by Jayhawkers and Indians from the Fort Cobb vicinity.

General Hudson immediately called three of his regiments, approximately two hundred men, into action, and he received the cooperation of Gen. Hugh F. Young, of the Fifteenth Brigade District (Grayson and Collin counties), for an equal number of men. This force, to be commanded by Col. W. C. Twitty, was all Hudson believed he could rely on to repel the invasion.[9] Governor Lubbock, having just complained to Gen. Paul O. Hebert about the dismal conditions on the state's northwest frontier, believed this threat to be so serious that he offered to turn the direction of the militia over to Confederate leadership. The order, unprecedented as it applied to defense of the frontier, came by Lubbock's direction; the militia came under Hebert's authority during the emergency.[10]

The impending invasion turned out to be nothing more than rumors and tall tales; but the rumors spread, as always, and their effect on the state of mind of the populace created a crisis in northern Texas during the fall of 1862. Since the first months of the war, Unionist sentiment in the region of Texas between Dallas and the Red River had been strong, particularly in the counties of Cooke, Denton, Wise, and Collin. Of the eighteen counties in Texas that voted against the ordinance of secession in 1861, seven were Red River counties or contiguous.[11]

As early as January 15, 1861, settlers circulated a document that called for northern Texas to form a separate state and remain in the Union. The disaffections subsequently intensified with opposition to Confederate conscription laws passed in April and September of 1862. In North Texas, discontent centered in Cooke County, and it was here, during the excitement of the supposed invasion, that the "conspiracy of the Peace Party" took place. Internal turmoil led to murder, mass hangings, and a cloud of unrest that plagued this portion of the Indian frontier until the war's end. The episode helped to determine the nature of defense on the northwest frontier.[12]

The forces and attitudes that fostered the Peace Party conspiracy and subsequently the Great Hanging at Gainesville were bound together by the prevalent anti-secessionist or ambivalent feelings of citizens who owned no slaves and had few ties to the social and economic system of slavery. Yeomen farmers of the region had no reason for supporting slavery, other than the ideology of racism, instilled with growing frequency into every argument for secession on the eve of the war by pro-slavery writers and speakers. For so many, morale declined from the opening months of the war. Bitter feelings were further engendered by the demand for conformity to southern rights by outspoken secessionists who controlled the military. A rising tide of dissent against Confederate laws of impressment, taxation, and conscription became evident among an increasingly alienated population.[13]

The conspiracy of the Union League, or Peace Party, in North Texas was discovered in September, 1862. Initially, the organization consisted of men with Unionist sympathies who secretly banded together to discuss political views with others of similar inclination. Members swore oaths to remain loyal to the United States Constitution and often communicated by secret signs, handshakes, and passwords, while leaders of the organization boasted of thousands of members and sympathizers in the region. Their activities included the accumulation of arms and ammunition that might aid a Union invasion of Texas, and it was said that Cooke County members established communications with Jayhawkers to the north.

Scant evidence convicted some of the condemned, and mob executions of more than forty men in October in Cooke and Wise counties, on mere suspicion, left a mark on the northwest frontier that lingered for the duration of the war. Not surprisingly, this part of Texas became, in the last two years of the war, a sanctuary for Confederate deserters, renegades, active Union sympathizers, and draft dodgers; they were to find covert sympathy from those whose anti-Confederate feelings crystallized during these days of October in 1862. The concomitant circumstances began, by late 1863, to overshadow even the Indian menace. Frontier defense began to mean the protection of frontier settlers from foes often as ruthless as the Indians, that is, each other. Hereafter, any discussion of frontier defense along the line of western settlements in Texas must take into consideration the increasingly complex dilemma that forced civil and military authorities to deal with the internal problems of desertion and resistance to conscription, as well as the ever-present Indian raids and threat of federal invasion.

The increase in Indian raids that everyone expected in the autumn of 1862 did not materialize until the first months of the following year, about the time of the reorganization of the Frontier Regiment by Governor Lubbock and the legislature. Cooke, Denton, Montague, and Wise counties suffered severe attacks in February, 1863, by a force strong enough to repulse a Frontier Regiment detachment sent in pursuit. In February and March of 1863 settlers on the northwest frontier inundated Lubbock's office with requests for additional assistance. The militia enrolling officer for Wise County maintained that

> the Indians have almost entirely ruined the frontier counties. Montague and Jack Countys are broken up and all North & West of Decatur in this County are gone except a few of the more firm class. Some of the renegades which escaped from this & Cooke Countys on account of being associated with the so called Peace Party have joined the Indians and are assisting them in the depredation of this frontier.[14]

On February 23, 1863, a petition by citizens from Wise, Parker, and Jack counties implored Lubbock to send an additional force to their section to help stem the rising tide of Indian depredations. Three weeks later a family living near Fort Worth confirmed rumors of conditions on the frontier: "Times are very hard here, every thing scarce but money. The Indians are depredating heavily all above us. They are now in Parker, Jack, Palo Pinto, Erath, and other frontier counties in large bodies, stealing and killing. I fear we are going to suffer greatly from the Indians."[15] From Gainesville sixty-two-year-old William C. Twitty, son-in-law of Texas pioneer Daniel Montague, informed the Confederate commander of Indian Territory, Gen. William Steele, that "the Indians are plenty all along the line of the frontier, killing and stealing," and implored him to send troops to help, or the frontier "will be entirely broken up."[16]

In the midst of the Frontier Regiment's reorganization, General Hudson, of the Twenty-first Brigade District, tried desperately to hold the Red River line together. During late 1862 and early 1863 he called militia companies into constant service along the northwest frontier, including a volunteer company from Montague County. All of these he stationed at points along the Red River with orders to daily scout north of the river for Indian signs. With General Magruder at such a distance in Houston, Hudson found his nearest support to be the units fighting under Col. Douglas Hancock Cooper in Indian Territory. Cooper's troops included the Choctaw and Chickasaw Mounted Rifles, and he agreed to cooperate with them in defending against Indians and Jayhawkers. Now, in March of 1863, in the face of increased Indian incursions, Hudson begged Governor Lubbock, General Magruder, and Colonel Cooper for aid.[17]

Help was on the way. In February two Cooke County residents, James J. Diamond and James Bourland, journeyed to Houston and Austin to consult with General Magruder and Governor Lubbock on the subject. Bourland wished to raise a command to be used exclusively along the Red River for frontier defense, but Magruder could give no such commission. Instead, he suggested that General Steele be consulted as to the formation of such a command through Indian Territory headquarters. The news in Austin was more encouraging; Governor Lubbock promised to do his best to pry appropriations from the legislature, then in special session, to fund a frontier defense force under Bourland's command for the northwest frontier. Lubbock failed in his objective when the legislature appropriated only $800,000 for the Frontier Regiment, with no provisions to raise additional men exclusively for frontier service. Lubbock was successful, however, in obtaining General Magruder's cooperation in providing additional forces for the region. Magruder agreed to authorize General Hudson to raise up to five companies for frontier service and to station four companies of De Morse's Twenty-ninth Texas Cavalry in Cooke County, with General Cooper's permission.[18]

With the exception of General Hudson's militia, the only additional permanent force assigned to the threatened northwest frontier was a cavalry battalion assigned to Col. James Bourland. Bourland's command arrangement may have been the most unusual in the Trans-Mississippi Confederacy. By the end of August, 1863, he styled his command the Border Regiment, but it was a unit under the jurisdiction, initially, of General Steele's Indian Territory. By October his regiment was located on both sides of the Red River, officially as part of the Second Brigade, First Division, under Gen. Douglas Cooper's command, with headquarters at Fort Arbuckle.

While Bourland was at Fort Arbuckle, in Indian Territory, the commander of the Northern Sub-District of Texas assigned him the command of all Confederate troops in the Texas counties of Cooke, Montague, Clay, Archer, Young, Stephens, Palo Pinto, Parker, Wise, Denton, and Jack. Thus spread over 150 miles, north to south, his command was thus charged with defending the frontier of Texas while he coordinated his activities with district commanders in Texas and Indian Territory. The strain was eased somewhat in January of 1864 when he moved his headquarters to Gainesville, Texas, and came under the authority of the Northern Sub-District of Texas, but he still maintained at least two companies on detached service near Fort Arbuckle in Indian Territory. Although Bourland's regiment never received the recognition that was given the Frontier Regiment by contemporaries or historians, his force was a permanent unit charged specifically with frontier defense, and it served in that capacity for the last two years of the war.[19]

Bourland, once referred to as "the hangman of Texas" for his participation in the Gainesville hangings, was a small, quick-tempered man known as a strict disciplinarian. He remained a controversial leader for as long as he commanded his regiment, known as Bourland's Border Regiment. The qualities that first drove him to pursue disloyalists without mercy never quite left this man, whom one observer called "a good fighter and a good hater."[20]

The problems inherent in establishing an effective defense in 1863 for the northwest frontier were exacerbated by lack of a command structure for the entire region. In the extreme western counties Buck Barry commanded the Frontier Regiment companies from Camp Colorado north to the Red River, with Colonel Bourland's command soon to be scattered east of Barry's, from north Texas to Fort Arbuckle. The nearest Confederate commander with authority over all of north Texas was in Houston, headquarters for the District of Texas, New Mexico, and Arizona. The reorganization that occurred on the Texas frontier in the late winter and spring of 1863 stemmed from several factors. As mentioned earlier, the Frontier Regiment underwent its reorganization during the attempt to transfer it to Confederate service. On a grander scale, the Trans-Mississippi Department itself received a new commander when, on March 7, 1863, the newly appointed Gen. Edmund Kirby Smith, a veteran of the Texas Indian frontier, arrived in Louisiana and established his headquarters at Shreveport on April 24.[21]

A restructuring of Confederate authority in Texas soon took place. The reasons differed, depending on the perspective—frontier Texans, or Confederate military leadership. As Governor Lubbock and frontier settlers had long wanted more effective means to defend the northwest frontier, Lubbock promptly notified General Smith of the continuing Indian problems, as well as the new problems emerging with deserters and conscription in the northwest counties. A quick response resulted in the creation, on May 30, 1863, of the Third Military District of Texas, later known for the duration of the war as the Northern Sub-District of Texas.[22]

General Magruder appointed Col. (now acting Brig. Gen.) Smith P. Bankhead, a Tennessean and former artillery officer at Fort Pillow, on the Mississippi River, to command the Northern Sub-District. Texas previously had been divided into Eastern and Western sub-districts, with headquarters at various locations, but normally near the coast. The new sub-district now had its headquarters at Bonham, in Fannin County, not far from the Red River. District boundaries were as follows: north and east of a line running along the southern boundaries of Panola, Rusk, Cherokee, Anderson, Freestone, and Limestone counties, then to the Brazos River just west of Marlin, in Falls County. The line went up the Brazos to Fort Belknap, then due northward to the Red River. Although assigned to the position on May 30, not until July 9 did Bankhead actually reach Bonham to assume command of the new sub-district.[23]

In August of 1863, just as Bankhead was assessing the problems of his command, a fresh wave of Indian incursions inundated the northwest frontier counties. Attacks occurred from Montague County along the Red River, southward to east of Weatherford, in Parker County, less than twenty-five miles from Fort Worth. During the entire month, defense against such raids fell primarily upon local citizens and militia of the communities involved and upon the small force of the Frontier Regiment stationed at Fort Belknap and Red River Station.

The command structure of the Northern Sub-District offered little assistance. In late July three of James Bourland's best companies of the Border Battalion left the region, along with a company of the Thirtieth Texas Cavalry, to reinforce Confederate forces north of Boggy Depot, in Indian Territory. Throughout August, Bankhead continued to direct his attention chiefly to the military situation in Arkansas and in Indian Territory. In July, Gen. James Gillpatrick Blunt had led a

Union offensive in Indian Territory southward from Fort Gibson on the Arkansas River. His objective was to seize the Confederate supply base at Honey Springs and to strike Gen. Douglas Hancock Cooper's force before it could be reinforced by Gen. William L. Cabell from Arkansas. The ensuing battle of Honey Springs (or Elk Creek), fought on July 17, 1863, was the largest single engagement of the war in Indian Territory, a decisive battle that secured for northern arms the upper section of the Texas Military Road that ran from Bonham, Texas, to Fort Gibson. It threw the Confederates on the defensive in Indian Territory for the remainder of the war and led to the final phase of the Union offensive, the capture of Fort Smith on September 1, 1863.[24]

These events distracted Bankhead's attention from Indian depredations, which mounted in August. On August 20 he confirmed to Magruder's headquarters that Gen. William Steele, then in overall command of Confederate forces in Indian Territory, had fallen back to cover Fort Smith, with the result that no organized force stood between Blunt and North Texas. Bankhead explained that he was preparing to move with all available force to Boggy Depot, as the best means of defending his sub-district. Just one week later Bankhead had the Fourth and Thirtieth Texas Cavalry regiments, as well as four full companies of James Bourland's Border Battalion, on the march to Boggy Depot in Indian Territory. He commanded approximately eight hundred men in person. On Friday morning, August 28, Lt. Col. Samuel A. Roberts replaced Bankhead as acting commander of the Northern Sub-District and held the position until Gen. Henry McCulloch assumed command in mid-September. During his interim command no evidence exists that Roberts afforded any aid to citizens in the Indian-ravaged counties; rather, his duties consisted almost entirely of forwarding supplies and reinforcements to Bankhead's brigade in Indian Territory.[25]

For much of August and early September, as would happen just two months later in October, the perceived federal threat diverted attention from the quite real peril of Indian attack. The series of raids first began in Parker County on Saturday, August 1, when a small party of seven Indians captured two children from their home near Spring Creek. A group of men from the small community immediately set out in pursuit, came upon the party two days later, and found the young boy and girl together on a horse at the rear of the Indian column. Remarkably, the children were rescued during the chase, in one of the few instances when captives were retaken so swiftly by pursuing Texans. Nine days later a raid, possibly conducted by some of the same band, occurred at Patrick's Creek approximately nine miles south of Weatherford. The marauders killed, scalped, and mutilated two sons of a local minister and wounded two other men.[26] On the same day, just a short distance away, the warriors struck near the home of Mrs. F. C. Brown, whose husband was away in Confederate service, killed one of her daughters, wounded one, captured another, and then killed Mrs. Brown before riding away. Wise County suffered similar attacks during the same period when, just west of Decatur, a force of approximately twenty-five Indians killed a young boy and two sons of Parson Vernon and wounded two others. On the same day raiders killed and scalped a man near the present community of Paradise, in southwestern Wise County, and put two arrows into the back of another.[27]

Word of these latest attacks, so near Decatur, Weatherford, and Fort Worth, spread quickly across the northwest frontier. In Tarrant County state militia of the Twentieth Brigade, under Gen. Nathaniel Terry, then in the process of organization, attempted to break for home to ensure the safety of their families. They did stay long enough to complete the enrollment, and then their officers quickly sent them in organized units to clear the counties of Johnson, Parker, Palo Pinto, and Erath of the invaders.[28] A despondent Weatherford resident wrote Governor Lubbock: "The country is absolutely full of Indians, some of them have guns, but for the most part bows & arrows. They are doing great mischief! Consternation pervades the entire frontier which is constantly receding."[29] Another citizen of North Texas, disheartened at recent news of a Union push toward the Red River across Indian Territory, spoke for the frontier settlers as well when he asserted that "things *look gloomy indeed*, and I am fearful we are a used up people. I am not generally despondent, but taking every thing into consideration it is impossible to be otherwise."[30]

Any additional efforts to meet these sudden and devastating raids were feeble in the extreme. With an eye on events in Indian Territory and anxious to lead a force against federals on that front, Bankhead heard of the first attacks on August 6. Threatened settlers soon poured petitions into his office. He responded by sending one squadron of Bourland's cavalry on a sweep through Wise and Parker counties. Bankhead also disarmed a company of the Fourth Texas Cavalry, a unit made up of men from the devastated counties, who began to desert so they could return to protect their loved ones. After only a short while in command, Bankhead grew weary of "this God-forsaken country" and complained to Magruder that "I wish myself anywhere but here."[31] Bankhead received only one suggestion from Magruder concerning the Indian manace. Magruder's adjutant sent word for Bankhead to move to Indian Territory to assist General Steele and then added, "You will, if you can do so, drive the Indians from the border as you go, and if not able to do so (and it is feared you will not), you will proceed with dispatch to comply with above order."[32] Bankhead ignored the unrealistic advice concerning the Indian threat and quickly made his way to Indian Territory.

By late August, with almost all of Bourland's force on the move toward Boggy Depot, in Indian Territory, only four small squadrons of his cavalry remained to cover the Indian frontier: one in Wise County; one at the town of Montague, in Montague County; one at Minor's Bend of the Red River; and one in northern Cooke County.[33] This thin line of protection, however, would be ineffective if the northern division of the Frontier Regiment, then patrolling the region between Fort Belknap and Red River Station, faltered in its efforts to cover their portion of the line. In August, the Frontier Regiment failed to respond to the crisis. With a single exception, its units failed to detect any of the raiders or to find and punish any of them on their return trips with stolen horses. Bankhead, now flustered by events in the western section of the sub-district, informed Magruder that he had "asked as to the whereabouts of the Frontier Regiment, but no answer has been received." He then commented that settlers along the frontier desired the removal of the regiment because it provided little protection.[34]

Direct responsibility for Frontier Regiment performance on this sector of the frontier fell to Lt. Col. Buck Barry. His officers reported a number of Indian signs during this period, but his men failed to confront raiders. Barry attributed this situation to "the drouthy season," which resulted in few visible tracks, and to the poor condition of the Rangers' horses, particularly those used by troopers of Capt. John T. Rowland's critical post at Red River Station.[35] A brief season of relief from the onslaught came in September, but it was only the lull before the storm. Twice more in 1863, in October and in December, the Comanches and Kiowas returned, more confident and bolder than before.

These renewed raids in the fall, however, often held an additional motive other than the traditional "murder raids" or horse stealing; for the first time cattle raids on the frontier became commonplace. Agents of the U.S. government had attempted to restore relations with the Comanches and Kiowas in early 1863, and they had actually succeeded in coming to an agreement with two Comanche and four Kiowa chiefs in Washington, D.C., although the Senate later failed to ratify the treaty. The temporary stabilizing of relations between these tribes and the United States enabled the Indians who raided the Texas frontier to trade their stolen cattle to U.S. Army contractors in New Mexico and Indian Territory. It is estimated that approximately ten thousand head of cattle were thus driven from Texas in late 1863 and 1864.[36]

Bankhead's command was meant to be temporary until a brigadier general from Texas could be assigned, an appointment that came in August of that year. On August 16 General Magruder ordered Henry McCulloch to relieve General Scurry as commander of the Eastern Sub-District, but shortly after he made the new assignment, Magruder received instructions from Kirby Smith to appoint McCulloch to the position of commander of the Northern Sub-District. Kirby Smith stressed that the new position was the most important and difficult command in Magruder's district, one for which he regarded McCulloch as having the necessary "tact, experience, energy, and good sense."[37]

Governor Lubbock immediately sent congratulations, glad that Mc-Culloch was now "in charge of the Indian frontier."[38] This statement indicates that the state government and frontier settlers viewed the new sub-district primarily as a means to best combat the problem of Indian depredations and only secondarily to resolve the desertion-conscription dilemma. General Magruder, and to a large degree, General Smith, rarely saw it that way. While their correspondence simply does not mention the Indian menace, those who lived in that part of Texas were never able to forget it. Particularly for the first eight months, McCulloch's command represented to Confederate officials a way to coordinate the defense of northeast Texas against federal offensives, to enforce Confederate conscription laws, and to control a growing disaffection among the civil population of the Red River counties.

One of the first works to chronicle the role of Texas in the war stated simply that McCulloch's object in taking command of the Northern Sub-District was to ensure "by either forcible or pacific efforts to get men out of what was called 'Jernigan's thicket,' which had been made a place of refuge by deserters and others that avoided conscription."[39] McCulloch, undoubtedly briefed on his new assignment by General Magruder, did not allude to the Indian threat in his first proclamations and orders. In his first address to the people of his sub-district, tendered in Bonham on his first day in command, he stressed the problems of conscription and desertion. In colorful language he decreed that "Lincoln's dastard hirelings," whose aim was to "insult our wives and mothers, our sisters and daughters; and commit outrages upon them worse than death itself," must be kept from invading the region.[40]

After putting forth his views on the Indian frontier to McCulloch, Governor Lubbock still expressed doubts that Confederate leadership would give the proper emphasis to the issue. The day after McCulloch made his initial address in Bonham, Lubbock wrote to Rip Ford: "The Indians on our frontier, incited by Jayhawkers, Renegades, and our savage, brutal and vindictive enemy, have become more cruel and bold than at any former period of our history. The force on our frontier is inadequate to its proper protection, and . . . I fear the Confederate Commander will not feel that he can give to that Country the aid that I have solicited from him."[41]

Nevertheless, six weeks later when Lubbock gave his last address as governor of Texas, he expressed the belief that the formation of the Northern Sub-District established the best basis to initiate "the general protection of the frontier."[42] It now fell to General McCulloch to organize his command structure as quickly as possible to deal with the myriad difficulties that would soon beset the northwest frontier of Texas.

5

The Northern Sub-District and Frontier Defense

August, 1863–January, 1864

Gen. Henry McCulloch reached Bonham in mid-September of 1863 and assumed formal command of the Northern Sub-District of Texas. As public clamor over the recent Indian raids subsided, McCulloch set out to meet the herculean task of organizing his command for its many responsibilities. He gave primary attention to Indian Territory and the threat of a possible invasion of North Texas by Gen. James Blunt's Union forces. This action required him not only to provide for troops and route them through Bonham to the front, but also to arrange his sub-district to be the principal source of supplies and equipage for all southern soldiers throughout the Trans-Mississippi Confederacy.

While pursuing these administrative goals, he was to enforce the Confederate conscription laws, to root out the growing number of deserters, draft dodgers, Jayhawkers, and bushwhackers in the region, and to maintain the confidence and morale of the people of North Texas. In the west, the relentless raids of Plains Indians placed a never-ending pressure on the northwest frontier counties. This urgent situation called for the presence of soldiers that McCulloch usually could not provide because of the priority often given to the sub-district's other problems.

In the face of these difficulties, McCulloch also contended with a command dilemma. The Northern Sub-District embraced much of the area assigned to the Frontier Regiment for protection, yet that body answered to the State of Texas, not to McCulloch's Confederate jurisdiction. To compound matters, Bourland's Border Regiment, operating on either side of the Red River, would remain answerable to General Steele, in Indian Territory, until January of 1864. It would require a vast endeavor of cooperation to achieve anything like a concerted effort on this portion of the Texas frontier.

The Indians returned in October with raids just as severe as those of August, though devastation did not occur as far southward. The first strikes came in Montague County during the second week of the month. Four settlers died and two were seriously wounded at the George Porter home, approximately five miles east of Head of Elm, now Saint Jo, close to the Cooke County line. One of Bourland's squads under Captain Totty quickly picked up the trail, followed it for the rest of the day, and received reinforcements from a detachment of Company G of the Frontier Regiment stationed at Red River Station. In the brief fight against some twenty-five Indians, the soldiers lost one killed, and the Indians made good their escape.[1] Later that month Parker County was again the target. Mann D. Tackett, out rounding up his cattle, found himself surrounded by fifteen to twenty Indians, but he managed to kill one and wound at least one before his attackers killed and scalped him. Not far away, the raiders killed at least two more and captured nine women and children.[2]

McCulloch soon heard of these latest attacks and expressed concern to Bourland that so many families of men serving their country should be left at the mercy of the Indians. He also reported a movement of settlers from Parker County into the interior counties to seek shelter, an action that should not be necessary, he stressed to Bourland, if the frontier received adequate protection. As Gov. Francis R. Lubbock expressed it, in somewhat uncharacteristic terms for one so sensitive to the needs of the frontier, the movement of so many settlers away from the northwestern counties meant that they took their cattle with them into the more heavily populated areas, where marauders were sure to follow. It was better to protect these settlers on the frontier, where the Indians could find livestock without threatening the more populous regions.[3]

In the meantime, Bourland and Barry continued to adjust their forces in order to offer adequate protection. Near the end of October Bourland described his efforts to detect raids long before they reached the threatened counties. He had recently returned from a scout north of the Wichita Mountains, in Indian Territory, and neither that scout nor one that journeyed as far as the South Canadian River, north of Fort Cobb, had discovered any Indian signs. His Indian spies indicated that they did not believe an attack on Texas was planned for the near future, but Bourland promised to keep the Frontier Regiment informed of any sign of hostile movements. Meanwhile, he kept one company at Fort Arbuckle and two on the Red River, just north of Clay County, to scout the land in between. At the same time, the Frontier Regiment companies of Barry's command withdrew their scouts and concentrated their strength to strike swiftly, as a large raid was rumored to be imminent.[4]

From his headquarters in Bonham, McCulloch saw a sudden increase in the troop strength of the Northern Sub-District during October. On October 9, General Magruder informed Kirby Smith that "I propose to send re-inforcements to Brigadier-General McCulloch, who represents this command (the Northern Sub-District) in the greatest danger." Magruder made good his word. McCulloch reported that he anticipated no Union threat to North Texas from Indian Territory, yet the rapid buildup of forces gave no relief to settlers fearful of Indian attack. No reinforcements were ordered to the frontier to assist Bourland or Barry in detecting Indian incursions.[5]

To understand why this relief for the frontier failed to materialize is to discern the scope of the complexities that befell frontier defense from late 1863 until the end of the war. The great numbers of men who hid out in the "brush" in the Northern Sub-District threatened the integrity of the entire region.[6] Their presence suggested an overt Unionist sentiment, and after the "Peace Conspiracy" of the previous year, Confederate authorities believed that to ignore it was to see it flourish. If men could avoid conscription by hiding out or desert their commands without fear of reprisal, military officials believed that the specter of their example could lead to widespread disaffection and plummeting morale.

Generals Smith and Magruder saw this problem in late 1863 as the greatest facing McCulloch's command. The dilemma grew more serious as many of those brush men robbed and pillaged their neighbors, cooperated with Jayhawkers, and forcibly resisted those sent to bring them in. Eventually, the frontier forces themselves—that is, the Frontier Regiment, the Border Regiment, and the Frontier Organization of the following year—began to be used largely to track down and arrest such men, rather than to conduct badly needed operations against Indians. Leaders such as Bourland and John R. Baylor relished the police duty. Frontier soldiers probably never would have been called upon so extensively for such work had McCulloch been able to maintain the large troop strength of October, 1863, but the federal seizure of Brownsville and the lower Texas coast in November, and Union general Nathaniel Prentiss Banks's Red River Campaign the following spring, stripped the Northern Sub-District of nearly all forces but state militia and frontier guards. Never again would McCulloch have the strength to clear the malcontents from the brush as in the fall of 1863. His inability to do so affected the nature of frontier defense until the war's end.

The move to do something about the pressing problems of desertion and resistance to conscription began just before McCulloch's arrival in Bonham. On August 26, in accordance with Pres. Jefferson Davis's recent proclamation on the subject, General Smith granted a "general pardon of amnesty" to all officers and soldiers in the Trans-Mississippi Department who should willingly return to duty by September 30, 1863. Texas was then in the process of organizing a ten-thousand-man force of state troops, called for by General Magruder the previous June and acceded to by Governor Lubbock. McCulloch's duty, when he took command, was to facilitate the recruitment and organization of the militia, to enforce the Confederate conscription laws, and to take action against those in the brush who would not report.[7]

It soon became evident that the amnesty deadline set by General Smith for the end of September should be extended, as that would give McCulloch a bare two weeks to gather the recalcitrants from his entire sub-district. Magruder relented and moved the deadline to October 31. McCulloch first attempted to use the olive branch, rather than the sword, a decision that ran counter to the wishes of some of the citizenry. After only a few days on the job, McCulloch reported that he possessed a number of pleas that urged him "to take steps to arrest deserters and conscripts that have gone into the brush in large numbers in some portions of the district. These men live off the property and produce of the people near their camps, and are a terror to the country about them."[8] In his conciliatory efforts McCulloch sought the help of two prominent men of the region who, in the secession crisis of 1860–61, had voiced Unionist sentiments, but who both later served the Confederacy faithfully: James Webb Throckmorton of McKinney, and his close friend and political adviser, Benjamin Holland Epperson of Clarksville. McCulloch called upon Epperson to seek out the brush men and urge them to do their duty:

I am satisfied that these men do not desire to do wrong, they cannot
be opposed to our holy cause, they cannot be friendly to our enemies,
but that they have simply come to wrong conclusions about their duty
to Country. I cannot believe that they are willing to brand themselves
as traitors, deserters or Tories, or that they are willing to destroy the
happiness of their Mothers, wives, and daughters . . . by having such
disgrace heaped upon them.[9]

Epperson was convinced that McCulloch's policy was to go into effect
"by kind, and gentle means, and he will not resort to sterner, until
these are exhausted." Throckmorton, discharged from the Confederate Army in mid-September, returned home and likewise attempted
to encourage the spirits of those of North Texas who were losing faith
in the war effort.[10]

McCulloch and three of his trusted volunteer aides, Samuel A.
Roberts, Elijah Sterling Clack Robertson, and John Henry Brown, all
journeyed to various sections of the sub-district in peaceful attempts
to persuade malcontents to report for duty. Robertson's tour took him
to the counties of Cooke, Denton, Grayson, and Tarrant, over three
hundred miles in eight days, after which he reported that he found
a positive sentiment throughout the region. As McCulloch's "confiden-
tial adviser," Roberts accompanied the general on trips to speak to the
state militia as they came in to enroll; Roberts said the talks seemed
to inspire the men. Brown gave well-received speeches to hundreds of
men at Honey Grove and Paris and likewise received praise, from no
less than the state commandant of conscripts, that his work and speeches
had a positive effect on the region.[11]

McCulloch, normally a patient and kindly man, nonetheless slowly
began to advocate more ruthless means to get the men out of the brush
after these optimistic days of late September and early October. He
left no doubt that the men were going to come in one way or the other.
He preferred it to be a peaceful transition, but he informed his staff
that military power would be used if results were not quickly seen:

> . . . and when driven to that—any hope of pardon and reconciliation
> ceases, and that I will hunt them down as the enemies of my Country,
> and her people, that I will send an armed force to take them dead or
> alive. Tell them I offer them peace, pardon, and friendship, and if they
> refuse, warn them of the consequences.[12]

General Smith, who always urged upon McCulloch a policy of ruth-lessness toward the men in the brush, wrote from Shreveport in a simi-lar vein, encouraging severe measures: "The deserters must be arrested and brought back to their commands or exterminated. The question now is whether they or we shall control."[13]

It was not long before McCulloch admitted that his pacific policy was about to fail. By late October he estimated that approximately one thousand deserters remained in the brush, including the ones who avoided conscription. Most of these men were hiding in those coun-ties which voted against secession in 1861. He estimated that the area bounded by Bonham, Dallas, and Gainesville harbored three armed camps of deserters, each numbering more than two hundred men who regularly patrolled roads leading to their encampments. The largest such encampment was located in Collin County; it may perhaps have been five hundred strong at one time — a "gang of deserters, skulkers and bad men generally," under the leadership of a "desperate character" named Henry Boren.[14] James W. Throckmorton tried his best but failed to talk Boren and his men into surrendering, although Boren appeared willing to negotiate with McCulloch. The authorities could only prom-ise the renegades that the safety of their families and property would be guaranteed if they went into the army — nothing more. It appears that Boren first wanted his men to be given arms, ammunition, provi-sions, and time to put their affairs in order before the reporting date. This leeway McCulloch absolutely refused to give; weapons would not be provided in advance. He made a fortunate decision, for a month later he learned from an informant that Boren's real intention was not to enter the service but to have his men seize Bonham and "wipe out secession in this part of Texas."[15]

General Smith once more urged McCulloch to adopt a firm course of action. Smith's adjutant, prominent Texas politician Guy Morrison Bryan, strongly insinuated the methods that might achieve success; he noted that in Louisiana, after two officers captured and executed ten deserters, over four hundred were taken quickly or turned themselves in. To even contemplate such action, McCulloch had to have the nec-essary force. One unit originally designated to fight against Indians along the frontier instead spent nearly its entire length of service in the sub-district confronting the deserter problem. The company was Ladies' Rangers, commanded by the experienced frontiersman John R.

Baylor. It was McCulloch's option to send Baylor to service against either Indians or deserters, but even in the midst of daily reports of the Indian raids of October, McCulloch believed the deserter problem to be more serious. By this time McCulloch had an effective force of approximately fifteen hundred to two thousand regulars in his sub-district, a total that included Bourland's command but none of the Frontier Regiment. The unexpected reinforcements he received in October, however, remained the most controversial.[16]

In mid-October a band of Confederate guerrillas under the notorious William Clarke Quantrill crossed the Red River at Colbert's Ferry and established winter camp along Mineral Springs Creek, about fifteen miles northwest of Sherman, Texas. Their camp was made approximately forty-five miles from McCulloch's headquarters at Bonham.[17] This winter camp was necessary, in part, for Quantrill's men to escape retribution for two of their recent affairs, the first being the infamous sack of Lawrence, Kansas, on August 21, 1863. During this escapade they looted the town and shot down approximately 180 men and boys.

Weeks later, while on their way to Texas, Quantrill's well-mounted and armed force of four hundred men came upon the headquarters escort of General Blunt. Then in the process of transferring his flag from Fort Scott to threatened Fort Smith, Blunt had an armed escort of approximately one hundred men with an accompaniment of assorted administrative personnel. Quantrill's band attacked on October 6 and nearly annihilated the escort; they killed eighty, wounded eight, and reported the death of General Blunt, although that officer managed to escape. Quantrill made his report on October 13 from General Cooper's headquarters at North Fork Town, near the junction of the North Canadian and South Canadian rivers; he then reached North Texas sometime in the next few days.[18]

Quantrill, preceded by some of his men two days before, reached Bonham late Sunday night on October 25 and conferred with McCulloch the next morning.[19] McCulloch had earlier heard accounts of the Lawrence raid and the affair at Baxter Springs, and the old Indian fighter already had fixed opinions about Quantrill and his manner of combat:

> I do not know as much about his mode of warfare as others seem to
> know; but, from all I can learn, it is but little, if at all, removed from
> that of the wildest savage. I appreciate his services, and am anxious to

have them; but certainly we cannot, as a Christian people, sanction a savage, inhuman warfare, in which men are to be shot down like dogs, after throwing down their arms and holding up their hands supplicating for mercy.[20]

On the other hand, General Smith commented enthusiastically about Quantrill's men being available to seek out those in the brush, and he stated that no better soldiers could be employed than Quantrill's Missourians. To dispel any notion of sending Quantrill away, and perhaps to better control Quantrill's men, Smith ordered McCulloch to keep them together as a unit under Quantrill, preferably to collect stragglers and deserters.[21]

It was probably sometime in the first week of November that McCulloch authorized Quantrill to proceed to "Jernigan's Thicket," located in northeastern Hunt County and in the western part of present-day Delta County, to apprehend and arrest, but not kill, those in the brush. Quantrill ingratiated himself with some of the malcontents and discovered a fact that was later confirmed to McCulloch in November: many of those in hiding planned to surrender, to be outfitted and assigned to local units, and then to desert to the federals. It seems that Quantrill captured but few of those in the brush and killed several, whereupon McCulloch quickly detached him and sent him to report to Kirby Smith in Shreveport. Quantrill disagreed with McCulloch's policy of leniency and said as much to Smith.

The commanding general agreed with Quantrill and recommended to McCulloch that "the only thing to be done now is to go vigorously to work, and kill or capture all those who refuse to come in. The commanding general thinks the ringleaders should have no quarter." Upon Quantrill's return from Shreveport McCulloch determined to use other troops for the job at hand. He sent Quantrill's band to track Comanches retreating from a recent raid; the troopers trailed for nearly a week, with no success.[22] They were, at least, a brief reinforcement for the hard-pressed settlers on the frontier, and McCulloch, at least, removed Quantrill's men from the populated areas for a short while.

With the Quantrill problem temporarily out of the way, McCulloch continued his policy of persuading the deserters to come in, enforcing the conscription laws, and organizing the militia. By the first week in November McCulloch indicated that large numbers of deserters led by Henry Boren were ready to report. A number of men in other parts of the sub-district also came out of hiding, thanks to McCulloch's use of "soft words better than hard ones to bring the young ones back to their duty."[23] Most of these men came in from areas east of a line from Gainesville to Fort Worth, but it was still difficult to get them in from the frontier counties farther west. McCulloch requested that Bourland pull whatever force he could spare from the Indian frontier to sweep through the counties of Wise, Jack, and Parker, where severe problems from brush men existed. He then added a fateful concluding paragraph: "Extend pardon to all that you believe come in voluntarily, arrest all others alive wherever found and let them all understand that they must go to the army and stay obedient [to] the Country or be killed."[24] This order went to a man who saw little difference between the conspirators hanged the year before at Gainesville and those now in the brush. In a letter to one of his company commanders Bourland thus interpreted McCulloch's instructions: "If you find those Deserters and Traitors in the brush shoot them down. We must rid the country of all the Bad Men. If any of them comes in and gives up with out being arrested you will send them to these Head Quarters and I will forward them to Gen. McCulloch and let him dispose of them."[25]

In Houston, General Magruder, unaware that McCulloch was rapidly collecting deserters, on November 6 instructed McCulloch to immediately break up the armed camps of deserters and then forward his militia to Houston. His order was no less emphatic than that of Kirby Smith: "You will, of course, use every exertion to effect their extermination as soon as possible."[26] One day before Magruder wrote this letter, McCulloch had designated the fifth day of November as absolutely the last date of voluntary amnesty in the Northern Sub-District. In a broadside printed at Paris, Texas, and distributed across the sub-district, McCulloch proclaimed: "No deserters will be permitted to remain in this Sub District. It may be well to say that the policy of pardoning deserters, has worked badly, has injured the service, and must be stopped; and that those so lost to honor as to desert, need expect to find no shelter in this Sub District, all will be hunted down and brought to justice."[27]

On this same day McCulloch succeeded in his efforts to get the most dangerous camp of deserters to come in voluntarily. Approximately 300 men surrendered, but only after he promised them a furlough of about fifteen days to take care of affairs at home before they had to report for enrollment. In addition, 335 men had come in during the efforts of the previous three weeks; some of these were immediately sent to their commands, while others in need of equipment were ordered to report on November 22.[28]

This was the origin of a most singular outfit simply called the "Brush Battalion."[29] Initial command of the unit went to Capt. John R. Baylor, who recruited the first deserters to help his own men root out those in the brush. Baylor's ruthless methods brought forth an outcry, but he soon left for Richmond to serve in the Confederate Congress. He was succeeded by Maj. John R. Diamond. On November 21 General Magruder, in response to the federal invasion at Brownsville three weeks earlier and the seizure of much of the South Texas coast, ordered all state and Confederate troops in the Northern Sub-District to report to Houston, with the exception of three mounted companies and one battalion of organized militia. Possibly unaware of the nature of the Brush Battalion at the moment, or unsure of just what promises Mc-Culloch had made to its members, Magruder made no mention of them.[30]

Under these circumstances, McCulloch by necessity now saw the Brush Battalion as a much needed force to supplement frontier defense in his sub-district. In October and November he collected deserters from numerous outfits, but chiefly from seven Trans-Mississippi regiments. During his preliminary organization of these men in early November he specified the ones that could rejoin their commands, but he then agreed that approximately four hundred volunteers could fill up four companies for Brush Battalion service on the frontier. When McCulloch met the men of the proposed battalion on Sunday, November 22, the appointed date for those furloughed to report, he came upon a scene of confusion and marked unpreparedness. Only three companies were present, rather than four. In addition, one hundred men who either had refused to report to their regular commands or just recently had come in from the brush volunteered for frontier duty. To complete the scene, the men came in with little more than the clothes they wore, thus being utterly unprepared for campaigning.[31]

Even with this many men reporting, McCulloch informed General Steele that approximately one thousand men still remained scattered in the brush about his sub-district. With the frontier in need of added protection, and with the federals relatively inactive in Indian Territory, McCulloch prepared to supply and equip the battalion as best he could. He intended to send it off the following Saturday, November 28, to serve under Bourland's jurisdiction on the frontier—that is, all but one company, the one that contained Henry Boren and his brothers. These "Jernigan's Thicket" men balked when they heard it was Bourland they were to serve under; they simply did not trust him. As for the rest of the Brush Battalion, McCulloch recommended that Bourland post up to one-half of them on patrol duty and keep the rest busy making shelters for the winter. The battalion left as scheduled from McKinney, in Collin County, and after a short march westward Bourland ordered them to encamp at Denton to await supplies and the necessary equipment for Indian service in the field.[32]

McCulloch planned for the men of the Brush Battalion to advance to positions where they could form an integral part of the defense of the Indian frontier. Initially, he intended for them to help Bourland fill the gap between Frontier Regiment units at Fort Belknap and Red River Station, but Bourland had grander plans. On December 11 Bourland assigned the men to their new posts. He ordered Major Diamond to post one company along the upper Little Wichita River, in Archer County, nearly due north of Fort Belknap, and to station two companies farther north on the Wichita River.[33] The last two companies were to be stationed still farther north, in Indian Territory, approximately thirty-five miles northwest of Warren's Trading Post, which was located on the Red River at the mouth of Cache Creek in present Love County, Oklahoma. There they came under the command of Capt. C. L. Roff, of Bourland's Border Regiment. The battalion quartermaster appointed by McCulloch, Lieutenant Merchant, had the thankless job of furnishing transportation, supplies, and forage from frontier counties already woefully short of provisions and vehicles.[34]

When the Brush Battalion received orders to reinforce the frontier in mid-December, they soon had their chance to encounter the Plains Indians. For the largest Indian raid of 1863, one of the largest and most devastating raids since the early days of the Republic, hit the Northern Sub-District within two weeks after Bourland assigned the troopers to the line. The great raid into Montague and Cooke counties in late December should have come as no surprise, as officers of the Frontier Regiment and Border Regiment had early warning that such a raid was imminent. Captain Rowland, from Red River Station, reported indications of such a raid to Lieutenant Colonel Barry during the first week of December; then Rowland sent his men in regular patrols to scout in the Cache Creek vicinity, north of the Red River and approximately fifty miles to the northwest of Red River Station. At the same time, Bourland learned "from reliable sources" that hostile Indians on the Canadian River, north of Fort Cobb, were prepared for a heavy raid into Texas. In response, he ordered the Chickasaw Battalion, then attached to his forces, to occupy Fort Arbuckle; he also ordered Capt. A. B. White's company at the fort to move westward to extend the line expected to be filled by the Brush Battalion. In addition, the colonel could count on the support of Baylor's company of Rangers and a small mounted company of militia under Capt. Samuel P. C. Patton, which had been recently attached to his command.[35]

Early in the afternoon of December 21, 1863, a force of approximately three hundred Comanches crossed the Red River east of Red River Station, entered Montague County, and then rushed toward the Illinois Bend region near the Montague-Cooke county line. This was no cattle raid. They first struck the Anderson, Willet, and Hatfield homesteads at Illinois Bend. Here they killed a man, two women, and a child, wounded three others, burned the homes, and moved on. Captain Rowland, with less than thirty men (the rest were scouting or hauling supplies to Cache Creek), reacted to news of the attack at Illinois Bend and set out from Red River Station. Just before reaching the Wallace settlement, near Sadler Bend, with Rowland's men in hot pursuit the Indians recrossed the Red River near the mouth of Mountain Creek, probably to deceive their pursuers into thinking the raid was over.[36]

Rowland's men rested their horses that night at the Wallace settlement, determined to begin their pursuit early the next morning. As they did so, word of the raid spread quickly to nearby settlers at the Elmore settlement on Fish Creek, about six miles to the east, and to the Potter settlement, four miles southeast of Elmore's. The news reached Gainesville that night. A detachment of Captain Patton's company, some twenty-five strong, left immediately and reached Wallace's before daybreak. Back at Sadler's Bend, the settlers forted up and hoped that the Indians were really gone.[37]

Early the next morning the confident warriors recrossed the Red River between the Wallace and Elmore settlements to complete what they had started the day before. When they reached the first house at Elmore, the settlers hiding there became so terrified to see such a great number of Indians that they bolted and tried to run for safety, rather than stay and be burned out. The Comanches soon killed several, chased others for miles, plundered the home, and stole the horses.

As the raiders swept on unimpeded, settlers living close by the Elmore and Potter settlements could tell the Indians were getting closer by observing the smoke of burning homes. As they destroyed and plundered whatever was in their path, the main body moved south to the Bonner home on Elm Creek, located only six miles west of Gainesville, which led fleeing settlers to later exaggerate the extensiveness of the attack to include Gainesville itself.[38]

As the large party of Comanches moved with their plunder, the force of Rowland, Patton, and volunteer citizens finally confronted them. They found little problem in tracking the invaders—just following the smoke of burning homes solved that—but the Indians moved rapidly, with extra mounts as usual, while the men with Rowland frequently had to rest theirs. Finally, the soldiers overtook the war party near a ridge overlooking a large field at Potter's settlement, some ten miles northwest of Gainesville. The Indians, full of the confidence born of a fighting heritage and superior numbers, continued to move at a leisurely pace. They showed little regard for the force behind them, until Rowland began forming his men for a charge. These Comanche warriors may have felt many emotions when faced by the charging Texans, but fear was not one of them. Rowland's men had scarcely started their attack when the Comanches to their front broke quickly into two wings and began circling to both flanks of the Texans. One did not have to be a veteran of Indian warfare to see what was happening. Rowland's men halted, fired ineffectively at long range, and then began to break for the rear. Several Texans were shot down in the pursuit, but most made it to the protective safety of a nearby fence and kept the attackers at bay. As the warriors trotted off the field, Rowland tried to get his men to move once more to the attack, but the demoralized defenders refused to budge. The only thing left was to wait for reinforcements and begin pursuit the following day.[39]

A contemporary source put white losses during the raid at thirteen killed and thirteen taken captive. Bourland's first report of the action to McCulloch, written on the night of December 22, estimated fifteen Texans killed "and some 2 or 3 young women carried off." Two days later his report to McCulloch confirmed losses of twelve killed and seven wounded, with ten homes burned and numerous horses stolen. It was a devastating raid. The Comanches lost only a few men, and the pursuit by ultimately hundreds of Texans never overtook the raiders after they crossed the Red River.[40] Repercussions were immediate; foremost in everyone's mind was the question of how such a large band of Indians had penetrated the screen of patrols and traveled undetected into the midst of the settlements.

Upon examination, it appears that Comanches unwittingly began the raid at precisely the right moment, just before Bourland completed the defensive preparations for the northwest frontier. It will be recalled that on December 11 Bourland ordered Major Diamond to post the Brush Battalion over a seventy-five-mile line, from the Little Wichita to north of the Red River. These orders, however, were not expected to reach Diamond until the fourteenth, while the Brush Battalion was still near Denton. One of the officers who brought reinforcements and joined in chasing the raiders was Major Diamond, who presumably commanded some of the better men of the Brush Battalion. This indicates that Diamond was still in Denton awaiting supplies before the battalion could move out. The raid hit from the northwest before the Brush Battalion could fill the gap between the Red River and Captain White's company, ranging to the west of Fort Arbuckle. Captain Rowland's Frontier Regiment company, at Red River Station, was in closer touch with Bourland than with his superior, Buck Barry, and undoubtedly coordinated his movements with those of Bourland for defensive plans north of the Red River. The scouts he had out toward the mouth of Cache Creek, thirty-five miles south of an expected Brush Battalion outpost, probably were too far to the south to detect the Indian penetration.[41]

It may also be that overconfidence by Bourland contributed to the December disaster. His own regiment bolstered by the five-hundred-man Brush Battalion, General's Cooper's Chickasaw Battalion, and the companies of Baylor and Patton, Bourland believed he had the strength to take the war to the enemy. He planned to take the field as soon as possible, in cooperation with the Frontier Regiment, to "make a move against the Indians & Federals" in Indian Territory.[42] It was in the midst of such preparations that the thunderbolt struck Cooke County; thirteen months would pass before Texans on this part of the frontier could carry out such an offensive expedition reminiscent of those of 1858.

General McCulloch did not delay to remedy a frontier defense that could allow such a raid to take place; he knew manpower was always needed, but he believed a change in methods might accomplish as much. In January Bourland lost his force of Chickasaws, and in the process he joined McCulloch's command in the Northern Sub-District.[43] Normally not one to chastise subordinates by post for their failures, McCulloch nevertheless wrote to Bourland: "I am unwilling to censure anyone unjustly but it seems rather strange to me that the Indians should be in the country in such large numbers before they were discovered. Several scouting parties may escape the observation of the vigilant but certainly such a body of men could have been discovered if there had been anyone on the watch at all."[44]

When he continued to receive reports that settlers were leaving the frontier for the interior because they could no longer count on the frontier forces for protection, McCulloch wrote to Bourland to propose a change in the plan of operations for the northwest frontier. Bourland should institute the familiar patrol system, station at least one company on the Red River near the Clay-Montague county line, post two companies betwen that point and Fort Belknap, and leave one company on the Red River, in Cooke County. A portion of Bourland's force would remain in the vicinity of Fort Arbuckle to scout westward for Indian signs. These changes, McCulloch noted, would have three major advantages: they would help solve the logistical problem of hauling supplies to the greater distances of Bourland's earlier positions, afford closer cooperation with the Frontier Regiment elements stationed at Fort Belknap, and just as importantly, bring a defensive line closer to the settlements to instill greater confidence among the settlers.[45]

The problems of the Brush Battalion, widespread disaffection in the Northern Sub-District (that would lead to the breakup of a plot that rivaled the "Peace Conspiracy" of 1862), and mounting difficulties with Quantrill's band were all on the horizon for the northwest frontier of Texas. Before examining their resolution, it is imperative to describe the origins and implementation of the last major organizational change in the defense of the Texas frontier, the establishment of the Frontier Organization. This final attempt by the State of Texas to provide the best possible protection for settlers who lived along the Indian frontier merits special attention, as it became the nucleus of frontier defense in the last eighteen months of the war.

6

Creation of the Frontier Organization

The final modification of the system of frontier defense in Texas began after the election of the state's last wartime governor. On August 3, 1863, Pendleton Murrah defeated Thomas Jefferson Chambers and took office three months later. Murrah placed particular emphasis on frontier defense in his inaugural address. Like former governor Lubbock in his last speech to the legislature, Murrah believed that the establishment of the Northern Sub-District went a long way toward strengthening the northwest frontier and, like Lubbock, he also believed it the responsibility of the Confederate government to ensure the defense of the Texas frontier.[1] Murrah too faced the question of state support for the Frontier Regiment, a force that came under considerable scrutiny by its critics in late 1863. Predominant, however, in the renewed movement to transfer it to Confederate service was the question of the financial burden upon the state treasury. In addition, legislators were reluctant to release the regiment to Confederate command without an alternate provision for frontier protection.

In November of 1863 Gen. John Bankhead Magruder, Confederate commander in Texas, became exceedingly impatient to obtain the services of the Frontier Regiment as an additional force to help meet the Union invasion of South Texas. He wished initially for the regiment to be turned over to Gen. Henry McCulloch so that Confederate units in the Northern Sub-District could be forwarded to the coast. By the end of the month Magruder proposed to Murrah that the Frontier Regiment be equally concentrated in two sites, at Fort Belknap under General McCulloch and at Fort Clark under Western Sub-District commander James Edwin Slaughter. The troops at Fort Clark would be used primarily to guard against a Union thrust either at San Antonio

or along the Rio Grande. Murrah, however, expressed rightful concern that such a concentration would leave too large a gap unprotected
along the Central Texas frontier. If authorities transferred the Frontier
Regiment to Confederate service, the three-hundred-mile line between
the two forts would be unprotected, thus causing the interior of the
state to suffer. With first-hand knowledge of the Texas frontier, Gen.
Edmund Kirby Smith concurred, and while he normally left the post-
ing of troops to his district commanders, he at least recommended that
General Magruder accede to Murrah's request to station a portion of
the regiment at Camp Colorado and along the Llano River as well,
possibly at Fort Mason.[2]

The subjects of frontier defense and the fate of the Frontier Regiment played a major role in deliberations of the Tenth Legislature in
November and December of 1863. While the governor and legislators
seemed willing to transfer the regiment to the Confederacy, even with
no restrictions, they hesitated to do so without assuring the best protection possible for the frontier counties. The resulting plan resembled
one proposed by Governor Lubbock during the previous session of the
legislature. The new law, entitled "An Act to Provide for the Protection
of the Frontier, and turning over the Frontier Regiment to Confederate States Service," represented the last major modification of frontier
defense by the State of Texas during the Civil War.

The new plan created what became known as the Frontier Organization, structure that functioned in the frontier counties not only until
the surrender of the Trans-Mississippi Confederacy but also for some
months afterward. Enacted by the legislature on December 15, 1863,
the law declared that all persons liable for military service who were
actual residents of the frontier counties of Texas were to be enrolled
and organized into companies of no fewer than twenty-five and no more
than sixty-five men. The act defined the frontier line as all the following counties, and included all those located north and west of the line:
Cooke, Wise, Parker, that part of Johnson west of the Belknap and
Fort Graham road, Bosque, Coryell, Lampasas, Burnet, Blanco, Bandera, Medina, Kendall, Atascosa, Live Oak, McMullen, La Salle, Dimmit, and Maverick. On the following day the lawmakers amended the
bill to include that portion of Karnes County lying southwest of the
San Antonio River, and that part of Bee County lying southwest of
the Medio River.[3]

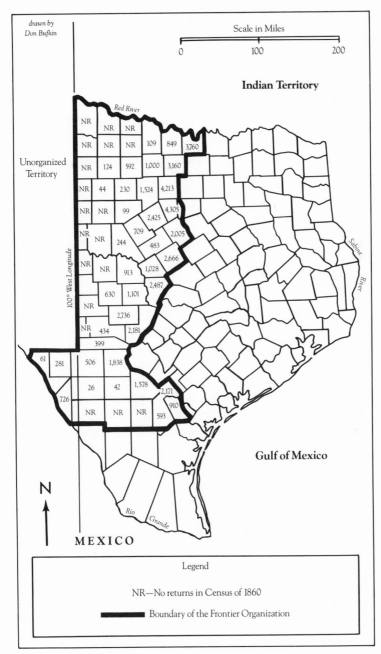

MAP 3. Population of the Frontier Organization region by county

The law instructed Governor Murrah to divide the designated counties into three districts and to appoint a suitable person with the rank and pay of Major of Cavalry to take charge of the organization of mounted companies within the district, said person to be charged with the district's defense. The law based the organization of the companies upon the minutemen pattern familiar to the Texas frontier. A captain and two lieutenants led each company and, typical of instructions long used by Ranger companies in Texas, the law required each man to have at all times a horse, gun, ammunition, ten days' provisions, and necessary equipment for service in the field.

Of the entire force raised in this manner, the major of each district was to require that one-fourth of his men, on a rotation basis, be in service at any one time, with provisions that the governor could set forth extraordinary circumstances by which the entire force could be called out. That the Frontier Organization was to be used to protect the frontier from Indian incursions was not stated in the bill, but was understood. The law emphasized, however, that all members of the organization were to take an oath that they would use the best of their abilities to arrest and deliver to the nearest Confederate States authorities every person reported or known to be a deserter, from either the state or Confederate States army, including all persons who avoided conscription. For their actual service in the field, the daily pay of officers and men was to be: captains, $3.00; lieutenants, $2.75; sergeants, $2.50; corporals, $2.25; and privates, $2.00.

Section twelve of the new law stated that upon the completion of the new organization the governor was to turn over the Frontier Regiment to Confederate authorities. The legislators hoped that these measures would guarantee that the frontier would have adequate protection, even if the Confederate-controlled Frontier Regiment left to counter a threat elsewhere. Just as important, this protection would come from those who lived on the frontier, from men motivated to give their best effort to protect their families and property. When the legislators passed the Frontier Organization bill, they also appropriated $800,000 to pay deficits for the support of the Frontier Regiment, and they appropriated $1 million to defray the cost of defending the frontier in 1864 and 1865.[4]

The Frontier Regiment obviously could not be transferred immediately; the Frontier Organization had to be in place, serving effectively, before the transfer. It was hoped that the details could be worked out by early February. In the meantime, it is interesting to note Col. James McCord's views on the changes made in the status of his regiment. Upon his arrival in Austin near the end of the legislative session, Mc-Cord wrote to Lieutenant Colonel Barry:

> There seemed to be a strong disposition on the part of nearly all of the members to rid the State of the expense, and many, or at least some of the Frontier members, did all they could to get us away, and they have succeeded, or at least we will soon be at the mercy of the comding. Gen. . . . but so soon as I can I will try and get [Governor Murrah] to use his influence with the Comding. Gen. to keep the Regt. where it is.[5]

Although expressing disappointment over the effectiveness of the Frontier Regiment, including charges made by Colonel Bourland, a number of people living on the frontier complained about the consequences should it actually be withdrawn. On the northwestern frontier Capt. J. T. Rowland, at Red River Station, reported that citizens of the region petitioned General McCulloch to use his influence to retain the regiment on that part of the frontier, while an old friend informed Gen. Kirby Smith that should the Frontier Regiment be removed, the Central Texas frontier would be overrun by cattle thieves and bushwhackers.[6]

The transfer of the Frontier Regiment proceeded slowly and uncertainly throughout the first months of 1864. Part of the problem stemmed from the extended time necessary to complete arrangements for the Frontier Organization, but routine matters within the Frontier Regiment contributed as well to the delay. Because of the scattered condition of the reigment, it was a lengthy process to gather supplies and stores for the regiment's subsistence at its proposed stations, Fort Belknap, Camp Colorado, Camp San Saba (replacing Fort Mason), and Fort Clark, and to arrange for the transfer of commissary commitments from state to Confederate responsibility.[7]

Taking stock of the opinions of his men, McCord reported that his captains and most of the troops favored the transfer. In response to Governor Murrah's early suggestion that the regiment first be mustered out of state service and then enrolled into the Confederate Army, McCord replied that this option might tempt too many of the men to join other commands. He favored a simple transfer.[8] One company composed of many men from the northwest frontier, however, protested their removal to the Rio Grande rather than to Fort Belknap. They expressed doubts that the men of the Frontier Organization could be trusted to guard the frontier. They viewed this new organization as "composed of men from almost every section of the state and even from other states, as well as a considerable number of deserters who have fled from conscription & draft, a great many of whom have neither families, property nor visible occupation."[9]

The adjutant and inspector general of Texas, David Browning Culberson, directed that the transfer of the regiment take place on the first day of March, 1864. New company elections took place at the time, while the proposed locations of the companies were changed: Camp Verde, Fort Inge, and Fort Duncan were each to house two companies, while James "Buck" Barry took command of four companies stationed at Fort Belknap. In addition, the ten companies were reduced in number to only eighty men each so that two additional posts could be located at Camp San Saba and Camp Colorado, a move opposed by Colonel McCord, as he much preferred to keep the regiment concentrated rather than scattered along the line.[10]

The command structure of the Frontier Organization occupied the attention of the state government in early 1864. In the first week of January Governor Murrah appointed three men to the rank of major and charged them with the command of the three newly created Frontier Districts. The First (or Northern) Frontier District consisted of the counties of Cooke, Wise, Jack, Parker, Montague, Young, Palo Pinto, Knox, Baylor, Stephens, Shackelford, Jones, Haskell, Hardeman, Archer, Clay, Throckmorton, Wichita, and Wilbarger—the northwestern frontier counties with a combined 1860 population of approximately fifteen thousand.[11] The Second (or Central) Frontier District contained the counties of Erath, Bosque, Coryell, Hamilton, Comanche, Brown, Lampasas, San Saba, Mason, Eastland, Coleman, Runnels, Concho, McCulloch, Menard, Kimble, Callahan, Taylor, and that part of Johnson County west of the Fort Belknap road to Fort Graham, an area with an 1860 population of approximately twelve thousand.[12] The Third (or Southern) Frontier District included the counties of Burnet, Kerr, Llano, Gillespie, Blanco, Bandera, Medina, Frio, Live Oak, Atascosa, McMullen, Dawson, Maverick, Zavala, Dimmit, La Salle, Edwards, Kinney, that portion of Karnes County lying southwest of the San Antonio River, and that part of Bee County lying southwest of the Medio River, a region with an 1860 population of approximately fifteen thousand.[13]

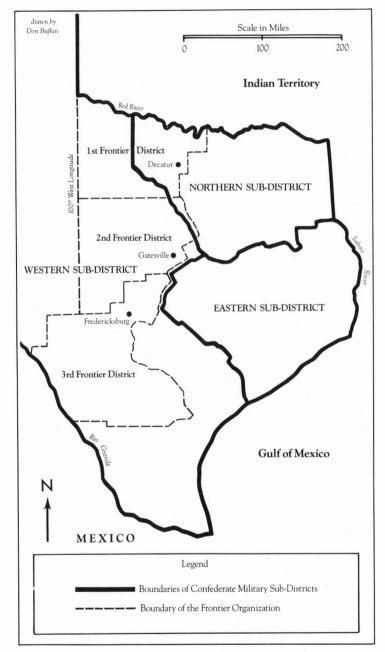

MAP 4. Command Organization, January–September, 1864

To administer these districts Governor Murrah appointed William Quayle as commanding officer for the First Frontier District, George Bernard Erath for the Second Frontier District, and James M. Hunter for the Third Frontier District.[14] In dozens of muster rolls for Frontier Organization companies one may glimpse something of the organization and of the men who served on the frontier during the last eighteen months of the war. Companies normally averaged between fifty and fifty-five in strength, usually with about fifteen men per squad for patrol duty. It should be recalled, however, that by law only one-fourth of the force was to be in the field at any one time, a requirement generally followed except in times of emergency. Thus, of the force of approximately four thousand men enrolled in the organization by the spring of 1864, one thousand remained constantly in the field. The length of service at any one time naturally varied according to the task, the presence of the enemy, and the availability of supplies, but most squads on patrol duty expected to remain out for about ten days.[15]

The men who joined the Frontier Organization, as might be expected, were older than the average men in the service of the Confederate Army. In his monumental study of the Confederate soldier, Bell Wiley concluded that approximately one-third of all the Confederacy's soldiers were between the ages of eighteen and twenty-five, while just under 17 percent were in their thirties. Similarly, Wiley reported that in the summer of 1864 the average age of a Union soldier was twenty-six and that more than 75 percent were under the age of thirty.[16] In contrast, an examination of the muster rolls of the Frontier Organization reveals that the average age of its soldiers was thirty-three, while approximately 15 percent of the force consisted of teenagers; the more than one hundred men who served as company commanders averaged thirty-nine years of age, and a number of them had served previously in the Frontier Regiment or in minutemen companies.

Although district commanders early expressed concern that adequate weapons might not be found to arm all who enrolled, the men soon obtained weapons of some sort, though the quality left something to be desired. In the most complete district-wide figures available for the spring and summer of 1864, each man of the organization owned, on the average, two weapons. The number of rifles was about twice the total number of pistols and shotguns, which were about equal in number. In the First Frontier District one company of forty-five Tonkawa scouts under their chief, Castile, went about their duties armed collectively with four rifles; bows and arrows served the rest. Correspondence from the Frontier Districts for the length of their existence chronicles a never-ending series of logistical problems. As earlier experienced by the Frontier Regiment, the lack of or poor quality of powder and percussion caps frustrated efforts until the war's end. The most common complaints stemmed from lead caps that were difficult to explode, caps that were too large and often dropped off the nipple of the gun before firing, and "slow-push" powder, crude homemade powder used when none other was available. All these factors more than once stripped the Texans of superiority over the bows and arrows used against them.

Almost without exception the commanding officers of the districts—majors and brigadier generals of state troops—gave the energetic leadership necessary for the arduous task of frontier defense during the last year of the war. Each brought different skills and experience to the office; and if some of them had seen little active service on the frontier, they at least knew the frontier people and the problems to be faced. The scores of captains who commanded the companies in the field represented a wide range of the best and worst the frontier had to offer. Each responded according to his gifts, and as in all such organizations, it was soon evident which captains and companies could be relied upon. Perhaps few of them would have served as Ranger captains in the 1840s or 1850s, but the best of them knew their jobs and went about their work with as little fanfare and as much expertise as any who ever took to the saddle on the Indian frontier of Texas. They may not have been called a Ranger Regiment, as were McCulloch's First Texas Mounted Rifles or the Frontier Regiment, but they met all the requirements of minutemen companies of Rangers that had served on the Texas frontier for over twenty-five years. Now, however, many of their friends who would have been by their side performed their duty eastward with the armies, and Indians were no longer the only enemy.

In January of 1864, when Governor Murrah divided the western counties to create the Frontier Districts, he appointed William Quayle, of Tarrant County, to command the First Frontier District. An Irishman who had immigrated to New York, this former sea captain had traveled extensively in Europe and Asia until recurring health problems forced him to seek a milder climate. Quayle came to Texas in the 1850s and settled near the community of Grapevine, northeast of Fort Worth. Always ready to serve his adopted state, he organized a company of cavalry in June, 1861. The first company to leave Tarrant County for Confederate service, the unit became Company A, Ninth Texas Cavalry, with Quayle elected as lieutenant colonel. He commanded the regiment at the battles of Pea Ridge and Corinth, but with his health broken by sickness after the latter battle, he returned to Tarrant County.[17]

Shortly after Quayle's return he won election to the state senate and took his seat in the Ninth Legislature in February, 1863. When the Tenth Legislature met in session in November of that year, Quayle began to assert his leadership. He served as senate chairman for the Joint Committee on Frontier Protection, the body that did so much to push through the bill to transfer the Frontier Regiment to the Confederate Army and to create the Frontier Organization. When Governor Murrah appointed him to command the First Frontier District, Quayle brought to the organization an enthusiastic support for its success, the experience of leading men into battle, and the proven ability to maintain discipline through leadership.[18]

Major Quayle reached his district in late January of 1864 and began to organize his forces. His task was to appoint enrolling officers, to present instructions to his captains, and most difficult of all, to try to raise the morale of the war-weary citizens of his district. He placed his headquarters in the town of Decatur, in Wise County, because it provided a central location easily accessible for the populated areas of his district.[19] He soon stated the objective of the Frontier Organization, which should not have been difficult for him to do, as he helped write the law that created it: "I believe this organization will be of great benefit both to the State and the Confederate States in keeping out the Indians & arresting deserters and those persons who are avoiding conscription and draft service and turning them over where they belong."[20] Quayle completed the preliminary organization of his district by March, and although he was not under Confederate authority, he extended to Colonel Bourland, an acquaintance from the war's early days, and to General McCulloch, whose Confederate sub-district encompassed half the First Frontier District, his earnest wish for his men to fully cooperate with Confederate units in the region.[21]

George B. Erath, oldest of the Frontier Organization commanders, was the only one who maintained the leadership of his district from inception to war's end. Erath had come to Texas in 1833; joining John H. Moore's Ranger company in 1835, he fought in the Battle of San Jacinto in 1836. Then he obtained a first-hand knowledge of the Texas frontier by service in Ranger companies in the 1830s and 1840s. During the early part of the Civil War he was a lieutenant, then captain, in Company I of the Fifteenth Texas Infantry. In late 1862 poor health forced him to take sick leave at home, in McLennan County, and brought about his resignation from the Confederate Army on December 2, 1862.[22]

In January of 1864 a courier surprised Erath by bringing him a commission from the governor to command the Second Frontier District. He accepted and on January 14 arrived at Gatesville, in Coryell County, his chosen headquarters for the district. He immediately authorized sixteen enrolling officers to begin their work, then saw to it that regular mail services and couriers connected his headquarters with Austin and the populated areas of his district. Erath never quite seemed to master the intricacies of administrative paperwork during his term of service (probably his staff was incapable of providing the necessary help), and he never wrote detailed reports of his patrols as submitted by Major Hunter. But he knew what it took to prepare men for battle, whether against Indians, thieves, bushwhackers, or deserters. He soon employed a chief scout, a man once held captive by Indians for ten years, promptly arrested those who refused to be mustered into the service, and personally supervised a number of patrols that set out in search of Indian signs or deserters—all this in just his first month of command while the companies were still reporting for duty.[23]

James M. Hunter, who received command of the Third Frontier District, had moved to Texas in 1851 to join his brother John, who lived in Fredericksburg. Hunter quickly learned something of life on the Texas frontier when he raised a company of eighteen men to protect the surveying parties led by Robert Neighbors along the Brazos and its Clear Fork tributary. Later, he carried mail on the San Antonio–Santa Fe run, engaging in three sharp fights with Apaches in the process. In 1859 he accompanied Earl Van Dorn's expedition against the Comanches in Kansas and Indian Territories. During the war Hunter served with the Frontier Regiment as first lieutenant and then as captain of a company based at Camp Davis, in Gillespie County.[24] The widespread Unionist sentiment that affected much of the region, particularly among the German population of South Texas, led to bloodshed earlier in the war. Hunter's approval by the German element and his knowledge of the land and people of the district made him Murrah's choice for the new command.

As the Frontier Organization prepared for war in 1864 along the cutting edge of civilization, the will and capacity for battle that had seemed so limitless in early 1861 began to give way with the rest of the Confederacy's hopes. In a corner of the war where men never talked of glory, it remained to be seen if this new organization of frontier defense could hold its own against increased assaults from within as well as from without.

An assault upon the Frontier Organization came almost immediately from an unexpected source, the Confederate government. Under the Texas Legislature's "Act to Provide for the Defense of the State," passed in December, 1863, Gov. Pendleton Murrah proceeded in January, 1864, to retain in the state militia for a six-month period all able-bodied men not in Confederate service or exempted by state law.[25] This stance by Texas, combined with the fact that the legislature exempted men in the fifty-nine counties of the frontier districts to enable them to enroll in the Frontier Organization, led inevitably to a state's-rights clash over the issue of conscription. This conflict, through subsequent debate between Texas and Confederate officials, held ramifications that affected the structure of the Texas state troops and threatened the existence of the Frontier Organization.

Gen. John Bankhead Magruder, from headquarters in Houston, responded with alarm to the state militia law. His initial concern dealt with that part of the law which proposed to offer three-month furloughs to one-third of the militia on a rotation basis. The general did not wish to see any reduction in the militia strength of ten thousand men, subject to Confederate control within Texas, that he had struggled so hard to gain from Gov. Francis R. Lubbock and the legislature in the summer of 1863.[26]

In early January of 1864, through his judge advocate general, Col. John Sayles, Magruder presented his views to Governor Murrah on the conflict between Confederate conscription laws and the new militia law. Murrah's spirited response left no doubt that he would not be as compliant on the issue of conscription and Confederate authority as had his predecessor. Murrah maintained that Texas called these troops into being under the sovereign will of the state. Therefore, the militia should be seen as volunteer aid to the Confederacy, and Magruder had no right to assume command over them unless the government of Texas gave him that right.[27]

The Trans-Mississippi Confederacy's commander, Gen. Edmund

Kirby Smith, likewise brought the issue to Governor Murrah's attention. Smith pointed out, in regard to the conflict between the legislature's actions and the existing Confederate conscription law, that only President Davis could suspend conscription in any locale, such as the frontier counties of Texas. Smith complained that "it is to be regretted that the Legislature should have passed an act so well calculated to produce an unpleasant issue between State and Confederate authorities." Not only did General Smith question the legality of suspending Confederate conscription laws in the frontier districts, but he doubted particularly whether the men of the Frontier Organization were even needed for frontier protection. Murrah had earlier estimated that between eighteen hundred and twenty-two hundred men would enter the Frontier Organization. Smith calculated that to add this number to the Frontier Regiment, soon to be transferred to the Confederacy, with service planned tentatively for the Indian frontier between Fort Belknap and Fort Clark, would give Texas a force of approximately three thousand men assigned exclusively to frontier defense.[28]

Smith's analysis, however, neglected two important points. The law in question called for only one-fourth of the men enrolled in the frontier districts to be in active service; if two thousand were enrolled, this would place only five hundred men in the field at any one time. There also remained the unalterable fact that once the Frontier Regiment became a Confederate Army unit, it was subject to recall at any time to meet emergencies elsewhere. That is exactly what happened only three months later when Magruder ordered Col. James McCord and the six southern companies of the regiment to the interior. It may have been somewhat of an embarrassment for Murrah, although not an unwelcome one, when he later reported to Smith that some four thousand men, twice the number expected, actually reported for enrollment in the frontier counties that spring.

In an attempt to clarify the position of the Texas militia, Generals Smith and Magruder met with Governor Murrah in Houston to try to arrive at an amicable arrangement. Instead, Murrah insisted upon state control of the "conscript element" and compromised only to allow those of draft age who wished to do so to enter either new or old companies in Confederate Army service.[29] To complicate matters the Confederate Congress at this time attempted to raise the number of men needed against the growing northern armies by passing a new draft law on February 17, 1864. The law in question conscripted for the duration of the war all white men between the ages of seventeen and fifty. Those in the army between eighteen and forty-five retained their current enrollment, while men of seventeen to eighteen and forty-five to fifty constituted a reserve corps to be used for military service within their home states.[30]

Chiefly a matter of semantics and interpretation of the Confederate Constitution, this debate in peacetime might have been merely an intellectual exercise. Now, however, in February and March of 1864 Union armies in the Trans-Mississippi began their spring offensives, the most serious of which was General Banks's Red River campaign, seemingly aimed at East Texas. In the face of pressure by Magruder to release the militia completely to his control, Murrah offered only to turn them over by brigades to the governor's six hand-picked brigadier generals of state troops, rather than by companies as prescribed by the Confederate Army. Magruder declined the offer as contrary to Confederate regulations.[31]

By the first week in April, 1864, Magruder was nearly frantic in his effort to solidify the defenses of Texas with the state militia in place of those troops forwarded to Louisiana. He daily expected to hear of the fall of Shreveport, Kirby Smith's headquarters, and of the occupation of most of northeast Texas by federal troops advancing through Louisiana and Arkansas. On April 5 Magruder made a last urgent appeal to Murrah to organize the state troops in the face of an emergency. Federal forces under General Steele in Arkansas were only sixty miles from Texas, while General Banks and his army were less than that distance away at Pleasant Hill, Louisiana.[32] Under these conditions Governor Murrah's objections gave way. "As you have declined receiving the State troops as State troops, I shall be forced, in view of the dangers surrounding the State and country, to cooperate with you in organizing them under the recent law of Congress. I shall take upon myself the responsibility, which I feel to be a very heavy one, of calling upon the State troops to look no longer to an organization under the State laws."[33] Magruder felt no ill will toward Murrah for his stand in the conflict, attributing the governor's actions to patriotic motives and to the belief that Murrah felt himself "trammelled by a law of the Legislature in relation to the conscripts." By the following month the Texas Legislature worked to conform the state's militia laws with Confederate conscription laws, by July transferring nearly seventy-five under-strength companies to Confederate service.[34]

The issue over conscription in Texas was not resolved by Murrah's April decision, for the governor did not admit that Confederate conscription laws were in force in the frontier districts. Here the enrollment of men for frontier service held priority, based on the legislative act passed the previous December, a point almost neglected by Smith and Magruder at the time and by historians ever since. In January and February of 1864, as the frontier district commanders took the men of their districts into service, they attempted to enroll only men who could prove citizenship in the frontier county in question and who were not then in active Confederate service. Even so, Major Quayle reported that the men were in "a continual state of excitement" that Confederate enrolling officers were about to enter the districts to take away those of conscript age not exempted by the Confederate law of February 17.[35]

Confusion over the conscript status of the men of the frontier districts mounted when Gen. Elkanah Greer, head of the Bureau of Conscription, Trans-Mississippi Department, issued Special Order Number 40. This order declared that men in the frontier districts could form "temporary organizations" for the defense of the Texas frontier, but that Confederate enrolling officers would also organize them into Confederate companies detailed for frontier protection "whilst their presence is necessary." This arrangement was not exactly what the legislature had in mind. State and Confederate authorities differed not only between each other, but among themselves, in interpreting how to proceed in the matter of enrollment in the frontier counties. General McCulloch gave specific conditions that applied to those parts of the First and Second Frontier Districts within his Northern Sub-District. He stated that all men enrolled as conscripts before the legislature passed the frontier protection bill should be sent to camps of instruction and taken into Confederate service.[36] Some of the more energetic Confederate enrolling officers, however, attempted to enroll all men not exempted by Confederate law. Major Quayle would have nothing of it: "I hereby notify you that I claim the conscripts in this Frontier Dist. they having been mustered into this service under the instructions of the Adjutant General of the State and I cannot give them up except by an order from the Governor of the State."[37] Quayle believed that to give up his district to Confederate conscription would be to remove from it all good men who could be counted upon to arrest deserters and fight Indians. Their removal would leave behind "a class of per-

sons" that would make the frontier "a resort of Disloyalty and Treason."
Likewise, in the Third Frontier District Confederate officers planned
to enroll men of the district into companies and to sever conscripts
from the Frontier Organization.[38]

In the midst of this state's-rights clash over the Frontier Organization, Pres. Jefferson Davis replied to a request by Governor Murrah
that the frontier counties be relieved from the operation of the Confederate Act of Conscription. Davis could give no such relief, but he
offered Murrah the next best thing, a move anticipated by General
Greer's earlier order. The president said that for the time being he would
direct General Smith to enroll the men of the frontier counties and
then have them detailed and left for the defense of the frontier. If not
a victory for Murrah and the legislature, this at least sounded like a
more permanent arrangement than found in the wording of Greer's
Special Order Number 40. During the special session of the legislature
in May, 1864, Murrah vowed that the officers of the frontier districts
would continue to exclude from their muster rolls all deserters and men
who left other parts of the south to avoid military service and would
embrace only those who were there in good faith before the passage
of the frontier protection bill. To promote that end, Murrah proclaimed
that further immigration into the frontier counties of Texas was now
forbidden, and all men found there between the ages of eighteen and
forty-five who were not residents of their district prior to July, 1863,
were to be turned over to Confederate military authorities.[39]

Over two months after the legislature met, Major Quayle reported
rumors from his district that the Frontier Organization was to be disbanded – rumors fed largely by General Greer's pronouncement months
earlier that led some frontier citizens to flee the frontier to avoid Confederate conscription officers.[40] Murrah assured Quayle that the districts would not be interfered with; he had General Smith's word on
that. In addition, Quayle should have felt encouraged because the governor had always taken a special interest in the Frontier Organization.
He then offered Quayle some advice on how to best keep the organization together, as well as a tip on public relations:

> See that the Laws are observed and obeyed. Make the Frontier Orga-
> nization so far as depends on you what it was intended to be by the
> State Law. Purge it of all the elements that does not properly belong
> to it, and in the faithful discharge of its duties it will do still greater

good to the country. You should be published from time to time, the good your organization is doing—their services—the satisfaction with it by the people—the protection it offers, etc. It will have a good effect. See to it.[41]

Good press notwithstanding, the Frontier Organization found itself assailed once more in the fall and winter of 1864-65. This time the critics were Trans-Mississippi army authorities who sought to break up the organization in order to call manpower from the frontier. If Governor Murrah thought that General Smith's relative silence on the subject meant acquiesence, he soon discovered otherwise. Kirby Smith's assistant adjutant-general, Charles S. West, opened the offensive in October.

Smith attacked the Frontier Organization as a structure that precluded conscription thereby producing an interminable conflict between Texas and Confederate authorities. There should be no reason, he said, to exempt anyone from conscription because of geographic location; he then pointed out that the Frontier Organization did just that for over three thousand men, who should be turned over at once to the Confederate Army. West then pointed out the standard argument against the organization, that it encouraged deserters and draft evaders to congregate in the frontier counties of Texas. By adding such men to the total, West estimated that approximately four thousand men on the Texas frontier should then be in Confederate service. He then repeated an aphorism quite familiar to Texans: "It is the duty of the Confederate Govt. & not of the State of Texas to protect the Indian frontier." West directed that the men of the frontier districts should be turned over to the Confederacy, whereupon General Smith would immediately order the Frontier Regiment to the Texas frontier, supported by local militia. According to West, this process would adequately protect the Texas frontier and release not less than three thousand men to fill the depleted ranks of the army.[42]

Murrah received West's letter while the Texas Legislature met in a special session considering the status of the Frontier Organization. Governor Murrah then placed General Smith's views before the legislature, but its members refused to change the law. Even when faced with a recent letter from President Davis stating that he could not continue to exempt men from the conscription law, the lawmakers provided necessary funds to continue the frontier districts. They maintained firmly that the Frontier Organization should not be interfered with by Confederate authorities.[43] Murrah wrote that Smith's plan to order the Frontier Regiment back to the frontier would not strengthen the frontier defenses of Texas but would only be an exchange of forces, an inequitable exchange for Texas. Such a move, coupled with ordering local militia to support McCord's regiment, would give barely two thousand men to guard a frontier over 500 miles in length and some 125 miles in breadth. An attempt to break up the Frontier Organization without substituting an adequate alternative plan could not be tolerated, Murrah said. With the firmness of conviction, Murrah defended the latest evolution of frontier defense in Texas:

> The testimony, as I am informed, is almost unanimous from the frontier counties, that the present Organization affords better protection to that exposed portion of the State, than any mode of defense ever before adopted. By its exertions and influence, disloyal combinations have been broken up, deserters arrested and sent to their post of duty, and quiet order and satisfaction restored to those counties. The Frontier Regiment did not afford to the Frontier that sense of security afforded by the present force.[44]

If "quiet order" in the frontier counties was more than a small exaggeration, Murrah and the Frontier Organization at least had the backing of legislators and people who lived on the frontier. James Webb Throckmorton urged the governor to "maintain it at all hazards & to the last extremity." He stated unequivocally that should the Frontier Organization be broken up, not only would Indians and Jayhawkers continue to do serious damage in the First Frontier District, but the entire frontier would be overrun by deserters, draft dodgers, and traitors, and the frontier line would be thrown back upon a new line of counties.[45]

After he arrived in Decatur to replace Major Quayle in December, 1864, Throckmorton modified his views so that he was at least willing to compromise the structure of the organization. He and General McCulloch agreed that the "young" men of the districts should be put into constant service, while the older men would remain at home, still organized and ready for emergencies; the frontier districts would then be maintained and supported by the Confederacy.[46] As far as is known, Murrah never viewed this alternative as a viable solution. As for General Smith, he worked no further to break up the organization, but he submitted his arguments to President Davis in February of 1865 and awaited a decision. Davis, caught up in the maelstrom of events that soon led to the fall of Richmond, never replied, and the Frontier Organization continued in existence until the war's end.[47]

7

Disaffection and Turmoil
on the Northwest Frontier

In January and February of 1864, just as the Frontier Organization began to install its procedure, Indian raiders once more struck the frontier settlements. Continuing throughout the spring chiefly in the First and Third districts, these raids consisted mostly of small parties. Several settlers lost their lives and many more their property. Throughout the spring and summer these two districts still suffered devastation from Indian incursions, but this familiar predicament paled in comparison with the growing dilemma of apprehending deserters and white renegades. The two problems restrained the district commanders from implementing a more comprehensive system of defense.

The masses of deserters, disloyal Confederates, apathetic citizens, and suspected Union sympathizers living on the fringes of settlement constituted a nearly insurmountable obstacle to frontier defense. A detailed examination of the military and social pressures brought to bear in the frontier districts presents a new, fresh view of the enormity of the problem. In the western sector of Gen. Henry McCulloch's Northern Sub-District, the Texas frontier's most troubled area, a large measure of the challenge of frontier defense consisted of coordinating the plans and process of the Confederate and state forces. An uncommon cooperation would be necessary to achieve internal security and to fend off Indian attacks. The new year, 1864, brought with it internal problems that disrupted and drew strength away from the primary task of defending the Indian frontier in the sub-district.

By January of 1864 that part of the sub-district north of an east-west line running through Dallas suffered more than ever from the presence of those in the brush. The renegades now were reinforced by deserters from Indian Territory who entered North Texas easily due to the inefficiency of the Brush Battalion. In early January a staff officer re-ported that the region was swarming with deserters and Union sym-pathizers, men who grew so bold as to even steal General McCulloch's horse.[1] The news was no better from Gen. Samuel Bell Maxey, sta-tioned in the Indian Territory. On the day after New Year's, Maxey reported that an entire company of Gen. D. H. Cooper's brigade de-serted, probably for the Northern Sub-District. A couple of weeks later Maxey's spies (after infiltrating deserter bands in North Texas) indi-cated that the men scattered about in the North Texas brush were de-termined never to come out, that they longed for a federal invasion.[2]

McCulloch bemoaned the fate that led him to command a district where disloyalty seemed to be so widespread. In the face of repeated encouragement by Magruder to shoot down the men in the brush with-out hesitation or mercy, McCulloch knew that he simply did not have the manpower to hunt down the numerous, strong bands of deserters who were once more gathering. He was under orders to send returned deserters to Houston, but he often had difficulty finding an escort strong enough to get them through his sub-district, as bands of brush men threatened to ambush any small patrol and free the prisoners.[3]

McCulloch assigned two principal military units to arrest and es-cort captive brush men. L. M. Martin's Cavalry Regiment was detached from General Maxey's department in Indian Territory, and companies of Bourland's Border Regiment were to be removed from Indian patrol duties for such tasks. So many men of Maxey's command deserted and made their way to the Northern Sub-District that Maxey kept a net-work of spies working there to infiltrate the groups, and he frequently sent additional military support to McCulloch to break up brush gangs. In early February, when McCulloch learned that approximately one hundred men led by a Dr. Penwell were about to cross the Red River and make their way north, he sent an urgent message to Maxey to be on guard, as there was no cavalry force in Texas available that could stop them before they reached Indian Territory. Maxey's men picked up their trail, captured Penwell and eight others, and killed seven more. Four of the men turned out to be deserters from Indian Territory; Maxey scheduled them to be executed by firing squad on February 18.[4]

The burden of such a command would have weighed heavily upon anyone, but for McCulloch, who still craved action as a field commander, the endless months of administrative difficulties with seemingly little good to show for it were especially galling. In late December, 1863, he wrote to General Magruder and requested a transfer to field command anywhere, even to a small cavalry detachment on the coast. By January the frustration and stress of his turbulent command seemed to overwhelm McCulloch. In a harsh letter to Magruder, he tried to explain the real situation in his sub-district. He stated that when he finally got the deserters out of the brush and ordered them to their state militia commands near Houston, they refused to go. Worse, he had insufficient force to compel them, nor could he induce them to report to their original commands, wherever located. With uncharacteristic bitterness McCulloch said that the best thing for the country would be to kill them; as traitors, they deserved death. His few infantrymen were used almost solely in guarding prisoners and protecting stores from thieves; his few cavalry units were engaged primarily in hunting deserters and escorting prisoners while trying to guard against Indian incursions. McCulloch noted that in recent weeks a dozen men had been reported killed or severely wounded, some by his men in pursuit of deserters, but most by bushwhackers. He concluded with this observation: "In addition to the deserters, absentees, and skulkers almost one-fourth of this population ought to be taken up for aiding and assisting deserters . . . and disloyal expressions and acts. I would be much gratified if I could be relieved and join you on the coast where the enemy is to be met and where there are loyal and true men to meet him with."[5] Dissatisfaction notwithstanding, McCulloch threw himself into his work with renewed vigor as spring approached, and he stayed in command of the Northern Sub-District until the war's end.

Command was made more difficult with the Brush Battalion still in the region. A Hollywood scenario might envision that these men "gone bad" would be transformed into paragons of frontier service, but such was not to be. Problems abounded from the day they left McKinney, and with few exceptions the men were more hindrance than help to the beleaguered frontier. Afterwards, McCulloch reflected that the men of the Brush Battalion behaved abominably everywhere they went, "committing petty depredations on the property of the people about all their camps." As reports of their poor behavior came in almost daily, McCulloch tried "to get the good men out from the bad by culling them." He endeavored to discover just which men could be depended upon, so that they could be placed with a company under Captain Ferrell. He vainly hoped to maintain at least one reliable unit for service out of more than five hundred men who marched off to serve in the Brush Battalion.[6]

Once looked upon as a way to reinforce frontier defense in northwest Texas, the Brush Battalion was now considered too unreliable to commit to Indian scouting duties. Instead, it was used in January and February of 1864 to meet the other objective of the Frontier Organization, to arrest all deserters in the districts and to work in securing others found hiding in the brush. This work also proved to be beyond the battalion's capacity. Even the influence of a good officer, Maj. John R. Diamond, failed to keep his men from "deserting constantly and going back to the Brush or to the Federals." The unit managed to break up a gang of bushwhackers in Jack County, but the battalion's presence in the First Frontier District and adjoining counties of the Northern Sub-District worked more harm than benefit.[7]

In late January of 1864 Colonel Bourland sent a detachment of men from Capt. Samuel Patton's Company of the Border Regiment to Elm Creek, approximately seven miles southeast of Denton, to break up a suspected hideout of brush men. In fact, over forty men known to be part of the Brush Battalion had been seen going into the thicket just four days earlier, and groups of Brush Battalion men were known to have been in contact with the Elm Creek group for some time. Bourland's detachment scouted the region and planned to move in at daybreak on Monday, January 25. McCulloch sent reinforcements, but the brush men received word of the assault in time, and most managed to escape. Of the hundred men known to be in the group, only fourteen were caught. By this time McCulloch reported that the Brush Battalion was down to a strength of only 209 men; with scores of deserters slipping off each week, the commander cursed a land which could harbor such men, adding that "I have never been in a country where the people were so perfectly worthless and cowardly as here."[8]

It seemed that men from the Brush Battalion were implicated in every new disturbance. Then, when Major Diamond learned that Henry Boren planned to lead a force of approximately three hundred brush men out of Texas to reinforce the federals, McCulloch determined to put an end to the Brush Battalion experiment once and for all. He disbanded it on Monday, March 21, thus ending the short history of a unit that was intended to be an example for others to come out of the brush.[9] On the day before McCulloch moved against the battalion he described the conditions of his sub-district to Governor Murrah:

> I can *assure you* that there is a *large* disloyal element here constantly at work in the army to get men out and keep them out of service. There are untrue men in *every* command . . . and many of them no doubt sought that service to avoid the conscript law and keep from meeting the Federal army. No man can know and understand the condition of this country unless he was in it to see for himself . . . and I will save the country or go down with it.[10]

Under orders from General's Smith's headquarters, the men of the Brush Battalion who wished to return to their old commands were to be escorted to Marshall, Texas, for enrollment, while all others were to be sent to General Magruder in Houston. Battalion commander Major Diamond, at least, was rewarded for his trials with the brush men; he received a promotion to lieutenant colonel of Bourland's Border Regiment less than two months later.[11]

In the midst of the unwelcome work of rounding up deserters and hunting down those who evaded conscription, McCulloch once more became involved with William Clarke Quantrill's band of men, who once again gave immeasurably more difficulty than aid. During the winter of 1863–64 Quantrill's men made a general nuisance of themselves by occasionally shooting up the town of Sherman and providing little assistance in rounding up deserters. Stories of plunder and robberies by Quantrill's men filtered into Bonham for some time, but when murder became commonly attributed to them, McCulloch knew he had to take action. He reported to General Magruder that he planned to arrest Quantrill and his men and send them to either Houston or Shreveport: "They regard the life of a man less than you would that of a sheep-killing dog. I regard them but one shade better than highwaymen, and the community believe that they have committed all the robberies that have been committed about here for some time."[12]

McCulloch planned to use men from Bourland's regiment to make the arrests, but just in case more force was necessary, he prevailed upon General Maxey for use of Col. Stand Watie's regiment, located just north of the Red River. McCulloch, however, failed to muster a force large or capable enough to take on Quantrill's band, so the general tried another tack. Having received word that Quantrill's men were ordered to report to the Texas coast for duty, McCulloch wrote to Gen. Hamilton P. Bee, in the Western Sub-District, just six days after telling Magruder of the plan to arrest Quantrill: "I . . . have advised Quantrill to ask for service west of Corpus Christi, where I think he will do us great good. There is no doubt about their being true Southern men, and, no odds what happens, will fight only on our side. They have been bad behaved in some instances, but have not been guilty of a fourth of what has been charged against them."[13] Now, Henry McCulloch, although toughened by a life on the frontier, was a gentleman of the old school, honest and true to his word throughout a long life of public service. The lone exception, seen here in the letter to General Bee, indicates just how desperate he was to rid the Northern Sub-District of Quantrill's influence.

Quantrill refused to report to Magruder on the coast; meanwhile, in March, Quantrill and another leader of his unit, "Bloody" Bill Anderson, had a falling out. When Anderson reported to General McCulloch that he was willing to testify as to Quantrill's guilt in recent crimes, McCulloch requested that Quantrill report to Bonham. On Monday morning, March 28, 1864, McCulloch dispatched two hundred men from James Webb Throckmorton's militia and approximately one hundred from Colonel Martin's regiment to arrest Quantrill and his men. Not long after they got under way, Quantrill and about two dozen of his men rode into Bonham for the meeting with McCulloch.

When Quantrill entered McCulloch's office the general informed him immediately that he was under arrest. Visibly shaken, Quantrill said nothing and placed his guns on a nearby table as McCulloch explained to him that certain charges had to be investigated. When McCulloch left for dinner he invited the prisoner along; Quantrill declined, preferring to stay in the office, on his honor. Not long after McCulloch was out of sight, Quantrill grabbed his pistols, raced out the door, and called out to his men to break for safety or everyone would be arrested. The gang then dashed out of town and headed for their camp near Sherman.[14]

Although the pursuing troops outnumbered the guerrilla leader's force by three to one, they were unsuccessful, more from reluctance to press the issue with men of Quantrill's reputation than from inability to overtake them. As McCulloch put it shortly afterward: "I have not had troops that had the moral and physical courage to arrest and disarm them."[15] Quantrill and his men soon crossed the Red River, thus ending their reign of terror in the region.

With the Brush Battalion broken up and Quantrill forced out of the territory, all in the last ten days of March, 1864, McCulloch may have expected his sub-district and the First Frontier District to be somewhat calmer. Instead, activities in the month of April caused the break-up of a disloyal combination that threatened to rival that of the Peace Conspiracy of 1862. On Sunday evening, April 10, William Quayle, commander of the First Frontier District, was at his headquarters in Decatur when one of his captains, James M. Luckey, rode into town and wished to have a private talk with him.

In the course of conversation Luckey casually asked Quayle if he still held anti-secession sentiments, as he had before the war began. The major cautiously replied in the affirmative, whereupon Luckey asked him to put official capacity aside and speak with him as one citizen to another. Suspecting that something was afoot, Quayle gave his approval; then Luckey suddenly inquired if he could talk treason. Quayle took the plunge and told Captain Luckey to say what he had on his mind.

Quayle was stunned by the story that Luckey unfolded before him. Luckey, it appeared, only pretended to be an ardent secessionist; actually, since the beginning of the war he had been working for the overthrow of the Confederacy. He was suspected of disloyalty, however, by a Sons of the South vigilance committee in Weatherford. He had recently learned that this group planned to seize him the following Saturday. Thinking he found a sympathetic ear in Quayle, Luckey requested the immediate assignment of his company to patrol duty farther west, where he would proceed to organize all resistance in the First Frontier District. He said he could already count on the support of two companies of Barry's Frontier Regiment troops and two hundred men of the Frontier Organization under himself and three other captains, as well as numerous deserters known to be in the region. Luckey proposed to establish a base out west, initiate communications with the federals in Indian Territory, and prepare to aid a Union invasion of North Texas.[16]

General McCulloch learned of the plot on the morning of the fourteenth but could scarcely believe that such a scheme was being hatched. He soon learned the story was accurate and began making plans, but in a manner so as not to cause alarm. No doubt reminded of Bourland's zeal in stamping out disloyalty in Cooke County in 1862, McCulloch did not want to be responsible for a repeat performance of that bloody affair. He replied to Bourland to keep an eye on the men of his command but not to precipitate action in the First Frontier District unless Quayle requested aid. McCulloch suggested that Quayle, if the story were true, should take careful steps in gathering proof of guilt before the ringleaders and their men should be arrested. If the investigation showed substantial evidence of treason, McCulloch proclaimed, "pounce on them and kill or capture the whole of them and better kill than capture them."[17]

In one sense, at least, the conditions in which this Frontier Conspiracy of 1864 transpired resembled the situation of 1862. Then, the Peace Conspiracy took place in the midst of rumors of a federal invasion; now, however, Union forces were in fact converging on Texas through Arkansas and Louisiana. They would be turned back. A Confederate Army threw back Banks's invasion force at the Battle of Mansfield two days before Luckey held his fateful dialogue with Quayle, but the news had not yet reached Bonham. The state and Confederate officials who set out to break up the conspiracy did so in the belief that the conspirators, if left unchecked, would soon be aiding Union invaders.

Meanwhile, Colonel Bourland's blood was up; not willing to wait for Quayle to request aid, he fired off suggestions on how the major should handle the situation. Indelicately, Bourland told Quayle that he knew all along that a great number of the soldiers of Quayle's Frontier District were traitors; now was the time to bag the lot of them. Bourland proposed to send spies from his command to gather information by pretending to be deserters. He then recommended that Quayle first inform the Sons of the South, at Weatherford, not to take action against Luckey but rather to stall as long as possible while pretending compliance. For his part, Quayle wasted no time. He immediately consulted with Judge J. W. Ferris, then holding district court in Parker County, about Luckey's story. Judge Ferris knew enough about the implicated parties to recommend their swift arrest by military, rather than by civilian authorities.[18]

The arrest order came soon enough. On the following day, April 15, McCulloch gave orders for Colonel Bourland to direct the arrests and send the traitors immediately to General Magruder in Houston. He instructed Bourland to take only his most reliable men and to make all arrests simultaneously, as designated by Major Quayle. McCulloch also called upon four companies of Col. Tilghman Good's Confederate cavalry from the vicinity of Paris, Texas, for support, although he did not place much faith in them. For this action Bourland's and Quayle's most trusted men were the ones counted upon. On the fourteenth, McCulloch dispatched a spy of his own from Bonham, a double agent of sorts, to find out what he could of the leaders and intent of the conspiracy. The man was L. L. Harris, a boot- and shoemaker by trade, whom McCulloch often used as an agent to obtain information from behind Union lines as well as from men in the brush. Previously, Harris had convinced Luckey that he was actually a clerk at McCulloch's headquarters and would keep Luckey informed of developments on that end. Now Harris headed west to allay suspicions and to help Quayle ferret out the leaders of the conspiracy.[19]

As the net was about to be drawn over the conspirators, Bourland, who did not accompany his force in the upcoming arrests, sent along advice on how to handle the operation. He sent three companies, approximately one hundred men, and suggested that Quayle send away his unreliable troops, retain only "true and loyal men," and then secretly arrange the arrests simultaneously, as McCulloch suggested. Only the officers should know the nature of the mission until the force arrived at the "different homes of those traitors." "Major, you must manage this affair in the same way we did in Cooke [County]," was Bourland's parting remark.[20]

The morning of Tuesday, April 19, was targeted as the day to spring the trap. As Quayle prepared to move in, the security lapse that inevitably accompanies such missions enabled a large number of those implicated to escape. They ultimately joined the federals or deserters in the brush. As the arrests began taking place on the nineteenth, principally in the counties of Parker, Wise, and Jack, many of the populace envisioned a repeat of the hangings of 1862. A "stampede" took place in Wise County when the rumor went out that Confederate troops were arresting everyone who voted "the Union Ticket" and who opposed secession in 1861, and many of them fled to the interior and as far away as Mexico.[21]

In Parker County the arrests came under the direction of a trusted officer and citizen of Weatherford, Capt. Joseph Ward, who commanded a company in the Frontier Organization. His lieutenant, Jackson F. Floyd, arrested three of the suspected ringleaders, James M. Luckey, A. F. Corning, and David O. Norton, and then took down their statements as written testimony. The men were taken to Decatur the next day, where they soon joined others arrested at the same time. From there authorities sent them to Fort Worth, where they could be placed under a more secure guard, with little hope of being rescued.[22] At Fort Worth Major Quayle arranged to send Luckey and seven others in irons to Houston, "charged to commit treason and with disloyalty." The few others taken with them were identified as deserters and sent to General McCulloch. The prisoners sent to Houston, particularly Luckey, expected to be executed for their activities. Surprisingly enough, authorities released the men that summer because of lack of evidence, whereupon Luckey joined his wife at her parents' home in Bell County. The outraged people of Parker County, particularly those of a local vigilance committee headed by Captain Ward and Judge A. J. Hunter, had Luckey arrested in Bell County on a writ issued by the judge. On August 1, when Luckey and his escort approached Weatherford, a group of men suddenly rode up, took Luckey away, and hanged him from a post-oak limb about fifty yards from the roadside.[23] Arrests continued to be made, about thirty in all, by the Parker County vigilance committee of the Sons of the South. All save one were acquitted before a tribunal in Decatur, and the one was merely sent to serve in the Confederate Army.

This incident bears so many similarities to the Peace Conspiracy of 1862 that it is curious that the mass executions of those days did not occur again in 1864. The old ardor of the war's early days had faded. The northwest frontier of Texas had suffered too many hardships, had seen too much misfortune and death; the mood of the populace to take action was no longer there as before, and the appeals of Bourland and other officers failed to change matters. No Union army had ravaged the land, but a war-weariness lay upon this portion of the Confederacy. Men would still react to protect lives and property from bushwhackers, or to fight against Indians, and a few would still rally to hang a suspected traitor, but the call to fight intangible rumors of conspiracy no longer moved the people.

8

Organization of the
First Frontier District

April–September, 1864

Even with the turbulent Frontier Conspiracy at an end, military leaders in the Northern Sub-District found no respite. An attempt to coordinate the activities of the Frontier Organization, Border Regiment,
and Frontier Regiment was disrupted by the proposed removal of Lt.
Col. James "Buck" Barry's Frontier Regiment companies from the Fort
Belknap region. In response to General Banks's federal offensive up the
Red River in Louisiana, a move that threatened East Texas, General
Magruder ordered the six southern companies of the regiment to the
interior. Here they would replace the mounted regulars who had earlier moved eastward to reinforce Gen. Richard Taylor's effort to stop
Banks. These companies concentrated on Onion Creek, near Austin,
in May, 1864, to prepare for their move eastward.[1]

While the regiment was split, several months passed before it could
be ascertained just who was in overall command of Barry's detachment
at Fort Belknap. In the spring of 1864 the Western Sub-District encompassed all the frontier counties, except the populated ones along the
extreme northwestern frontier, but its successive commanders always
focused their attention on the coast and Rio Grande defenses rather
than on the protection of the interior.

Gen. Henry McCulloch, of the Northern Sub-District, was the logical choice as the Confederate commander to best direct Barry's battalion of the regiment, but he labored for some time without specific
instructions to do so. He could only request that Barry's men and the
Frontier Organization companies cooperate with Bourland's Border Regiment to maintain frontier defense. As late as April 26 McCulloch wished
to move two companies of the Frontier Regiment farther west, but, as
he complained to General Magruder, he doubted his authority to do

so. Finally, Magruder confirmed in May that Barry's four companies at Fort Belknap were, indeed, subject to McCulloch's orders. When Gen. Thomas F. Drayton took command of the Western Sub-District that summer, the boundaries were changed to make him responsible for only that portion of Texas west of the Colorado River, a move that implied the extension of McCulloch's authority to include all of the First Frontier District and Barry's Confederate companies on patrol there.[2]

When Buck Barry's four Frontier Regiment companies of the northern division also received orders in early spring to report to the interior, adjustments had to be made quickly to cover the gap that would be left. Barry managed to have the orders revoked and remained until August, when his troops pulled out, not to return for nearly three months. Nevertheless, much of the planning done in April to cover the removal of Barry and his companies reveals the strategic situation on the northwest frontier at this time, a condition that existed in fact several months later when Barry actually left.

In April Barry discovered that his battalion was to be concentrated at Fort Belknap prior to a move toward the coast. He believed that such a move would open up to Indian invasion all of Clay and Montague counties, as well as parts of Cooke, Wise, and Jack, and at the same time would expose approximately 150,000 head of cattle in the First Frontier District to Comanche and Kiowa raids. As it was, Captain Rowland's Frontier Regiment company, at Red River Station, was some fifty miles west of Bourland's nearest Border Regiment outpost on the river. To withdraw Rowland would be to open a floodgate of enemy activity against the northwest settlements. Barry estimated that the four companies of his command already covered a line over 250 miles in length; he did not see how Bourland could possibly extend his forces to plug the gap. General McCulloch prepared for just such an eventuality in May when he ordered Bourland to initiate the process to extend his companies to cover the region between Fort Belknap and the Red River upon the removal of Barry's companies.[3]

Bourland proceeded to make plans that would actually take effect in August. Throughout the latter months of 1863 Bourland had frequently moved the site of his headquarters, but he had tended to favor locations along the Red River or even farther north near Fort Arbuckle. In 1864, however, he directed operations from his office on the west side of the courthouse square in Gainesville, located approximately five miles south of Red River, in Cooke County. Throughout the spring and summer of 1864 Bourland's companies constantly shifted to new locations, attempting to offer the best protection against Indians while at the same time trying to maintain the region's internal security. Throughout the spring months Bourland handled these duties with only six companies at hand; four of them were detached for service on the coast for some time, and one, Company A, maintained a permanent post near Fort Arbuckle, in Indian Territory. When the Frontier Regiment companies left in August, Bourland once more had ten companies to use, and he proceeded to station them to protect the northwestern frontier.[4]

By mid-summer, 1864, Bourland's companies and commanders were located at the following stations: Company A, Capt. C. L. Roff, Camp Simons (southwest of Fort Arbuckle); Company B, Capt. James J. Diamond, Fort Arbuckle; Company C, Capt. A. J. Nicholson, Fort Arbuckle; Company D, Capt. A. B. White, Fort Belknap; Company E, Capt. F. M. Totty, Victoria Peak (west-central Montague County); Company F, Capt. S. F. Mains, Fort Belknap; Company G, Capt. S. P. C. Patton, Gainesville; Company H, Capt. James Moore, Hubbard Creek (eastern Shackelford County); Company I, Capt. J. B. Anderson, Buffalo Station (Buffalo Springs, southeast Clay County); and, Company K, Capt. William C. McKaney, Camp Twitty (near Spanish Fort, just east of Red River Station). Captain Roff soon became major of the regiment, in charge of the small battalion at Fort Belknap, while Lt. Col. John R. Diamond commanded the battalion that operated out of the Fort Arbuckle vicinity. Regimental quartermaster was Capt. William C. Twitty.[5]

On a straight line, Bourland's patrols covered over two hundred miles, from the scouts west of Fort Arbuckle to the patrols that extended out of Hubbard Creek as far south as Camp Colorado. Of course, in any discussion of Civil War military operations it is superfluous to speak of any line as the crow flies. No roads connected many of the posts held by Bourland's companies, but eventually a regular courier service developed between Confederate commanders at Fort Belknap, Gainesville, and Bonham. Regular communications between First Frontier District commanders at Decatur and Bourland's headquarters led, in the absence of a telegraph, to as efficient a communication system as possible by post, one more rapid than the postal service of today over the same area.[6]

Colonel Bourland, as always, chafed under orders to keep his companies on patrol duty near the settlements. He preferred instead to take the initiative to scout out Comanche and Kiowa encampments in Indian Territory and strike them first. In April his scouts west of Fort Arbuckle sent along information that a large force of hostile Indians had passed recently near Fort Cobb and was headed in the direction of the Wichita Mountains. Bourland immediately called upon Major Quayle to provide a force to cooperate in a preemptive strike against them, but the Frontier Conspiracy uncovered by Quayle just a few days afterward canceled such plans. In July Bourland prepared to concentrate his companies for a move north of the Red River, but once again he was forced to cancel the operation in order to extend his companies to cover the line vacated by Barry's companies in August.[7]

In the midst of these plans by Bourland's men, the effort of the Frontier Organization to protect the Indian frontier should not be ignored. While state troops of the Frontier Districts came to act primarily as the police organization of the frontier counties, with specific orders to round up deserters and enforce conscription laws, they were charged as well with protecting the frontier against Indian encroachment. No closer cooperation between Confederate and state forces in guarding the Indian frontier existed than in the First Frontier District. When in July, 1864, Bourland began to extend his forces over a wider area than ever before, he depended upon the cooperation of Major Quayle's companies to supplement his own to help fill the gaps between the companies of the Border Regiment. He asked Quayle to send regular detachments to patrol the Red River crossings, from the well-known rocky-bottom ford at Sivells Bend, in Montague County, westward to various points along the river as far as Clay County.[8]

When Quayle organized the First Frontier District earlier in the year, he set forth the procedure by which Indian patrols would be carried out. Men of each company were divided into four squads for service of ten days at a time to search for Indian signs along the boundaries of the counties where they mustered.[9] In actual practice the companies rarely confined their activities to only their counties of organization. Commanders in all the Frontier Districts often called upon more reliable companies as fire brigades to rush to points of crisis, and they also used such units to concentrate their strength in critical areas.

In August Barry finally received orders to transfer his command to the coast. The departure of his four companies left only a small remnant of the regiment on the frontier, a two-company battalion stationed at Camp Colorado under Capt. Henry S. Fossett. For nearly two months Barry and his companies remained on duty at various points near the coast until Gen. John G. Walker, who succeeded Magruder, ordered them back to Fort Belknap in October. The six southern companies never again returned to frontier service, even though Colonel McCord continued to work toward that end. In November, after word came of renewed difficulties on the frontier, not the least of which was the great Elm Creek Raid by Comanches and Kiowas near Fort Belknap, McCord appealed to General Walker for permission to return his regiment to frontier service. Walker refused; he told McCord that "he had but few troops in this vicinity and if he needed any at all he would be likely to want them this winter."[10] For the rest of the war this contingent of six companies remained chiefly in the newly created Central Sub-District, stationed at Bastrop, at Columbus, and at various points near the coast.

With the Frontier Regiment in such a state of flux for much of 1864, and with the permanent removal of half its strength from the frontier by late spring, the heaviest burden of defense in the First Frontier District fell upon the Frontier Organization, Bourland's Border Regiment, and one small, unlikely, band of reinforcements. As ready as Texans were to fire upon any Indians found south of the Red River, there remained one welcome tribe—the Tonkawas.

This central Texas tribe, formed in the early nineteenth century by the merging of remnants of various Tonkawan bands, had long been an enemy of the Comanches who held sway over much of north-central Texas for so long. In the early days of the Confederacy, even before Fort Sumter, Henry McCulloch had requested that Tonkawas be allowed to serve with his force on the Texas frontier, and several such scouts accompanied him into Indian Territory shortly afterward. Most of these Tonkawas were not located in Texas at the onset of Civil War; they, like the other tribes of the Brazos Indian agencies, had left the state in the forced exodus of 1859. A small remnant, however, remained in Texas under Castile. Approximately three hundred more under Chief Placido, who had done so much to aid the Ranger and Army campaigns against the Comanches in 1858, had moved to the Anadarko Agency in Indian Territory near Fort Cobb. There on October 25, 1862, a force of pro-Union Shawnees, accompanied by Comanches, Kiowas, and Caddoes, attacked the Tonkawas and massacred nearly half, including Chief Placido.[11]

The survivors of the massacre made their way to Fort Arbuckle and then, with the help of Buck Barry, journeyed back to Texas in 1863. They located in two groups, one near Fort Belknap and the other near Camp Colorado. Here a Tonkawa tribal council agreed to accept the leadership of Castile. Colonel McCord authorized Barry to provide them supplies and suggested to state officials that they be used as spies and scouts for the Frontier Regiment.

Soldiers and citizens of northwest Texas welcomed the Tonkawas because of their past help against the Comanches. Even John R. Baylor, who is probably identified more than any Texan of the period with a hatred of Indians, requested the use of several Tonkawas to spy for his company. After much debate over the responsibility of providing for the Tonkawas, in December, 1863, the legislature responded to an impassioned plea by Governor Murrah and appropriated $20,000 to provision them until such time as the Confederate Government could assume the task. Murrah concluded with forceful logic: "They are in our midst; they are friendly; they are willing to fight for us; they are desolate and without a home." The same measure also directed the Frontier Organization to employ the Tonkawa warriors at the standard pay for troopers.[12]

In February, 1864, Major Quayle indicated to General McCulloch that the small group of Tonkawas near Fort Belknap would serve as excellent scouts and spies for the First Frontier District forces. Major Erath concurred concerning the Tonkawas at Camp Colorado. Throughout the next several months Texas authorities continued to discuss ways to best utilize the Tonkawas, places to maintain their camp, and means to provide for them. In May Castile paid a visit to Governor Murrah in an attempt to resolve some of the problems. Barry tried to help by sending along a written introduction:

> Allow me to introduce to you the Tonkaway [sic] Chief, Castile, who visits you for the purpose of securing a home in Texas. They suffered a massacre rather than act traitorous to us; they say they are now weak and not able to contend with more powerful tribes north of Red River is why they ask a home in Texas, that they have been on the frontier of Texas some thirty years fighting its enemies until the once powerful tribe is now dwindled down to about 180 souls, but that they are yet willing to do all they can for Texas.[13]

By late summer Castile and forty-four of his warriors enrolled as one of the Young County companies of the First Frontier District. The company first appears on a muster roll of August, 1864; Castile is listed as captain of a company having a complement of three officers and forty-two privates. The troopers were armed collectively with four rifles and "bows and arrows."[14] Major Quayle sent word to Governor Murrah of their organization as a company and mentioned their lack of proper weapons, but the official reply hardly lived up to expectations. Inspector General David B. Culberson wrote that Governor Murrah thought it best to use the Tonkawas exclusively as spies and scouts for the military, rather than as a separate company. As he stated the potential problem: "The propriety of arming so large a body of Indians, and allowing them to roam over the Country, appears doubtful and may be productive of bad results."[15] Quayle agreed. Since Colonel Culberson stated that guns could be provided to the Indians if they remained attached to white companies as scouts, Quayle requested that at least twenty rifles be sent as soon as possible to arm them. When Gen. James W. Throckmorton left Austin in November to replace Major Quayle, he brought along with him the twenty guns as well as a keg of powder, ammunition, percussion caps, cooking utensils, and a promise, later fulfilled, to obtain for the Tonkawas cloth made at the state penitentiary in Huntsville.[16]

The officer directly in charge of providing for the Tonkawas was Capt. Y. H. Isbell, detailed in June of 1864 as acting state agent for the Tonkawa Indians. The convoluted story of just who had authority to manage the affairs of the Tonkawas, particularly in regard to supplying them, involved Gen. Samuel Bell Maxey, in Indian Territory, Lt. Col. Buck Barry, Col. James Bourland, Gen. Henry McCulloch, and the commanders of the First Frontier District. Finally, Throckmorton had charge of providing for them until January, 1865, when he reported to the state inspector general that he was at last successful in an effort "to get the Tonkaway Indians off our hands," by transferring the responsibility permanently to Confederate command.[17] The Tonkawas, although few in number, provided able service by their invaluable scouting and trailing abilities, a welcome addition to the hard-pressed Frontier District forces.

The officers and troopers on the frontier now needed all the help they could find. During the next few months an unprecedented flurry of activity in the First Frontier District resulted in the pursuit and arrest of numerous deserters. By the first of April Major Quayle reported that a number of armed gangs of deserters existed in the First Frontier

District. Some of these groups were thirty strong or more, and one band had a known strength of at least 120. The breakup of the Brush Battalion in March and the dispersal of the Frontier Conspiracy in April set in motion a general movement of those in the brush. Many of the renegades headed for the western limits of the Northern Sub-District, about midway across the breadth of the First Frontier District, where they reportedly planned to raid the settled areas. Others of the brush men gathered their families in preparation for leaving for California.[18]

Reports from spies indicated that many deserters and draft evaders were congregating along Hubbard Creek, in Stephens County, where, as General McCulloch put it, "the impression is all over the country that there is no war in California and if there they could live in peace."[19] To add to the problem, men from Bourland's Border Regiment and James "Buck" Barry's Frontier Regiment battalion deserted during the spring at an alarming rate. In fact, the Border Regiment at this time had an effective strength of only 365 out of a total of 602 on the rolls. McCulloch by now believed Quayle to be an able and efficient officer, but because the men of the Frontier Organization depended largely upon their own means for forage and supplies, their scouts in search of deserters were of limited duration. McCulloch believed that the Border Regiment had to provide more efficient service, but because of the scattered nature of the command and its other role of scouting for Indian signs, its efficiency was less than peak. McCulloch wanted Bourland to recruit two more companies, with Quayle's and Governor Murrah's permission, from the First Frontier District. Also, owing to Colonel Bourland's age and feeble health, McCulloch desired a younger officer to take his place.[20] McCulloch failed to achieve either of these objectives for the time being; the work went on with the men and officers available.

During April and May the military quickly closed on the scattered gatherings of deserters. Bourland reported reliable information on deserter groups in Denton County, between Elm Creek and Clear Creek north of Denton; in Shackelford County, near the valuable saltworks; in Indian Territory, between the Red River and the Wichita Mountains; in Jones County, near Fort Phantom Hill; and in west-central Texas, in the Concho River vicinity. The greatest threat, however, came from a group of renegades and deserters known to be at Victoria Peak in western Montague County.[21] Approximately three hundred men reportedly had congregated there with the intention of joining forces with a group just beyond the Red River and moving to Union lines in Kansas. Bourland proposed to use part of his own force and three of Quayle's companies to root out this bunch; there was no time to waste in gathering supplies for a long march. He told Quayle: "We can live on Buffalo and Beef for a short time. Take a little salt; we must catch them and let us lose no time."[22]

The expedition started out on Monday, May 9, with about 250 men of the First Frontier District under Capt. Joseph Ward. The captain intended to rendezvous with two companies of the Border Regiment, but they arrived too late and found only a deserted camp. They should have known that surprise would have been nearly impossible, because the high elevation of Victoria Peak provided sentries a commanding view of any approaching forces. Bourland grasped this point, at least; for the rest of the war he kept one of his own companies posted there. When the expedition first moved out, word came from one of Buck Barry's spies that Capt. H. J. Thompson, of the First Frontier District, who commanded a company at Buffalo Springs in southeastern Clay County less than twenty miles west of Victoria Peak, was actually a leader of the band of deserters. It was said that he planned to drive a large herd of cattle west, join deserters along the Big Wichita River, and then drive the cattle to Kansas.

These military forces converging at Victoria Peak used this information to begin their pursuit over the country west to the Big Wichita and northward in the vicinity of the Wichita Mountains. With a combined force of approximately 450 men, in the largest expedition of its kind since the creation of the frontier districts, Capt. James J. Diamond, of the Border Regiment, and Captain Ward, of the Frontier District, led one column to scout out the south side of the Big Wichita, while Captain Roff of the Border Regiment covered the north side. They shortly received additional reinforcements from the Frontier Regiment in the form of Captain Rowland's small force, which left Red River Station about eight days after the others headed west. By the time Rowland's men reached the Big Wichita the combined forces of the Border Regiment and state troops were already north of the Red River scouting the area between Cache Creek and the Wichita Mountains; therefore, Rowland kept his men to the south.[23]

For all its efforts this extensive operation never came upon the main body of deserters and renegades, but they did fall upon some of its stragglers. Bourland's men allegedly killed one man who surrendered, while twenty-two men of Capt. S. F. Mains's Company sent word that they would return voluntarily if they could be reunited with their old company. Bourland replied that if they turned themselves in he would send them to General McCulloch's headquarters, according to instructions, and he also warned them that if they refused to come in, he "would take and kill the last one of them." Most of the deserters at this time were taken in this fashion, not through capture, but by voluntarily turning themselves in. In May and June Major Quayle reported that his frontier forces captured thirty deserters from Confederate service while eighty turned themselves in, a ratio that seemed to hold true for the rest of 1864.[24]

Whenever Quayle's men procured any deserters they were required to send them directly to Colonel Bourland's headquarters in Gainesville, whereupon the colonel would then forward them to General Mc-Culloch in Bonham. McCulloch usually routed them under guard to Magruder's headquarters in Houston, though on occasion he sent them to the Bureau of Conscription in Marshall. The road from Gainesville to Bonham, however, turned out to be a rough one, in more ways than one. Beginning early in the year, charges abounded that Bourland's men frequently murdered some of their prisoners, not in the act of capturing them, but after they were taken and under guard. A muster roll for a First Frontier District company records tersely: "Ransom Graves, age 27, taken by Col. Bourland's men and killed, April 25."[25] When Captain Rowland, of the Frontier Regiment, mentioned in May that Bourland's men had murdered a deserter, Rowland commented about the colonel: "I believe he is doing very good service towards capturing deserters. And they find or meet but few favors from him which makes them dread to fall into his hands."[26]

So many reports began filtering in to McCulloch's office that when word came of a series of murders in May and June, he sent a strong reprimand to Bourland informing him of complaints about the cold-blooded murder of prisoners:

> I do not desire men shot after they throw down their arms and hold up their hands nor after they are captured unless they undertake to make their escape, and then there should be no doubt on the subject. There is no one in the land more anxious than I am to rid the country of such men as by their actions deserve death, *but I cannot in any manner* agree to make myself Judge Jury and Court Martial to decide their cases

and execute them without trial and if such things have been done let
them occur no more.[27]

In fact, McCulloch sent one of Bourland's letters to Governor Murrah; in the letter Bourland implied that perhaps the shooting of a few
more men of Quayle's Frontier District would help curb desertion.
Quayle bristled when he learned of Bourland's statement. The colonel
wrote that he only meant such a fate for the "bad" men of Quayle's
command, then added indignantly, "I think that 27 years in Texas, and
a part of the time was helping hang and whip rascals out of the country, surely ought to give me some ideas of Mankind."[28]

Eventually, Bourland's own men attempted to put a stop to the practice. In October of 1864 charges and specifications were prepared to
be used against Bourland in court-martial proceedings. Four charges
of incompetency were minor points; the charges on conduct unbecom-
ing an officer and a gentleman lay at the heart of the matter. The charge
stated that Bourland "ordered, permitted, or connived" in the murder
of prisoners; then it proceeded to list details. It told of the deaths of
two men in January and February and then detailed the murders in
May and June that had attracted McCulloch's attention. While passing through Sherman on their way to Bonham with nine prisoners
in leg irons, men of Bourland's "special guard" had borrowed shovels
for a burial detail, even though no one was yet dead. Then that night
they shot two prisoners and buried them. A short time later, concerning a Mr. Pitman being taken to Bonham, Bourland instructed his guards
that if Pitman happened to be killed before they reached Whitesboro,
fourteen miles away, his horse was to be returned and given to Bourland's assistant quartermaster. It was so done. The charges related not
only stories of such deaths on the road to Bonham, but also of men
taken out of custody by the colonel's "special guard," marched outside
of Gainesville, and hanged.[29] The twenty-eight men of the Border Regiment who signed as witnesses included five of his captains.

No evidence exists that a court-martial was ever held, but it is known
that Bourland remained in command of the regiment for the duration
of the war, save for a leave of absence in early 1865 when Lt. Col.
John R. Diamond took his place. It is quite possible that the leverage
offered by such charges, combined with McCulloch's strict accounting
for future deaths of prisoners, ended the practice. After the late summer of 1864, Bourland's correspondence contains none of the familiar

rhetoric about shooting brush men, nor can any instance be found again of prisoners killed while in his charge. It hardly requires a leap of imagination to suspect a declining morale in the First Frontier District in the face of such behavior by Bourland's command, or to wonder why so many deserters tried to return directly to their old units rather than to be forwarded to Bonham by Bourland.

General McCulloch's impatience with Bourland also stemmed from the actions of Bourland's men across the heart of Quayle's district. These actions included the arrest, without proof, of men assumed to be deserters if found alone, and outrages against citizens of the district. Bourland thus defended his methods to Quayle: "I differ in opinion as to making these arrests without sufficient evidence—doing good for I am satisfied that where we know a man to be disloyal and can't get such evidence as we can get at him with, we can at least trouble him enough to make him keep his sentiments confined to himself and probably drive him from our midst."[30] McCulloch had heard enough by this time to ease Bourland out of the business of bringing in deserters. As of September the only forces charged specifically with actively searching out renegades were those of the Frontier Organization. McCulloch informed Bourland that his command was to concentrate on the Indian problem; because of numerous "acts of rashness" by the Border Regiment, internal security was to be handled by Quayle's men only.[31]

As winter approached, General McCulloch had to remove the patrols from the First Frontier District in order to guard against a greater threat to the eastern portion of his sub-district. The danger was not from federal invasion. In October and November deserters once more began to come into northeastern Texas in large numbers, as did irregular bands of bushwhackers who wished to refit and winter there. "Deserters, absentees, and skulkers must be kept out of the country, or it will be ruined this winter," McCulloch wrote to Bourland. He felt compelled by necessity to modify his previous instructions to the colonel and once more turn him loose in Quayle's district to hunt down deserters, with a strong caution to arrest only men liable for military service, not those suspected of disloyalty or of harboring deserters.[32]

Kirby Smith was aware of the situation, and he blamed it on the fact that counties of the Frontier Organization were exempt from Confederate conscription laws: "The frontier counties . . . are . . . a grand city of refuge where thousands of able-bodied men have flocked to escape service in the Confederate Army." McCulloch meant to shut off that refuge. He received aid in the process from Governor Murrah who, after receiving petitions from citizens in northeast Texas, requested Smith to send reinforcements to the counties along the Red River.[33]

By late fall McCulloch received the troops he needed to stem the tide of renegades, deserters, and war-weary men moving westward to the Frontier Districts. McCulloch's force now consisted of five cavalry companies and two infantry companies, representing nearly eleven hundred men in the eastern portion of his district. His force within the First Frontier District totaled approximately six hundred under Bourland and Barry.[34] General Maxey, as always, provided prompt support by trying to keep men from drifting across Indian Territory to north Texas. He published McCulloch's General Orders Number 33, which stated that "should any party be found in the brush . . . they will be fired upon at once and shot as long as they resist or try to escape." Maxey reinforced this goal by issuing his own orders to keep north Texas free of such men.[35]

Such efforts only partly explain why so few stragglers and deserters made their way to the First Frontier District during the winter of 1864–65. An additional reason lay in the increase in Indian raids during the late fall and winter. Hostilities by Kiowas and Comanches not only served to restrict the movement of deserters and conscripts in the First Frontier District until spring, but also limited the problems caused by brush men along the entire line of the First Frontier District. The number of deserters along the northwest frontier may not have decreased, but most of those at this time came from Confederate or state units already on the frontier; they were not from Confederate units across the Red River.

9

Later Days of the
First Frontier District

October, 1864–May, 1865

Throughout the spring and summer of 1864 Maj. William Quayle struggled to maintain order in the First Frontier District, the most complex and difficult district to manage in the entire Frontier Organization. By summer's end he prepared to step down as commander of the district. Quayle needed time off to improve his health and to put his own affairs in order; lying just below the surface, however, was the relentless pressure of his job, made impossible in August and September by continual difficulties with the men of Bourland's command. He wrote to Governor Murrah on September 8 and requested to be relieved, a request the governor granted on September 26. It is not known if Quayle recommended anyone for his position, but he heartily approved Murrah's choice, James Webb Throckmorton of McKinney.[1]

Throckmorton was one of the state's most distinguished politicians, a member of the state senate, and one of the influential voices of north Texas. He represented Collin and Grayson counties at the regular session of the Tenth Legislature and chaired the Military Affairs Committee. His cordial acquaintance with William Quayle stemmed from this period, when he and Quayle served together on the Committee on Frontier Defense.[2] For the rest of the war these two friends were on the best of terms, each supportive of the other and each willing to aid the other's attempt to preserve and perfect the Frontier Organization.

At the same time that the legislature created the Frontier Organization, it also passed "An Act to Provide for the Defense of the State." An effort to reorganize the State Militia, this law called out the militia for a six-month period, subject to Confederate command while in service within Texas. It created a reserve corps that in time of emergency would keep two-thirds of the militia in the field for as long as needed to meet a threat. On March 1, 1864, Governor Murrah appointed Throckmorton as a state brigadier general to command Brigade District Number 3, one of six militia districts created in the state.

Throckmorton issued the necessary instructions throughout his district and began assembling militia by the third week of March. He selected Bonham as his headquarters, where he could work in close cooperation with General McCulloch, and he established his brigade encampment in the southwest corner of Fannin County. As for the eight hundred to one thousand men that he assembled by the first of April, he hoped to have them ready to meet Union invasions of Texas by way of Louisiana or Indian Territory, to guard Confederate commissary stores, to help round up and guard deserters found in the brush, and to detach two companies for frontier service in Quayle's district.[3]

When the first called session of the Tenth Legislature met in May, both Throckmorton and Quayle attended; this time Quayle was a member of Throckmorton's Committee on Military Affairs. The Committee strongly recommended the continuation of the Frontier Organization. Governor Murrah agreed, stating to the legislature: "If thoroughly systematized and faithfully executed, it promises better protection against the peculiar warfare waged upon the frontier by the Indians than any plan heretofore adopted. It seems to harmonize well with the habits, the peculiar interests and pursuits of the people of those counties."[4] This session of the legislature also passed a law that made Throckmorton's succession of Quayle a natural one. The lawmakers gave the governor discretion to assign one of the state brigadier generals for duty in a Frontier District "to make more efficient the frontier organization."[5] Quayle's competent administration of the First Frontier District brought no need of a change; only his desire to be relieved altered the command structure.

Throckmorton did not travel immediately to Decatur to take charge on the frontier. He wished first to attend the second called session of the legislature, October 15 to November 15, 1864, a session that Quayle did not attend because of the renewed threat of "Indians and renegades" in the First District.[6] Throckmorton was an excellent choice to replace Quayle, and in the fall of 1864 the First Frontier District needed all the help it could muster. On October 13 the wartime era's most destructive Indian raid took place; it was one of the largest ever seen on the Texas frontier.

The celebrated Elm Creek raid, in Young County in October, like the Cooke County raid in the previous December, took place at a most inauspicious moment for the settlers of the region. It occurred during the three-month interval when Barry's Frontier Regiment companies were on assignment near the coast, while Bourland's Border Regiment, spread out over a two-hundred-mile line, attempted to fill the gap left by Barry's companies. The raid also took place after Governor Murrah designated Throckmorton as Major Quayle's successor, but before the general's arrival. In addition, the raid took place in General McCulloch's Northern Sub-District just after McCulloch left Bonham for a two-month leave of absence, while Col. George Sweet replaced him temporarily.[7]

The Elm Creek raid had its origins in the disturbances that rocked the plains to the northwest earlier in the spring of 1864. A renewal of conflict on the south-central plains initially involved Cheyenne and Arapahoe tribesmen, joined later by various bands of Comanches and Kiowas, in warfare against Union forces along the Kansas-Colorado frontier. Destructive raids by various parties of these tribes virtually halted travel along the Santa Fe Trail and sent a wave of terror across the Kansas frontier. Throughout the summer bands of Comanches and Kiowas accumulated stores for the coming winter at their camps along the Canadian River, in the Texas Panhandle. As Union commanders prepared plans to reclaim the western military routes that had been cut by the raids, they devised a strategy to pressure the Kiowas and Comanches to the south.[8] The five hundred to seven hundred warriors of these two tribes led by the Comanche warrior Little Buffalo, probably saw the Elm Creek raid as a way to secure needed horses and cattle for the upcoming winter warfare.[9] The Comanches, many bands of whom had no part in the treaties signed in 1861 with Confederate commissioner Albert Pike, surely needed little incentive to strike once more at the hated "Tejanos" south of the Red River.

Under the full moon of October 12, a large force of mounted Comanches crossed the Red River near present Burkburnett and moved to the area northwest of Young County. Ready to strike the next morning, they concentrated on the small area of settlements near Fort Belknap in west-central Young County. The community of Belknap, located about one-half mile south of the fort, had boasted in 1858 a population of approximately one hundred fifty, with a number of stores, shops, and even a hotel. Settlers had more than twenty-five hundred acres under cultivation in the county, where the Cross Timbers merged with the state's north-central plains to the northwest. By 1864 only a dozen or so families, fifty to sixty settlers in all, clung to the area just north-west of the fort, along either side of the Brazos River about twelve miles northwest of Fort Belknap. These hardy people who stubbornly stayed on the bare face of the plains had spent part of the previous year build-ing defensive palisades of logs, placed picket fashion in the ground sur-rounding the homes. The two strongest of these fortified homes were small stockades: Fort Bragg, a home on the Bragg ranch, along Elm Creek just south of the Brazos; and the stronger of the two, Fort Mur-rah, thrown together in February, 1864, and named after Governor Murrah.[10]

The warriors reached the area about noon on the thirteenth, split into several groups, and then fell on the surprised community with a ferocity that so characterized conflicts between Comanches, Kiowas, and Texans. Most of the hardest fighting and deaths occurred along Elm Creek as Indians struck the farms and ranches of the area. An account of a portion of the attack of October 13 gives an idea of what transpired during such raids. At the Fitzpatrick ranch, in a two-story house once known as the Carter Trading Post, a band of women and children tried to hold off their attackers. Mrs. Milly Durkin, age twenty-one, fired away with her shotgun as Indians broke down the door. She was thrown to the ground; "while one Indian split her skull and scalped her, another Indian struck Mrs. Fitzpatrick with his spear to force her to look upon her daughter's torture." A seven-year-old boy was shot down when he ran out the door, and an infant boy found hidden in a box under a bed was killed. Two women, one of whom was a mulatto named Mary Johnson, who was pregnant and whose husband, Britt, was away on business, along with five children, were tied to horses and led away. When the Indians started back with them that night, they rode for nearly two days in the direction of the Pease River before mak-ing camp. When the warriors saw that one of the thirteen-year-old cap-tives was too ill to sit up and travel, they tied the boy to a brush heap, set fire to it, and forced his mother, Mrs. Elizabeth Fitzpatrick, to watch him die.[11]

The smoke of burning buildings soon alerted settlers on both banks of the Brazos, and as many as possible tried to make it to either Fort Murrah or the Bragg stockade. Lt. N. Carson, in command of a de-tachment of Company D of the Border Regiment, had twenty men posted about thirteen miles west of Fort Belknap when the attack began. When he received word of the attack, he left immediately with fourteen troopers and headed toward Elm Creek. They rode until they reached a point just north of the Bragg Ranch, scene of the heaviest fighting of the day; there they confronted approximately three hundred warriors who broke off from the main party and headed for them. The soldiers fell back to the north and headed for the McCoy Ranch, in a running fight of about two miles. The Indians killed five of Carson's men during the pursuit and wounded the horses of five others. Just ahead of the Indians, Carson's men rescued two women at the McCoy ranch and scrambled across the Brazos to the safety of Fort Murrah.[12]

Meanwhile, for some six hours Comanches and Kiowas surrounded the Bragg stockade, where the Bragg family and a host of their neighbors crowded in fear and successfully withstood all efforts by the Indians to drive them out. During the exchange a rifle shot killed Little Buffalo, and the attack broke off shortly afterward. As the Indians moved northward, the soldiers and settlers who huddled together in Fort Murrah saw two large parties, each two hundred to three hundred strong, ride by to the east and west of the stockade with their captured livestock in tow. The thirty-two able-bodied men at Fort Murrah expected a dawn attack, but most of the soldiers refused, understandably, to make a twelve-mile night ride through the host of Indians to Fort Belknap. Finally, Francis Peveler and one of Carson's men agreed to try. They made it through and arrived to find that a few settlers had arrived before them with the news of the attack. Approximately twenty-five soldiers remained to guard the fort, but the rest had been ordered away on a scout before the Indians attacked. Riders then headed east to find reinforcements for the beleaguered frontiersmen. Major Quayle received the awful news in Decatur at dawn the next day.[13]

Quayle saddled up the post guard, gathering company detachments and volunteers as he rode out. Soon he had more than two hundred men riding for Fort Belknap, some eighty miles away. Colonel Bourland did not receive the news at his headquarters in Gainesville until the morning of the fifteenth. He then sent word to Quayle that three of his companies, those under Captains Anderson, White, and Moore, would soon converge on the area. This force represented three of the four companies that he had concentrated near the Red River to strike a blow at Indians coming south.

Intelligence reports just in from Gen. Douglas Cooper, in Indian Territory, indicated that officials expected three large columns of Plains Indian warriors to appear at any time along the northwest Texas frontier. Supposedly, the Elm Creek raid was only the first. That a raid took place after a moonlit night in October came as no surprise; in fact, just six days before the attack Quayle wrote to Austin that he anticipated Indian movement bearing in from the northwest. The expectation of a major raid caused Quayle to cancel all plans to attend the upcoming special session of the legislature.[14] The Texans were astonished at the huge number of Indians that actually arrived. The massive party moved so rapidly and carefully that Bourland's and Quayle's scattered patrols never detected it until the blow fell along the Brazos.

When Quayle's men were still approximately twenty miles east of Fort Belknap, a rider met them with the news that the Indians had cleared out; there would be no dawn attack. Quayle pushed his men and arrived at Fort Belknap at sundown. There he learned that a force of about sixty, combined mostly from Captain White's Company D and volunteers, had pursued the Indians toward the northwest. The Texans broke off the chase after approximately one hundred miles; the Indians simply had too much of a head start, even though laden with booty and livestock.[15]

Although the Texans suffered heavy casualties, they might have fared worse but for the heavily fortified stockades of Bragg and Murrah located nearby. At least five soldiers and seven settlers were killed and mutilated, and seven women and children were carried off. Although the Indians, as usual, carried off their own dead, Carson believed that his men killed seven or eight in the running fight. Most of the Indian casualties came during the lengthy attack on the Bragg home; in all, it is believed that some twenty Indians died in the raid. This extraordinary number of losses occurred because the attack was pressed in uncharacteristic manner upon a fortified position. The Indians burned eleven homes on October 13, after looting them of everything of value; all horses that could be found were taken, and the cattle not driven off were killed.[16] None of the other attacks anticipated by Bourland took place, but damage enough was done; such a destructive raid never again took place on the northwest frontier of the state until after the end of the war. Nevertheless, the citizens of Young County and other counties nearby prepared as if a major attack might come at any moment. The practice of forting up, that is, settlers drawing in to live near heavily fortified stockades or ranch houses, became common procedure. In fact, General Throckmorton's first order, when he took command of the First Frontier District, called for the settlers on the frontier to fort up. Some left for the interior, but many who long had endured hardship on the frontier refused to be driven out.[17]

State and Confederate response took the form of two measured changes in policy to ensure that there would be no repeat of such a raid as had befallen Elm Creek. The disaster gave impetus to a once-proposed but unused plan that called for a preemptive strike upon concentrations of Comanches and Kiowas believed to be in the northwestern section of Indian Territory. Previously, in May of 1863, officials had canceled an ambitious three-month campaign north of the Red River proposed by Colonel McCord of the Frontier Regiment, but the plan was revived in 1864. Tentative preparations had begun in the summer of 1864, three months before the Elm Creek Raid, when Major Quayle requested Governor Murrah's approval of a ten-week scout of at least two hundred men for a sweep through Indian Territory as far north as the Kansas border. A month later he still hoped to receive permission for such an expedition, but by this time he planned to send a force of more than three hundred men. He received no reply, but none was necessary in the face of the impending departure of Barry's four companies from the northwest frontier; every man would be needed along the line of settlements. But help was on the way. Barry's command returned from the interior shortly after the Elm Creek Raid and reported to Colonel Bourland for duty. They were a welcome reinforcement for the First Frontier District. Bourland promptly recalled two of his companies, Moore's and Mains's, to Salt Creek Station, on the Red River, while Barry's men once more covered the western end of the line.[18]

Major Quayle never had a chance to organize his hoped-for expedition, but his successor did. After the legislative session ended in November, Throckmorton started for Decatur to take active command; by that time Major Quayle was already at home in Tarrant County, in poor health again. Throckmorton arrived in Decatur on December 13, 1864, set up headquarters in the old Howell and Allen store, which had been converted into an arsenal during the war, and officially assumed command of all state forces in the First Frontier District.[19]

Not until January of 1865 did Major Quayle return to Decatur as

Throckmorton's second in command. A testament of Quayle's efforts on behalf of the First Frontier District is seen in a letter that Throckmorton wrote to Governor Murrah: "I cannot close this communication without admitting to the very able service rendered by Maj. Quayle. The . . . organization has been immense. This with other labors has been herculean & I scarcely see how he has been able to discharge his office duties with so little aid, and at the same time perform so much duty in the field. This frontier & the state owes him more than can be known or appreciated."[20] Quayle's health continued to deteriorate, and he served in the district only until the end of March, when he obtained a furlough and ended his service to the frontier.[21]

When Throckmorton took command in December he expressed concern about renegades, Jayhawkers, and Indians and their theft of Texas cattle. Convinced that "the federal army at Forts Gibson & Smith have been largely supplied with Confederate beef," Throckmorton again proposed a sweep through western Indian Territory to Kansas.[22] This time the plan would go into effect. By the end of the year the frontier protection units of the First Frontier District numbered as follows: Frontier Organization (state), 1,436 (approximately 350 on duty at one time); Border Regiment (Confederate), an effective strength of 498, of which approximately 350 were included in the four companies stationed within Texas; and Barry's Battalion of the Frontier Regiment (Confederate), an effective strength of approximately 150 (with another 120 that patrolled the northern portion of the Second Frontier District).[23]

Not long after New Year's Day a meeting took place in Decatur between the military hierarchy within the Northern Sub-District, namely, General Throckmorton, General McCulloch, Colonel Bourland, and Lieutenant Colonel Barry. In their discussion of how to protect the frontier more effectively, all agreed to organize a winter campaign into Indian Territory in the vicinity of the Wichita Mountains. It was to be a major campaign involving more than four hundred men, of whom two hundred were to be contributed by the Frontier Organization, with Maj. Charles Roff, of the Border Regiment, in overall command.[24]

The expedition got underway on schedule on February 1, 1865, with fewer men than anticipated. Companies from the various commands made their rendezvous at the mouth of the confluence of the Big Wichita and the Red River in northern Clay County. Major Roff commanded the expedition as planned, while Captain Earhart directly coordinated Throckmorton's state troops. The men started out in good spirits. Even when the hardship of severe weather hit and cut short the campaign, the morale of the Frontier Organization men never seemed to sag, although there were problems within the Border Regiment companies. On the second day out some of the younger members of the Frontier Organization decided to have some fun with a few older men, some of the "scarry [sic] fellows" on the trip who may have had little desire to tangle with Comanches. A few of the boys made their way at dawn of the second day to where their victims slept, then banged away on their saddlebags and shouted "Indians!" as loud as possible. The handful of "scarry fellows" made a dash of over two hundred yards through thickets, briars, and thorns before they stopped running and returned to camp to face gales of laughter. The pranksters could not resist pulling a more ambitious stunt about a week later. One night the conversation turned to the numerous Indian signs seen that day and the expectations of meeting with Comanches before long. Soon after everyone bedded down for the night, three or four men slipped off to one side of the camp, and after making sure that all but the objects of the joke were in on the stunt, fired their rifles in the air and raised a yell. A nearby shallow lake did nothing to slow down the jittery ones: "Away went the scarry fellows, minus clothing but taking their rifles with them. Through the lake they went, lickety-split to the low ground and timber, some of them losing their guns in the water on the way. After discovering it was a hoax they came back very angry and very much on the prod."

These pranks were the highlight of the entire expedition, for nothing else of consequence occurred. After the men had been a few days out on the trail, the weather turned to an almost constant downpour of rain, sleet, and snow. Forage for the horses was in short supply, but the men ate well from buffalo and cattle killed along the way.[25] Indian signs abounded in the vicinity of the Wichita Mountains; the soldiers came upon abandoned Indian camps, but not an Indian was seen. As the weather grew more severe, Major Roff ordered "the great western scout" to return after barely ten days in the field. Disorder accompanied the return as the men straggled back in, walking their worn-out horses.[26] Although he saw no positive results, Throckmorton believed that the expedition was not in vain: "It will teach the Indians that even in mid winter, we intend to hunt them in their retreats. The expedition has prevented any raids of consequence during the present light moon."[27]

The officers who met in Decatur in January intended originally for this winter campaign to precede a larger and more extensive expedition to be conducted in the latter part of spring. They never carried out such plans. In just one month, from December, 1864, to January, 1865, Throckmorton reported a drop of approximately 250 in the effective strength of his forces. A corresponding drop in the Confederate companies through desertion, coupled with an attempt by Confederate authorities to deal once more with the Comanches and Kiowas by treaty, ended the prospect of any more extended campaigns north of the Red River before the end of the war.[28]

With prospects dim for additional offensive action in the spring, authorities implemented the second phase of a plan to prevent future Elm Creek affairs. This time, it was General Throckmorton who did so by a complete reorganization of his forces. In correspondence in January, 1865, with Governor Murrah and with Col. John Burke, the new adjutant and inspector general of Texas, Throckmorton outlined his proposal. He believed that the best possible plan for the Frontier Organization would be to organize a permanent force for service in the field. In fact, he believed that in his district he could organize between five hundred and six hundred men at no added expense; the men in reserve and in the field would donate three-fourths of their state pay for provisions and transportation. The scarcity of provisions, adequate arms, and transportation led Throckmorton to suggest that the Confederacy be charged with providing such essentials in return for Confederate commanders to direct any extensive, joint operations against the enemy.[29] Throckmorton never received orders for such a consolidation, but cooperation between his forces and McCulloch's Confederate troops allowed the plan to be put into operation during a joint punitive expedition in February, 1865.

Sometime after mid-February of 1865 Throckmorton divided his command into four battalions of approximately six companies each. The battalion commanders were Capt. C. Potter, in Cooke County; Capt. J. B. Earhart, in Wise County; Capt. Joseph Ward, in Parker County; and, Capt. J. J. Cureton, in Stephens County. These men maintained regular scouts, greater in strength now than previously, from the Brazos River to the Red River, at intervals of twelve to eighteen miles. For support, permanent outposts of company strength were maintained in the counties of Palo Pinto, Stephens, Young, and Jack.

Basically, Throckmorton's state troops filled the center of the line of defense on the northwest frontier of Texas. Barry's men covered the region west of Fort Belknap and southward to Camp Colorado, while the companies of Bourland's Border Regiment, on the right flank of Throckmorton's command, took up a general line from Buffalo Station, in Clay County, northeastward to Victoria Peak, Salt Creek Station, and Fort Arbuckle. After the Elm Creek raid Bourland usually maintained company posts at Buffalo Station, Victoria Peak, Salt Creek Station, and occasionally Spanish Fort. Salt Creek Station, in Montague County just south of the Red River, replaced the site for Captain Rowland's Frontier Regiment company, which had been stationed nearby for so long. Two companies were usually present at the station, and in January, 1865, it became temporary headquarters of the Border Regiment, under command of Lieutenant Colonel Diamond, while Bourland was on leave.[30]

This modification represents the last organizational change within the First Frontier District. As such, it represents the last attempt of a determined search to perfect frontier defense in the Northern Sub-District of Texas. During the short while that officials used this system, the northwestern counties suffered none of the ravages of Indian attacks of times past. Certainly, the combination of several companies into battalion strength for scouting purposes would allow a full complement of men to meet any major incursion that approached the size of the Elm Creek raid. Although Indian raids occurred infrequently in this region in the spring of 1865 and were not expected to intensify until late summer or fall, still the coordination of the minutemen companies of Rangers of the First Frontier District with elements of the Border Regiment and Frontier Regiment may have been the most effective combination to withstand the Indian threat. The rapid collapse of morale in Texas that came with military disasters across the Confederacy in April and May cut short this last effort in the evolution of frontier defense during the Civil War.

As northers rolled in, bringing on a harsh winter, the job of tracking down men in the brush came almost to a standstill in the First Frontier District. As talk of Indian incursions once again predominated, the officers prepared to renew their efforts with the advent of better spring weather. By late March of 1865 renegades were again rumored to be on the move westward, and the men of the Border Regiment and Throckmorton's Frontier District were soon on the trail. The last great roundup of armed deserters on the northwest frontier took place in the last days of March and early April of 1865. Throckmorton sent

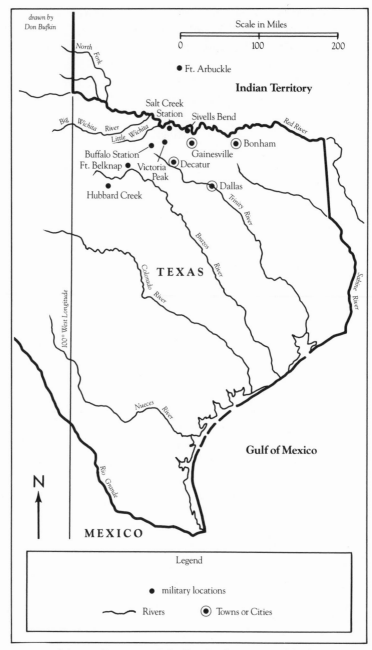

MAP 5. Outposts of the Border Regiment, 1864–65

word to thirty-two-year-old Capt. George Bible Pickett, at Decatur, that approximately one hundred deserters from Confederate service in East Texas were then in movement across the district on their way to New Mexico Territory. These fugitives were known to have been congregating for some time along Denton Creek, in Wise County. When Pickett and thirty of his men left Decatur on April 1 headed northwest, he learned that Lieutenant Colonel Diamond, of Bourland's Regiment, was already in pursuit.[31]

Companies from Jack, Wise, and Montague counties under the command of Captains J. B. Earhart, William H. Shoemaker, and S. Shannon joined Pickett's men en route. They picked up the trail in Wise County and followed it with little difficulty to a spot on the Little Wichita River, in western Clay County not far from the present city of Wichita Falls. At dawn on April 3 scouts found the deserters camped just over a ridge, near the river's edge. The combined state and Confederate force on the field was 134 strong, including 79 men from three companies of the Border Regiment and 55 state troops from parts of four companies. The deserters, approximately 100 in number, had superior mounts and plenty of supplies. Diamond, of the Border Regiment, by agreement in overall command, advised against an immediate assault; he preferred to wait for a night attack. Pickett, nevertheless, recommended an immediate surprise attack.

This joint effort was a cooperative one between state and Confederate troops, and as Diamond did not object, Pickett asked for volunteers for the mission. Two entire companies of the Frontier Organization and a handful of Confederate troops stepped forward to volunteer. About thirty of these men moved to the right (north) flank under Captain Shannon, while Pickett took the same number to the left. These two forces charged simultaneously, not to attack the deserters directly, but to drive off their horses before the brush men could react. With the alarm, as the renegades rushed about to see what was happening, Diamond and the rest of the force appeared at the top of the ridge as if prepared to charge. No attack was necessary. Without horses they were helpless; the deserters soon put up a white flag, and the action ended, save for a brief episode when the deserters seized Diamond and demanded that their horses be returned.[32]

The 98 men and 150 horses captured were then taken back to Buffalo Springs, in Clay County, to await transport to Houston.[33] The disposition of the prisoners' property deserves note. Just a week after Throckmorton assumed command in Quayle's place, he suggested that his troops be allowed to confiscate the property of those they captured, in lieu of pay from the state. This, he said, "will be a great stimulus to exertion."[34] The policy was adopted in 1865, but a dispute arose in April between Throckmorton's and Bourland's men over disposition of the spoils taken on the Little Wichita. McCulloch had to solve the disagreement. Divide the private property equally, he said, taking care to set aside stolen Confederate horses or arms; officers of each force could then jointly divide the remaining horses, saddles, bridles, blankets, and arms. He recommended that the most valuable portion should go "to those who acted most gallantly in the capture."[35] In the final act of this last drama the recently captured deserters were still within the district when word came of Lee's surrender to Grant at Appomattox. Such news did not mean the war was over for the Trans-Mississippi Confederacy, but to many it signaled that an end to conflict was in sight. The prisoners taken on the Little Wichita were released.[36]

There was, of course, no end in sight to the conflict between Texans and the Plains Indians, but Confederate officials attempted to change that. Before its fortunes collapsed in the spring of 1865, the Confederacy made one last attempt to bring peace to the Indian frontier, this time by negotiation with Plains tribes. Earlier that year Confederate officials learned that a number of the hostile bands north of the Red River desired friendly relations. Perhaps this entreaty for peace stemmed from renewed pressure exerted by federal military forces, but for whatever reason, in March of 1865 Gen. Kirby Smith, on the advice of Gen. D. H. Cooper in Indian Territory, appointed General Throckmorton as Confederate commissioner on the part of Texas to treat with the various bands of Comanches in an effort to come to terms with them. Throckmorton's first inclination was to turn down Smith's commission, but the latter's desperate tone persuaded him. He went into the job, however, with the attitude that "we know the Indian character too well to trust to their promises."[37]

Upon further reflection, General Smith in April modified Throckmorton's status; he was now to be one of two commissioners to meet with the tribes in May, the veteran Indian negotiator Albert Pike being the other. Smith diplomatically phrased the reason for the addition of Pike: "Owing to the many years of incessant hostility and predatory warfare that had existed between the Wild Prairie Comanches and the frontier settlers of Texas, that a deep distrust and bitter hatred of Texas had been infused into the breasts of these savages . . . it would not be well to give to Texas as a state too great a prominence in the negotiations."[38] Smith wished the treaties to be made along the lines of those of 1861, but this time he wanted a tripartite arrangement to bind together all Plains Indians hostile to the U.S. government, the Five Civilized Tribes of Indian Territory, and the Confederate government. Especially important was the agreement between the Plains Indians and the Five Civilized Tribes so that they could cooperate in a general attack on the Kansas frontier. Just before the negotiations began, General Cooper informed Throckmorton not to bring up the subject of the Indian move against Kansas until the Trans-Mississippi governors approved the plan, as rumors abounded that Confederate authorities might soon be negotiating the surrender of the Trans-Mississippi Confederacy.[39]

Governor Murrah appointed Maj. John W. Lane as substitute to command the First Frontier District, and Throckmorton left Decatur about the first of May to travel to Indian Territory for the council. With General McCulloch in charge of providing supplies and wagons for the trip, Throckmorton journeyed to the Washita River, near Elm Springs, for the scheduled May 15 meeting with the various tribes. Throckmorton and Col. W. P. Reagan, who replaced Albert Pike, met with numerous Indian leaders representing over a dozen major tribes.

The commissioners proposed that the Plains Indians agree never to enter Texas south of the Red River, a proposal that met with almost unanimous dissent. The Indians insisted that they be allowed to follow the buffalo into Texas as they had always done. On a more positive note, Throckmorton managed to meet with the chiefs of all the Kiowa bands and every Comanche band but one. By trade and negotiations he recovered white captives from them; he also laid the groundwork for further negotiations that later, in the Camp Napoleon Compact of May 26 and the Drying Grass Moon negotiations of August 15, implemented the release of nine white Texans from Indian captivity, including some of those taken during the Elm Creek raid the previous October. Having done all he could, Throckmorton returned to Texas the second week in June to find that the Trans-Mississippi Confederacy had surrendered to the United States government just two weeks before.[40]

10

Second Frontier District

1864–65

In the Second Frontier District Maj. George B. Erath hardly settled in at his headquarters in Gatesville before he recommended altering the system of patrol duty. Rather than keep one-fourth of the companies in constant rotation to serve in the field, as mandated by the legislature, Erath proposed to eliminate wasted motion by keeping one-fourth of the men permanently in the field. The remainder would work to harvest crops, forward supplies to those on patrol, and remain constantly ready to be called out in emergencies. The idea looked good on paper. No one could be found who relished the idea of permanent service on patrol, however, and the rotation continued.[1]

When he sent in the completed report of his district for the month of April, he praised the officers and men of his command for their zeal and energy. He set out on an inspection tour of the district and expressed satisfaction that all was running smoothly, with one exception; he strongly urged that at least one-half of his men be allowed to take the field to counter the increasingly active Indians and white renegades in the western counties of his district. If he could not get one-half in constant service, he hoped at least to be given discretion to order a majority of his force into the field, with the assurance that the state would pay them. To this end he urged state senator George E. Burney to persuade lawmakers in the forthcoming session to remedy such manpower problems so that his men could "drive rascalls [sic] and torys [sic] from the country." In this he partially succeeded. A law passed that session which allowed the frontier districts each to form two provost guard companies of sixty-four men for constant duty in the capture and guard of deserters.[2]

Indian incursions were the least of Erath's worries during the late spring and summer of 1864. By the end of June he reported confidently: "Although the organization was created principally for defense against Indians that part of duty has become in the greater part of the Dist. of minor importance since my last report. A feeling of security against the savage enemy and contentment on that account is becoming more evident."[3] Indian raids increased to some extent after Erath wrote this passage, but rarely did they take precedence over the wave of activity that surrounded the pursuit of deserters and outlaws in the district.

The most notable conflict with Indians during the first eight months of Erath's command occurred in August, 1864. Lt. Singleton Gilbert commanded an Eastland County company stationed at Nash Springs, three miles northwest of present Gorman. On August 8 he sent out a squad of eight men, led by James L. Head; they left camp for a ten-day scout and the next morning came upon fresh Indian signs between present Cisco and Eastland. Moving southward, they followed a trail made by an estimated thirty to fifty Indians for over twenty miles before overtaking the party at a ranch at Ellison Springs, several miles west of Gorman. Head quickly sent for reinforcements from the nearby company. Gilbert's arrival provided a force totaling twelve to sixteen troopers against thirty to thirty-five Indians.[4] It should have been an even match, as a number of the Indians were on foot, carrying blankets and bridles to be used on the horses they planned to steal.

Accounts vary concerning the brief struggle that ensued. One source states that Gilbert unwisely ordered a frontal assault against the Indians and then fell back before a withering fire that killed the commander and another man, wounded three more, and left no Indian casualties. This account records that as the soldiers left the field, the Indians continued unimpeded and stole more than fifty horses near Stephenville. In an interview several years later, a participant remembered a total of three soldiers killed, three wounded, and one Indian wounded, but he noted that the military unit pursued the Indians and recovered eighteen horses. Erath's comment that the Ellison Springs fight was "a most desperate struggle in which all the bravery of frontier life was brought to bear" did little to soften his bitter observation that this was also the only unsuccessful Indian engagement of the summer for the men of his command.[5]

While the defeat of Frontier Organization forces has been recounted in three published sources, the successful follow-up to the battle has never been told. Several days after Gilbert's men recaptured the eighteen horses, Sgt. A. D. Miller, in command of an eight-man squad in Stephens County, came upon a party of at least twenty Indians moving in a northwesterly direction. These Indians probably represented the main body of the party attacked earlier in Eastland County by Gilbert's men. Miller followed the trail approximately fifteen miles, overtook the hostiles, and attacked. As Capt. J. W. Curtis, of Stephens County, later described the battle to Major Quayle, the fight lasted about one hour. Miller's men had a total of four rifles and six pistols, while their well-mounted opponents had one rifle and one pistol plus the usual bows and arrows. This time the soldiers prevailed. At no loss to themselves, Miller's men killed two Indians, wounded three, and captured seventy-three horses, seven saddles, and an assortment of bridles and blankets, thus bringing to a close the brief campaign that began in Eastland County.

Just a week or so later an even larger party—numbering forty to fifty Indians—struck quickly just west of Jacksboro, attacking a five-man patrol of the First Frontier District. They killed two and wounded one in a desperate fight, but three Texans finally managed to escape. A Border Regiment detachment which reached the site the following day reported five dead horses and pools of blood scattered over the ground where the fight had occurred; 117 arrows picked up by some of the curious marked the violence of the brief encounter.[6] Such fights amply demonstrate the variable quality that made up the men of the Frontier Organization. Contemporary descriptions of Indian fights in the frontier districts, while noting the involvement of larger parties of Indians than was typical for the first nine months or so of 1864, represent the strategy and tactics used on the frontier at this time. Patrols tried to detect and prevent incursions or to punish the raiders on their return, and the charge and running fight characterized most of the clashes between such forces.[7]

In his memoirs of command in the Second Frontier District, Major Erath mentions the problem of Indians but ignores the problem of deserters. Yet the latter presented difficulties for his Central Texas district from its inception. In fact, in his first report to the adjutant general's office in Austin, Erath related that in his area great dissatisfaction emanated from members of the Frontier Regiment, many of whom threatened to desert if their units were ordered away from the frontier. By February of 1864 Erath reported gangs of deserters resisting arrest in his district. In Erath County an all-day battle between Capt. Silas Totten's company and deserters trapped in a fortified house led to the capture of eight men, while seven more in the vicinity gave up the next day.[8]

By the first of April, Erath's men accounted for the arrests of twenty-nine men, most taken from the eastern counties of the district. But the greatest difficulty stemmed from the large number of renegades along the western fringes of the district, far from the usual company patrols. Because the threat of Indian attacks in the spring and summer of 1864 was lesser in the Second Frontier District than in Quayle's district to the north, brush men, often with their families, congregated in the region between the Concho and Colorado rivers. As early as March reports came in that deserters were gathering in the region. In this situation Erath had the benefit of cooperation with troops of the Frontier Regiment stationed at Camp Colorado, located in Coleman County in the west-central portion of the Second District.[9]

Genuine aid from the Frontier Regiment, however, had to wait a month or so because the regiment's transfer to the Confederacy exacerbated the deserter problem for Erath's district. Not only did a large number of Captain Lloyd's men desert the Frontier Regiment at this time, but also, as one report asserted, "Capt. Whiteside's company have all deserted save himself and one man."[10] With the reorganization completed, two small companies created in the process remained at Camp Colorado under Captains Henry Fossett and G. B. Cooke.

Attempting to keep a closer watch on this western section of his district, Major Erath established a regular post of twenty men and a lieutenant on the Concho River. But a party of this size was no match for the growing numbers of renegades in the region. In late May the outpost reported that approximately two hundred disloyal men and deserters left the area for El Paso; it was said that they intended to flee to California. A large patrol from Camp Colorado pursued them along the upper Concho but arrived too late to stop the exodus. Captain Fossett estimated that five hundred men, women, and children were in the party headed west with forty loaded wagons, a herd of cattle, and an estimated thirty deserters from the Frontier Regiment. In order to stop the westward movement by deserters and those evading conscription, Governor Murrah prohibited further immigration to the unorganized counties of the state.[11]

Meanwhile, activity increased in the eastern counties. During an inspection tour of the eastern sector of his district, Erath learned of the citizens' low morale and heard much criticism of the government.

Discouraged, he dispatched a confidant to the capitol for the purpose, as he put it so quaintly, "of explaining to his excellency the Governor . . . the condition of affairs and present facts which Southern men would not like to commit to paper."[12] The major then ordered the trusted Captain Totten and fifty of his Bosque County men to go to Lampasas County, in the southeast of the district, to root out some sixty to seventy deserters who were causing problems. Sympathizers helped keep their positions a secret, and Totten's force turned back. He soon returned, this time reinforced by parts of three additional companies, with orders to stay until the job was done. The 120 state troops remained in the county for three weeks and made a number of arrests, with a total of 103 taken into custody since January. As for Lampasas County, "the Jayhawkers disappeared."[13]

In the northeastern part of the district a number of deserters from Confederate units in the Northern Sub-District made their way in considerable numbers to Erath County. Although the county lay outside Henry McCulloch's sub-district, as well as beyond Major Quayle's Frontier District, McCulloch called upon Quayle to send a force there to arrest the renegades, forward them to Colonel Bourland, and then ship them on to Bonham. Erath's district also seemed to feel the effects of any major enterprise that occurred in Quayle's district, a case in point being the Frontier Conspiracy broken up in April in Parker, Wise, and Jack counties. Numerous bands fled Quayle's district and made their way across Erath's. Rumors seemed to confirm that as many as three hundred "Jayhawkers" were soon to rendezvous along the San Saba River, and the presence of a well-armed gang of nearly fifty seen in San Saba County seemed to confirm the story. A small detachment that included Erath's son, Walter, pursued the renegades but soon turned back in the face of superior numbers, thus allowing this group of deserters to continue their journey unimpeded.[14]

There never seemed to be a conflict between Erath and McCulloch, or among the commanders of the First Frontier District. While McCulloch's Northern Sub-District included only a small slice of Erath's district for much of 1864, all of that changed in September when a reorganization of the state's military sub-districts took place. The Northern Sub-District more than doubled in size; it now constituted an area as large as the combined states of Virginia and Maryland.[15] It now also included the northern half of the Second Frontier District and all of the First Frontier District. Still, McCulloch had no authority to issue orders to the officers of the Frontier Organization. Nonetheless, he often called upon them for cooperation, and he always received it. With the added size of his district McCulloch sent a special admonition to Quayle and Bourland to cooperate fully with Erath to control the Jayhawkers and deserters. Then he indicated to Bourland that his men were free to cooperate with the Frontier Organization against known deserters anywhere in the Northern Sub-District west of a line from Bonham to Waco. McCulloch, in fact, had a much higher respect for the commanders of the Frontier Districts than for the men they commanded: "General McCulloch has every confidence in Majors Quayle and Erath, and think that they will discharge their duties as far as it is practicable for them to do so, with the material they have to operate with, but that a considerable number, both of officers & men, are entirely unreliable and would rather shield disloyal men and deserters than bring them to their just punishment."[16]

McCulloch indicated as much to General Magruder's chief of staff when he stated that the men of the Frontier Organization could scarcely be reliable, as many of them served with that force just to avoid Confederate service. Only strict enforcement of the conscript laws, he said, could bring the region under control. He made this statement before the expansion of his sub-district's boundaries and then concluded with this view of the First Frontier District: "If that country and the Frontier Regiment had been put under my command last fall I could have had it in much better condition now."[17]

Even before McCulloch sent word in October for Bourland and Quayle to cooperate with Erath, operations began that considerably overlapped the two Frontier Districts. On Friday morning, August 26, 1864, Company H of the Border Regiment, a force of about ninety men commanded by Capt. James Moore, left Gainesville. They were under orders to garrison an outpost on Hubbard Creek near the Shackelford and Stephens county line, site of a rumored haven for deserters and renegades.[18] The military authorities needed such a far-flung outpost of the Border Regiment to help cover that part of the line upon the removal of Barry's battalion of the Frontier Regiment in that same month. Anxious to get to the business of rounding up deserters, on their way Moore and his men surrounded a house where a known deserter allegedly was hiding. The troops opened fire, filled the house with lead, and got their man. They also killed an elderly couple who lived there.[19]

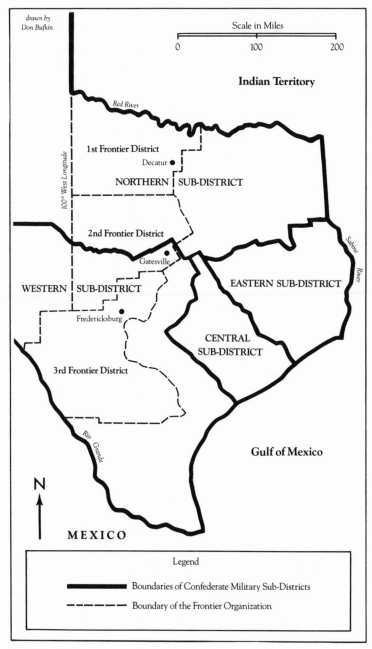

MAP 6. Command Organization, September, 1864–May, 1865

After this inauspicious start, the company continued without delay by way of Fort Belknap on to Hubbard Creek.[20] While posted there the company made a number of reconnaissance patrols into the neighboring Second Frontier District. They once reached as far south as Camp Colorado, over fifty miles away. As the patrol passed through uninhabited land and neared the fort, unoccupied at the time by Frontier Regiment forces, "men streamed forth . . . and ran away like rats from a burning barn."[21] The men of Company H had found their deserters, more than fifty, mounted and in flight; but with provisions low and the horses tired, the troopers decided against pursuit. The unit made similar scouts to the abandoned posts of Camp Cooper and Fort Phantom Hill but spotted no deserters or Indians. After aiding the Second Frontier District very little in clearing the area of deserters, the company made its way back to Clay County in November to the outpost at Buffalo Station.[22]

Shortly after Captain Moore's men left the Camp Colorado vicinity, Major Erath ordered a force of approximately one hundred men, commanded by Captain Totten, to patrol the territory between the San Saba and Concho rivers to search for deserters and Indians. Gen. John D. McAdoo gave the alarm that up to sixty deserters were heading for that region with a herd of approximately one thousand cattle. Totten's scout of the region discovered nothing, nor did he find any sign when his unit swung northward up the Colorado and then back to the settlements by way of the Clear Fork of the Brazos.[23] After Totten concluded this scout, little need existed to keep patrols so far west on the fringes of the Second Frontier District, as the weather and Indians would control the deserters until spring. For the next several months Indian activity dominated Erath's attention. The problem of lawlessness from renegades and deserters remained a secondary one in the district from the onset of winter until the breakup of the Confederacy in late spring.

There remained one more great drama to be acted between Indians and the men of the Second Frontier District, the tragic affair of January 8, 1865, known ever after as the Battle of Dove Creek. The Indians in question were not the Plains Indian raiders who so often plagued Texan settlements; these were more than six hundred men, women, and children of the Kickapoo tribe who fled hostile Indians in the Kansas-Indian Territory region by journeying across the Texas frontier to join others of their tribe who had migrated to Mexico over fifteen years before. The first report of the Kickapoo presence in Texas came from a scout led by Capt. N. W. Gillentine of the Second Frontier District. On December 9, 1864, he found the trail of what he believed to be about five hundred Indians near the Clear Fork of the Brazos, about thirty miles west of the abandoned Fort Phantom Hill. This was in a region far west of any Texan settlements and was at least seventy miles west of Camp Colorado. He informed Lieutenant Colonel Barry of the Indian presence, tribe as yet unidentified, then headed eastward to begin gathering companies from Major Erath's district.[24]

With Erath in Austin on business at the time, it fell to his senior captain, Silas Totten, to organize the coming campaign. Nearly 300 men of the Second Frontier District soon fell in. The force included companies from the counties of Bosque, Johnson, Comanche, Coryell, and Erath. Before his men left to intercept the Indians, Totten learned that Capt. John Fossett, commander of the Frontier Regiment detachment now stationed at Camp Colorado, wished to rendezvous at Fort Chadbourne so that a combined state and Confederate effort could be made. On December 31 Fossett reached Fort Chadbourne with approximately 50 men; 60 men sent from Barry's force soon joined them. In addition, a detachment led by Captain Cureton, of Stephens County in the First Frontier District, and a Brown County company of the Second Frontier District arrived to make a total strength of 161 men.[25]

Here the requisite coordination for such an extensive and sustained field operation began to break down. Totten decided not to meet Fossett at Fort Chadbourne as planned but to pick up the trail near the Clear Fork of the Brazos and follow it to the main body of Indians. Meanwhile, impatient that Totten's men had not reported, Captain Fossett set out with his force from Fort Chadbourne on January 3, 1865, found the Indian trail, followed it southward to the North Concho River, and camped there on January 7. When Fossett left Fort Chadbourne on the third, Totten's state troops, led by four Tonkawa scouts, also moved to the south, following Indian signs. They made camp on the North Concho on January 7, approximately thirty miles from Fossett's men. On that same day Fossett's Confederate scouts reported that they had located the main body of Indians thirty miles farther south along Dove Creek, just below Spring Creek, a tributary of the Middle Concho. Fossett then decided to move forward the next morning to attack, although the location of Totten's men and the identity of the Indians remained in doubt.[26]

On the march southward scouts from Totten's men came upon Fossett's force near the Middle Concho. In a field conference the leaders arranged for Totten's state troops to rendezvous with Fossett's men about a mile or so north of the Indian camp as soon as possible. A dawn attack was still in the plans. Captain Totten left a detachment with his supply wagons and moved ahead with approximately 220 of his men. The Confederate force, with a shorter distance to travel, reached the rendezvous point two hours after midnight, but the state troops did not arrive until nine o'clock on the morning of January 8. With a combined effective strength of approximately 380 men, the two forces rested in the cover of a ravine behind a hill that blocked the view of the Indian camp. The exact number of Indians remains uncertain, but the Texans estimated the opposing force to be approximately 1,000 warriors.[27]

The Indian camp was aptly situated for defensive purposes. Located on the south side of Dove Creek, inside a dense thicket of brush and live oak astride two dry creek beds, it was backed by a high bluff. The Texan plan was for Totten's command to move eastward to Dove Creek and ascend that stream in order to attack the camp from the north, while Fossett's Confederate command would move to the southwest of the Indian camp, drive off their herd of horses, and then attack from that quarter. Totten's Frontier Organization men, still exhausted from their hard ride to reach the field, initiated the attack just before ten o'clock that morning. They waded through Dove Creek and rushed forward into the thicket before them. It was no surprise attack. Already warned of the presence of nearby soldiers, the Indians waited in excellent cover. With many using the ravines as rifle pits, they opened fire. Though a few used bows and arrows against the Texans, a number of the Indians had Enfield rifles and used them with telling effect. The result was a bloody ambush of the state troops in a one-sided fight. The battle lasted just under an hour, ending when Totten's men fell or staggered some four hundred yards to the north to recover.[28]

When the ill-fated attack began, the Confederate force to the west initially succeeded; Fossett quickly ran off the Indians' horse herd. He then sent some seventy-five men to the south of the camp to cut off the Indians, should the state troops drive them in that direction. Fossett's main attack on the camp began at just about the time the state troops were being hurled back in confusion. From a vantage point on a nearby hill Fossett witnessed the disaster that befell the state troops.

When he then ordered his companies to the attack, they, too, met stiff resistance. Attacking from the west, Fossett's men fanned out along the banks of Dove Creek, with their right flank anchored to a small tributary. For nearly six hours his men kept up the fight until, riddled by unrelenting fire from Indians concealed in timber and ravines on the east bank of Dove Creek, the Confederates began to retreat just before five o'clock in the afternoon. Throughout this lengthy phase of the battle Totten's men stayed out of range of the fight, while most of the wounded and demoralized had fallen back to a position some three miles north of the battlefield. As Fossett's men began to move northward to disengage, always a delicate operation in the face of an aggressive enemy, they inexplicably made the mistake of crossing to the east bank of Dove Creek, north of the Indian camp, before continuing their northward retreat. A party of Indians crept up the Dove Creek channel and, as the Texans crossed, rose up and cut the Confederate column to pieces with sudden and destructive fire. The soldiers could endure no more. A wild panic ensued, officers lost control of their men, and as the Texans retreated northward before the onslaught of bullets, the Kickapoos rushed in and recaptured most of their horses.[29]

Battered and exhausted, the Confederates finally broke free to the north and reached the state troops, who had been inactive since the morning fight. The combined force camped along Spring Creek nursed their wounds and counted their dead. The final casualty count for the state and Confederate troops was twenty-six killed and twenty-three wounded, by far the heaviest losses suffered by Texans in any Indian conflict of the war. Fossett and Totten estimated that they killed perhaps as many as one hundred Indians, but when the Kickapoos reached Mexico, they reported that they had lost eleven killed and seven wounded.[30] By the morning of January 10 up to fourteen inches of snow blanketed the battlefield as the Texans began a slow trek back home. The victorious Kickapoos continued on their way to the Rio Grande without further interruption.[31]

The public severely criticized the military leaders' conduct of the battle; blame was directed even in some measure toward Lieutenant Colonel Barry and Major Erath. Gen. John D. McAdoo, who now coordinated all military activities by state troops in both the Second and Third Frontier districts, investigated the affair in February and particularly criticized both Fossett's and Totten's handling of the situation. Rumors immediately began to circulate, perhaps with some foundation, that not only were the Indians friendly, but they actually tried to make the Texans aware of that fact several times during the fight. One elderly Indian man, taken prisoner when the Texans captured the horse herd, had tried to explain that his people were peaceful; but Captain Fossett had executed him on the spot. In exaggerated form, rumors abounded that an Indian under a white flag had tried to convince the Texans not to attack. Less than three weeks after the battle General Throckmorton heard that "the Indians made demonstration for peace, and were charged three times before they fought."[32]

Though the Texans' malfeasance may not have been that blatant, the fact remains that sufficient reconnaissance could have prevented a needless battle. Even the ease with which the Texans made off with the Indians' horses should have strongly suggested that these were certainly not Comanches and probably were not Kiowas. In fact, the seizure of the horses made the Indians' position virtually untenable. Erath's adjutant could not believe that experienced frontiersmen would make such a mistake: "They ought to have known whether they were friendly or not."[33] General McAdoo later criticized the action because there had been no council of war, no communication of orders, no reconnaissance, and no suitable plan of battle.[34]

Some Texans were quick to point out that this tragic failure of military prowess indicated the ineffectiveness of the "flop-eared militia," as men of the Frontier Organization were sometimes scornfully called.[35] That Erath's best captain, Totten, had a major role in the affair, seemed to confirm the description. Such a blanket condemnation of the Texans who fought in the battle ignores the fact that the men had traveled over three hundred miles on the campaign in the dead of winter and endured hardships and heavy losses without complaint. The absence of effective tactical leadership on the battlefield, not the caliber of the men who fought, brought disaster. The Second Frontier District continued to feel the repercussions of the affair throughout the spring, as desertions increased among the men of both the Frontier Regiment and the Frontier Organization, a fact made bearable only by diminished Indian activity.

11

Third Frontier District

1864–65

Not surprisingly, Maj. James Hunter's Third Frontier District enrolling officers were slow in performing their duties; only gradually did they forward muster rolls to district headquarters in Fredericksburg, in Gillespie County. After all, this was a region where two years earlier German members of a Union Loyal League had formed militia companies to defend the area equally against Indian raiders and conscription officers. Here too, just six months before, citizens of German heritage had formed a volunteer company for service against Indians, with the stipulation that the volunteers would not be susceptible to Confederate conscription.[1] The major problems that accompanied Hunter's six-month tenure in command of the Third Frontier District are largely attributable to the opposition to the Confederate conscription laws by a sizable part of the German population of the district.

Political disaffection by a number of those of German heritage manifested itself quite visibly in 1862 and 1863. First came the controversial killing of some fifty Germans at the Nueces River in August, 1862, then came the military occupation and martial law in certain areas of south Texas in 1862–63, followed by the breakup of organizations hostile to the Confederacy. Military authorities responded quickly and firmly to suppress what they perceived as resistance to the Confederacy, but after January of 1863 this overt hostility to the new government faded away, only to be replaced by a passive resistance by many German Texans.[2] Within this atmosphere, Major Hunter, a friend to many of the German population in the Fredericksburg area, sent out his first patrols to enforce conscription and arrest deserters.

By late January of 1864 bands of deserters and outlaws terrorized much of the northeastern section of Hunter's district, particularly along roads leading to the more populous areas in the east. Twelve men were killed in January, including two soldiers, six settlers, and four bushwhackers. A patrol by Capt. Christian Dorbandt's Burnet County company attempted without success to flush some of the renegades out of the Pedernales River country. As they actually found a cave with signs of recent occupancy, the scout did not turn back with nothing to show for their efforts. They attempted to arrest two known deserters from the Frontier Regiment, were fired upon first, and then proceeded to kill the two after a sharp fight. There was still much work ahead, as Dorbandt put it: "Truly Blanco [County] seems to be in a pitiable condition. I could not order my whole company back to their aid for many of the horses are broken down for want of forage, but a few of my men have volunteered to go back and afford all the assistance possible."[3] This part of the country also lost one of its best protectors in January when Albert Walthersdorff left his Blanco County command to join Col. Rip Ford on the lower Rio Grande as instructor of tactics. Walthersdorff, an imposing figure of immense size and strength, led a militia battalion in protecting the region from late 1863 until his departure in January, 1864.[4]

It took Major Hunter longer to organize his district than it did Erath or Quayle, and the settlers of his region felt the delay. In fact, a petition signed by thirty-two citizens of Gillespie, Kerr, and Kimble counties indicated that they deplored the removal of Company A of the Frontier Regiment from Gillespie County, as they had no confidence in the ability of the men of the Frontier Organization to protect their property or families. These men then forted up in Camp Davis and at a location on Spring Creek and demanded protection "on account of the depredations of Jayhawkers and disloyal men who infest our frontier, burning houses and murdering the good citizens of the frontier, rendering the collection of our stocks of cattle too hazzardous [sic] for one, even 5 or 6 men to undertake."[5]

Fortunately, in February and March Hunter received help from another quarter. In December, 1863, General Magruder called upon Rip Ford to undertake a campaign in the lower Rio Grande Valley to drive out the federals and restore Confederate trade through Brownsville. Ford asked for those exempt from conscription to fill up his ranks, a process that took several months. As he gathered his force, men of the Frontier Organization guarded the supply base he established on Lagarto Creek, in Live Oak County. While Ford's expeditionary force consisted mostly of boys and old men, the presence and strength of its thirteen hundred men helped keep renegade activity in the San Antonio region at a minimum, at least until it left for the Rio Grande at the end of March.[6]

Not only did Hunter have to contend with lawlessness in the upper counties of his district, but he also faced a threat from a source over which he had little control. Just as McCulloch, Quayle, and Throckmorton often worried about Jayhawkers marauding southward from Indian Territory, Hunter faced a similar problem in his western and southern counties; gangs of renegades often raided northward from their strongholds in Mexico. Spies from the Frontier Organization estimated that as many as four hundred deserters had escaped just across the Rio Grande at Laredo and Eagle Pass; not even the offer of a pardon by General Magruder could induce them to rejoin their commands. So many armed gangs raided into Hunter's district from that part of Mexico, opposite Eagle Pass, that captains in the region felt compelled to keep in the field more than the standard total of one-fourth their numbers.

The captains soon discovered that small patrols were no match against the heavily armed gangs and parties of Indians they ran up against; commanders began to consolidate companies to form a more effective deterrent. One officer urgently recommended that a strong permanent force be posted west of the Leona River on the Eagle Pass–San Antonio Road "or the Frontier will be in the hands of renegades and deserters." As pressure from this quarter built, Hunter also saw to it that large patrols, from sixty to seventy-five in strength, combed the upper Llano River country for reported bands of deserters rumored to be heading for a rendezvous with those gathering along the Concho.[7]

By late spring another crisis caused a large number of citizens in the Third Frontier District to lose confidence in Hunter's leadership and prevail upon the governor for a change. A series of murders, robberies, and outrages perpetrated by bushwhackers, state troops of the Third District, and men of the Frontier Regiment excited the populace of Gillespie and Kendall counties into a frenzy.[8] While the legislature met in Austin, the height of the troubles came in May when Hunter arrested five men of the Frontier Organization and two of the Frontier Regiment, including William Banta, captain of Company A. Hunter wrote to the governor, explaining that he suspected the jail to be unsafe and requesting that he be allowed to send the men to prisons in

Austin or San Antonio. The request was denied. It was Hunter's opin-ion that the real danger lay with an armed party who might try to rescue the men from jail; he miscalculated. Less than two weeks later, two hundred armed men rode into Fredericksburg and overcame the twelve-man guard stationed at the jail. With no intention of freeing the men inside, the mob pushed their way into the stone jail and opened fire upon the prisoners, who were kept in two small rooms separated by a hallway. They killed one of the prisoners instantly and wounded four others critically; two died the next day.[9] All this occurred not long after a bold band of renegades left the vicinity but vowed to return and to "have the frontier in a blaze before any troops can get there."[10] The fact that in the midst of the commotion some twenty-two cap-tured deserters managed to break away and escape, along with their arms and horses, served only to embarrass Hunter further. These epi-sodes were in mind when Governor Murrah in May related to the legislature: "Major Hunter, though laboring [in] the midst of great diffi-culties, deserves great credit for the energy and address exhibited by him in prosecuting an inquiry into the facts connected with the horrid murders and robberies committed in Gillespie County."[11]

Major Hunter's problems also included Indian raids, but these usu-ally took a back seat to internal problems of lawlessness within his district. Citizens who lived along the western portion of his district, however, perceived the lack of adequate attention to the Indian prob-lem as symptomatic of not only Hunter's inability to provide leader-ship but also of the inferior quality of protection offered by the men of the Frontier Organization. Several citizens petitioned Maj. A. G. Dickinson, Confederate commander of the post at San Antonio, for the return of the Frontier Regiment company recently removed from Camp Verde. One of them described the situation:

> I have the honor to call your attention to the defenseless condition of that portion of the frontier between Camp Verde and the Rio Grande, which is being daily run over by bands of Indians and lawless white men with impunity. If these loyal citizens are not relieved from their present embarrassed condition by at least one well-organized company, to be stationed at some prominent point in said locality, they will be forced to move to the interior for protection.[12]

A similar petition signed by citizens from the counties of Mason, Menard, McCulloch, San Saba, Llano, Kimble, and Gillespie likewise pleaded for the return of the Frontier Regiment detachment to Camp San Saba as "the country seems to be literally swarming with Indians at present and has been so for ten or fifteen days."[13]

Hunter divided the companies of his district into four squads of about fifteen men each.[14] These men soon met the test of handling quick-hitting forays because the winter and early spring months brought a sharp increase of Indian raids into the Third District. No major attacks occurred, however. Most raiding parties consisted of only a handful up to two dozen Indians on horse-stealing raids, but the threat of large murder raids remained. One such band struck the family of George Todd, former paymaster at Fort Mason. Todd's fourteen-year-old daughter, Alice, was riding on the saddle behind him, while a young black girl was astride another horse with Todd's wife. Mrs. Todd and the girl tried to ride away when the Indians came upon them, but the attackers quickly killed them with arrows. Young Alice fell off the horse and before her father could turn to rescue her, the Indians swooped down to carry her away. George Todd survived but he never again saw his daughter.[15]

A typical example of the way in which Major Hunter's men responded to such raids is seen in another episode. On the night of April 15, 1864, a party of twenty-three Indians on a horse-stealing raid struck along the Hondo River, in Medina County, about thirty miles west of San Antonio. Approximately ten settlers and state troops soon engaged them; light casualties resulted on both sides. The Indians, probably Lipan Apaches, broke off the fight to continue their mission, while the Texans sent riders for help. As Indians in the area always retreated west-by-northwest, Capt. George Robbins, of Medina County, sent word immediately to the company in Bandera County, to the north, to be on the lookout, while Capt. John F. Tom ordered detachments to move at once to block the passes and river crossings west of Medina County. Tom's men took up the pursuit, relieved later by others with fresher horses. While the troops could neither bring the Indians to decisive battle nor recover any of the stolen horses, they at least killed the chief and wounded five other warriors; the soldiers lost but one killed.[16] Similar affairs constituted the great majority of conflicts with Indians along the entire Texas frontier in 1864–65, the notable exceptions, of course, being the Elm Creek Raid in October, 1864, and the Battle of Dove Creek in January, 1865.

All these problems during Hunter's administration set the stage for a change of command in the Third Frontier District. Thomas C. Doss, a prominent resident of Gillespie County, headed a delegation that met with Governor Murrah to urge that a "distinguished man" be sent to command the Third Frontier District. Murrah agreed; in fact, it is more than likely that the difficulties in the Third District played a role in the legislature's willingness, in the law of May 31, to authorize the governor to appoint higher-grade officers to improve the efficiency of the frontier districts. On June 20 he assigned brigadier general of state troops John D. McAdoo to command the district.

At the outset of war McAdoo had volunteered, and he served with the Twentieth Texas Infantry until 1863. From September to December of 1863 McAdoo was in Houston; holding the rank of lieutenant colonel, he served as assistant adjutant general of state troops. While in that office, in December General Magruder recommended him to a position with the state militia, under the legislative act that reorganized the force. The following March Governor Murrah appointed McAdoo to command Brigade District Number 6 as brigadier general of state troops. When McAdoo arrived to take charge of the district, one resident of Fredericksburg may have exaggerated when he said, "Since the Gen. has been here there has been several deserters arrested and sent off and such a thing as that was never heard of in this Co. before," but when a large number of the influential citizens lost faith in Hunter, Murrah made the change.[17]

After McAdoo assumed command in Fredericksburg on June 23, he made an inspection tour of much of his district. He later filed a report that best describes the conditions leading to his appointment in Hunter's place:

> I found almost the entire population of a large portion of the District laboring under the greatest excitement. Within a few months, twenty men had perished by violence. Some had been waylaid and shot; others taken from their homes at the dead hour of midnight and hung, and their houses robbed; and some had been mobbed and murdered in jail and in irons. No man felt secure—even at home. The Indians seemed to be the least talked of, the least thought of, and the least dreaded of all the evils that threatened and afflicted the Frontier.[18]

McAdoo tried to assure the people and to restore confidence, and in large measure he succeeded. He was well received throughout the district and made a good impression on nearly all he met.

As soon as McAdoo arrived to take command, he called a conference of all company commanders at his headquarters in Fredericksburg. There he spent two days reviewing the status and needs of his
district, along with plans to make defenses more efficient. After a satis-
factory conference McAdoo set out on his inspection, where he made
essentially the same speech at the various communities he visited:

> I addressed every argument within my grasp to them in behalf of pa-
> triotism to the *whole* country, unwavering devotion to the laws of the
> land, and the strictest preservation of social order; and against all dis-
> loyalty to the great cause of Southern Independence, . . . and against
> all violence and social disorder, destructive alike in their tendencies,
> to the peace and security of all, the good and bad, the innocent and
> the guilty.[19]

The morale of the Third Frontier District improved visibly, partly
from the confidence bolstered by McAdoo's arrival, but more from the
efficient work done by the troops under his command. By autumn the
companies of his district, by extraordinary effort, captured or drove
to cover many of the gangs that previously terrorized the countryside.
Soon, these outrages became scarce occurrences. With this major problem now minimized, McAdoo set out to reorganize his companies, chiefly
to make them conform to the directive that no one legitimately liable
for Confederate service be continued on the rolls. When this process
met its goal, McAdoo reported a strength of approximately fourteen
hundred men enrolled in his district. Every one of them would be needed
to fight Indians during the coming winter. Satisfied at the accomplish-
ments of his administration thus far, in the midst of rumors that the
Tenth Legislature might give in to Confederate pressure to break up
the Frontier Organization or reduce its forces, McAdoo defended it
with the most logical and practical argument possible:

> The people of the Frontier, under the existing Organization, are satis-
> fied. The system is better adapted to the purpose for which it is framed
> than any previously adopted on our extensive and exposed Frontier.
> At all times, and on all parts of the border, scouts are regularly on duty;
> and the Indians seen scarcely into the settlements anywhere without
> being immediately discovered and pursued. These scouts operate in their
> own vicinity, over a country well known to themselves.[20]

That summer, General McAdoo provided a firmer hand at the top,
alleviating many of the problems the Third Frontier District had faced

under Major Hunter. By the time McAdoo assumed command, so much chaos existed from white thieves, renegades, armed deserters, and talk of disloyalty, that the Indian threat receded. Nevertheless, McAdoo knew by experience that winter would likely bring increased Indian activity. He therefore set out to standardize regulations regarding company patrols that before had been met only at the option of the company commanders. He maintained the four-squad, ten-day patrol system with the requirement of prompt reporting to permanent camps for rendezvous at the start and completion of each scout. Patrols were no longer confined to county boundaries but were assigned to areas known to be favorite haunts or routes used by Indians, renegades, or deserters. A few men remained at camp at all times to act as couriers to inform adjacent counties of fresh trails sighted or impending action. McAdoo issued an order familiar to Ranger companies of decades past: should Indians penetrate the patrol line, their escape routes would be sealed off immediately to ensure absolutely their death or severe punishment. The general also began the practice of combining several companies into common camps to cooperate in battalion-strength scouting activities and to call upon a full complement of men in time of emergency, rather than on the one-fourth total mandated by law.[21]

Throughout McAdoo's successful first few months in command, he insisted that much of the credit go to his staff for their energetic efforts. Noticeably absent was any mention of Major Hunter, still officially second in command. McAdoo's correspondence never again mentioned Hunter's involvement in any major position of responsibility with the Third Frontier District. On January 19, 1865, Hunter tendered his resignation; Murrah accepted it immediately, and Hunter's official capacity with the district ended.[22]

In November the new Confederate commander of the Western Sub-District, Gen. James Slaughter attempted to usurp McAdoo's authority. Abruptly, in a rare instance of attention to the Third District, Slaughter appointed one of his subordinates, Col. A. C. Jones, who commanded the eastern division of the Western Sub-District, to take command of the Frontier Organization in the counties of Nueces, Duval, McMullen, Live Oak, Bee, Goliad, Refugio, and San Patricio.[23] Slaughter claimed that since he had it on good authority that no Indians had been seen in the designated region for seven years, the Frontier Organization there was unnecessary, and its existence was merely a pretext for many to remain out of the service. He further pointed out to Governor Murrah that Confederate military units could protect the frontier counties far better than could the Frontier Organization, whose leaders engaged men "in hauling cotton to different points on the Rio Grande—those men certainly are not protecting the frontier."[24] Needless to say, Slaughter's invective came to naught; Murrah and the legislature had struggled to maintain and perfect the Frontier Organization too long, even against the wishes of General Smith and President Davis, to see its integrity diluted by the maneuver of a sub-district commander.

Yet another change in the command structure of the Third Frontier District came when Major Hunter resigned in January of 1865, a change that altered McAdoo's role as commander. On January 19 John Henry Brown accepted Governor Murrah's appointment as major of the Third Frontier District. When the Civil War began, Brown served as a staff officer for Gen. Ben McCulloch. When McCulloch died at the Battle of Pea Ridge, Brown returned home in poor health, but he soon returned to work, this time on Gen. Henry McCulloch's staff as major and as McCulloch's assistant adjutant general in June, 1862.[25] Poor health, "bloody flux and severe affection of the chest," forced his resignation in November of that year, with this endorsement by McCulloch on Brown's resignation request: "Approved and respectfully forwarded. This is one of my oldest and best friends, selected from among them as *the man* to go with me through this war. It is natural that I should hate to give him up."[26] Once more he joined McCulloch's staff at Bonham, in the Northern Sub-District; but his broken health, this time requiring surgery, forced his departure from Bonham in May, 1864. Undaunted by his physical disability and determined to do all he could for Texas, Brown commanded a company of San Saba County men in the Second Frontier District until Murrah appointed him as major in the Third District.[27]

The command arrangement of both the Second and Third Frontier districts changed during the winter of 1864–65. In December, General McAdoo began to specify all his correspondence written from Fredericksburg as "Headquarters, 2d & 3d Frontier Districts," signed "Brigadier General Commanding." From January of 1865 until the end of the war, both Brown and George Erath endorsed their correspondence as the commanding officers of the Third and Second districts, respectively. Brown was not simply a second in command, as Hunter became, but was the major in command of his district, with McAdoo in the role probably intended by the legislature, to coordinate the efforts of all frontier forces in the region and to work in harmony with the Confederate military. This role by General McAdoo lessened the administrative burdens on Brown and Erath and allowed them to concentrate more on the military proficiency of their commands.[28]

As in the Second Frontier District, the problem of desertion and disaffected elements of the population faded as Indian activity increased during the winter. With the coming of spring McAdoo knew that once again men would try to slip away to the west. In the spring of 1865, McAdoo attempted to coordinate the defenses of both the Second and Third Frontier districts through Erath and John Henry Brown. While local companies remained in readiness along the eastern counties, McAdoo issued orders on March 10 for Major Brown to organize a major military campaign to leave from Camp Verde in one month.[29] Brown left Fredericksburg on Friday, April 7, and arrived at Camp Verde three days later, where he met his captains and their assembled troops. Originally, General McAdoo proposed the use of one-fourth of the effective manpower of the Third Frontier District, a force 400 strong, but the companies reporting totaled less than half that number. Parts of twenty-two companies eventually participated in the operation, with some woefully underrepresented. A company from Frio County sent but one man, a company from Kerr dispatched 2 men, and only 3 men showed up from a Kendall County company, "one of them a half-witted boy as a substitute." Camp Verde now had a total strength of 183 men and 243 horses and pack animals. Brown divided this assorted group of "Americans, English, Irish, French, Poles, Germans, and Mexicans" into four columns commanded by John Files Tom, C. Herring, John Lacey, and James M. Tomlinson. Contrary to previous orders, some men reported without pack animals and with only a few days' rations. Brown concluded that some hoped thereby to be sent home. He did not oblige them.

The mission proposed to sweep the region between the upper San Saba and Concho rivers. The troopers would attempt to locate and bring to battle a large party of renegades and "disbanded Federal soldiers" reported to be on the verge of attacking the frontier settlements. Brown's unimpressive-looking battalion moved out on the eleventh, preceded by two ten-man scouting parties commanded by Capt. C. R. Perry and Lt. Henry Smith. The entire force went north through Kerrville, then west along Johnson's Fork of the Guadalupe, and north to the Llano River valley. Brown deemed it too difficult to proceed through rough chaparral country to old Fort Terret as planned, and with scouts out in front and on the western flank, the party made its way instead directly to Fort McKavett on the San Saba River in western Menard County. They arrived on April 21 with some twenty-two men fewer because of desertion and courier duty. Two days later Brown's men took up the march again, this time to the headwaters of Kickapoo Creek, a tributary of the Concho, at the west-central fringe of the Second Frontier District.

Here the men finally saw some action. Lieutenant Smith's scouts surprised a group of fifteen or so "Jayhawkers" on a brushy hill, charged, and put them to flight in the direction of the South Concho. Brown then dispatched Captain Tom and some sixty men to make a night march to overtake the outlaws before they got away. Troopers caught them the next day, but the twenty-three captives turned out to be deserters from the Frontier Regiment, not members of the gang spotted the day before. To trap the latter, Brown had his men move off to the north so that spies would think they were moving on, while in reality he planned to double back at night on a forced march and hopefully catch the gang hiding out at Fort McKavett. It was a long shot. After nearly three days of hard traveling, Brown's men managed to pull it off, only to find five men at the fort; three they let go, and two they identified as known horse thieves. They came upon three more soldiers that day, one from the Frontier Regiment and two from Confederate commands; Brown paroled them back to their units.

Brown ordered his men to scout for the next few days, the last three days of April, along the upper Guadalupe and the Llano. While there, Lieutenant Lacey and his detachment came upon a party of bushwhackers amidst the thick undergrowth of a creek bottom. A fight ensued, with Lacey's men reinforced throughout the day by the rest of Brown's command. It is uncertain how many opposed them, but Brown's men arrested seven, killed two, and unwittingly allowed two to escape. Major Brown then gave the word to head for home. The command rode wearily back to Fort Mason, reaching Fredericksburg on May 4 after three and one-half weeks of hard campaigning. Even though the foray did not prove as successful as he hoped, Brown expressed his satisfaction at the way the men kept up their spirits and responded to adversity: "They readily yielded to all my wishes and orders and showed a zealous desire to do good service for the country. I should rejoice to have such men on every campaign. Discipline and concert of action will render this frontier organization most effective for good."[30] If discipline was ever needed, it was needed now. The men returned to hear about Richmond's fall, General Lee's surrender, and President Davis's flight.

12

Frontier Defense in Retrospect

Texans went to war in 1861 against two foes: the armed forces of the United States, and the Plains Indian raiders. Some Texans believed the conflict with the former would be short and successful, while those on the frontier knew they would have their hands full with the Plains Indians. Before the war approximately one-fourth of the strength of the U.S. Army was stationed in Texas, with additional protection provided by Ranger companies on patrol. This combination severely punished the Comanches and Kiowas in the late 1850s, but not even this commitment could stop the almost constant Indian raids. In 1861 it was natural for the state to look to the Confederate government for protection of its Indian frontier, but recalling the difficulties of the U.S. Army in the same task, Texans quickly saw little to convince them that Confederate responsibility could solve the problem. Part of the difficulty, indeed, lay in the belief of most non-Texan Confederate authorities that the Indian menace did not really require the military might or expenditure that Texans demanded. Secretary of War Leroy P. Walker in 1861 echoed U.S. authorities of the 1850s when he called the Indian threat "merely predatory" and believed that one regiment of cavalry should suffice on the frontier.[1] This same attitude existed on the part of the Confederate leaders throughout the war. In one sense they were correct; if damage done to life and property were the sole standard upon which to base the degree of military force required, then one regiment should have been sufficient. One estimate gives a total of approximately eight hundred Texans killed by Indians from the summer of 1862 to 1868, which would suggest a total of nearly four hundred Texans killed, wounded, and made captive for the four years of the Civil War.[2] These losses scarcely compare with the total of Confederate casualties suffered in even a single medium-sized battle of the war, but those back east failed to appreciate the nature of warfare on the Texas frontier.

Texans who witnessed the results of countless Indian raids throughout the 1850s and 1860s could scarcely imagine more ruthless conduct than that practiced by their old adversaries; in this war so often the victims were women, children, and old men. After long years of conflict with Comanches and Kiowas, Texans cared little for motive or justification behind the action of their enemies. They perceived only that Plains Indians killed, mutilated, or captured settlers along the frontier. The image of this type of warfare, one that even citizens of eastern Texas could scarcely comprehend, drove Texans to persist in their efforts to solidify frontier protection and exterminate Plains Indians found in their midst. No quarter was asked, and none was given.[3]

Of a white population of over four hundred thousand, Texas placed approximately sixty thousand men into service during the war.[4] Of this total McCulloch's First Regiment, Texas Mounted Riflemen maintained a strength of eight hundred to one thousand while on frontier duty. When the Mounted Rifles left the field, the Frontier Regiment managed to keep its effective strength at around one thousand until the last months before its transfer to Confederate service in the spring of 1864. Bourland's Border Regiment added another five hundred or so men for its companies located on the northwest frontier and in Indian Territory. Not until the coming of the Frontier Organization was the strength of numbers found that might give protection, some four thousand, but by state law only one-fourth of this total was available at any one time. Texas thus had, for most of the war, the equivalent of about one and one-half regiments of mounted cavalry for frontier service, at a time when at least three mounted regiments were required. Edmund Kirby Smith, in the first month of the war, predicted that five regiments would be required to hold the frontier and the Rio Grande line, a figure he later reconsidered when he assumed command of the Trans-Mississippi Confederacy. The numbers were simply not available to enable the duplication of the large punitive expeditions of 1858 by Ranger and U.S. Army forces, but the attempt was still made on a smaller scale, even in the war's closing months.

Any attempt to discuss or evaluate the effectiveness of frontier defense during the Civil War brings forth a natural comparison with frontier defense in the years immediately preceding and following the war years. For the pre-war years, this comparison has been made within these pages. An in-depth treatment of the post-war years is outside the scope of this work, but several inferences may readily be made. A few historians have pointed out that the Texas frontier suffered as never before in the years immediately following the Civil War, particularly from late 1865 to 1869. For the first two years of this four-year period, incomplete frontier county records show more than 160 Texans killed by Indians, two dozen wounded, and more than 40 carried away into captivity. Added to these statistics were over 30,000 cattle and 3,600 horses stolen or killed.[5] Historians of the Texas frontier have elucidated the severity of these devastating raids directly following the Civil War and have noted that many of the new settlers were unprepared to meet them. One cause of inadequate frontier security undoubtedly stemmed from the delay in sending U.S. Army troops to the Texas frontier; the federal government chose instead to provide armed protection in the more populated areas of the state to prevent the persecution and mistreatment of Union men and freed slaves.[6]

The impression has sometimes been given that during the last year of the war the frontier crumbled as the settlement line receded approximately one hundred to two hundred miles, but a careful reading reveals that such an estimate always includes the years immediately following the war.[7] During the war there certainly was a depopulation of some areas because of problems from Indians or white renegades, or from men who left to serve in the army and who had their families moved to the interior; but the settlements were quickly reoccupied. An examination of the frontier fort line of 1860 and the 1860 census returns may also give a mistaken impression of what happened along the frontier during the war.

It would be a mistake to believe that the settled portion of Texas in 1860 extended as far west as the outer chain of U.S. Army posts on a line from Camp Cooper to Forts Phantom Hill, Chadbourne, McKavett, and Terrett. While a small number of settlers lived near the posts in the 1850s, their presence would be insufficient to label the area as a frontier line in Texas if one used the definition of a frontier as a density of two to six persons per square mile. The frontier line in Texas remained considerably east of this chain of forts. The Mounted Rifles maintained this general defensive line in 1861; but stating the fact that the Frontier Regiment redefined the area to be protected by withdrawing eastward by fifty to seventy-five miles is not the same thing as saying that the frontier was hurled back. The most serious threat and severe devastation to the Texas frontier came in the four-year period following the Civil War.[8] Within this context, comparison of the 1860 census returns with those of 1870 is also misleading, particularly in regard to the counties of the northwest Texas frontier. These exposed counties suffered from Indian depredations more than any others in the years immediately following the war. The population loss during the decade certainly cannot all be attributed to the Civil War years.[9]

As established in the preceding chapters, to see the issue of frontier defense in Texas from 1861 to 1865 solely in terms of the Indian threat is to misunderstand the nature of frontier protection for those years. By late 1863 the state of affairs in frontier counties reached a complexity unforeseen in the early, exuberant days of the war. As serious as was the constant Indian menace, the problem of deserters, draft dodgers, bushwhackers, and Jayhawkers eventually overshadowed even the Indian threat along much of the frontier. The immense commitment of men, time, and expense to combat such problems could do nothing but detract from what in 1861 was wrongly perceived as the frontier's only difficulty—fighting Indians.

Leaders on the Texas frontier also wrestled with a problem faced by most nations at war before and since, that is, how to deal with disaffection and how to distinguish between varying shades of dissent, patriotism, and growing war-weariness. These factors complicated the already fragile social fabric, as settlers living on civilization's edge faced an unrelenting foe to their front and a growing threat from within, made manifest by the decline of civilian morale that continued unabated from the war's first months.[10] In the face of such adversity it should come as no surprise that Texas leaders, particularly during the Murrah administration, clung to a state's rights concept that ensured protection for the frontier. It has been contended that the Confederate epitaph "Died of State's Rights," simply does not apply to the Trans-Mississippi Confederacy.[11] A more cooperative spirit shown by the Texas legislators and Governor Murrah would almost certainly have led to a reduction in military strength for frontier protection, a state of affairs that Texas leaders would not contemplate.

The present study concurs with the conclusions of one of the most perceptive historians of the Texas frontier, William Curry Holden, that the Texas frontier held its own during the Civil War. Before the war, not even the full might of the U.S. Army could stem the tide of Indian attacks on the Texas frontier. Texas Rangers companies in antebellum years, equal to any body of Indians, could not defeat what they could not find; the vast expanse of the Indian frontier, equivalent to the distance between Richmond, Virginia, and Lake Erie, was too great and the men too few. The celebrated punitive expeditions of 1858, intended to break the Indian threat once and for all, were followed by two years of unrelenting Indian raids.

Frontier defense in Texas during the Civil War, for all its difficulties and apparent failures, was equal to that of antebellum days and superior to that of the immediate post-war years. If protection against Indians had been the only problem, the combination of Frontier Regiment, Border Regiment, and Frontier Organization could have gone a long way toward securing the Indian frontier in 1864–65. The additional obstacles they were called upon to meet were never faced by the army or Rangers in the days before or after the war. It is difficult to envision what might have occurred had Indians been the only threat, and perhaps it would not be instructive to do so. The men who defended the frontier must be judged only by what was accomplished, and in that their shortcomings are apparent. It would probably have been little consolation to them to learn that they did as well as any men could have done under the circumstances.

During the long four-year conflict Texans defended their own frontier with relatively little support from the Confederate government. The leaders and men involved in this undertaking were no strangers to the situation. Most had served in Ranger companies before the war, and nearly all lived near the section of frontier in which they served. Unfortunately, it has been popular to denigrate the efforts of state troops on the Texas frontier, as done by Texas writer T. R. Fehrenbach: "Toward the end of the war, it was an axiom on the frontier that the state troops employed there were composed almost entirely of men who chose border service to escape the considerably greater dangers of death or dismemberment with Hood, Bragg, or Lee."[12] Even though some men of that description served in state units on the frontier, a blanket indictment should not apply to all. It is true that many of the best men in the state volunteered in 1861 for service in the eastern armies, as the lure of adventure called them to distant battlefields. However, many good men whose wives and children lived along the frontier remained to defend their homes as best they could.

For these men of the frontier, whether called Confederates, Rangers, state troops, minutemen, or militia, men who never went off to

war with flags flying, drums beating, or bands playing, it could well
be said:

> Not for fame or reward, not for place or rank,
> Not lured by ambition or goaded by necessity,
> But in simple obedience to duty as they understood it,
> These men suffered all, sacrificed all, endured all, and died.[13]

With a seemingly minimal amount of financial support and a constant
shortage of provisions and equipment, most of them gave their all to
guard the frontier of Texas with "ancient renown and disciplined val-
our."[14] Military and economic expediency served as the catalyst for the
evolution of the defense system from McCulloch's Mounted Rifles to
the Frontier Organization. By such changes the defense of the Texas
frontier during the Civil War exhibited a combination of organizational
policies that characterized the previous thirty years of Texas military
experience. The method and determination that held the frontier together against all odds during 1861–65 stood in marked contrast to the
rapid collapse of this same frontier at the Confederacy's end.

In the late spring of 1865 the Frontier Districts could hardly escape
the disintegration that generally accompanied the last weeks of the war
in Texas. Desertions from the Frontier Regiment and the Frontier Organization increased during the last months of the war, especially in
the Second Frontier District after the Dove Creek disaster.[15] When word
reached the Frontier Districts of the May 26 surrender of the Trans-
Mississippi Confederacy, there was no laying down of arms and going
home as occurred in other parts of the South. These men were already
home; they knew that some type of organization had to be maintained
to guard not only against Indian incursions, but also against the lawlessness that seemed pervasive. In the Second and Third Frontier districts Major Brown and Major Erath saw to it that volunteers of their
commands would continue to provide at least temporary protection
for the frontier; then they headed for Mexico along with a number
of other high-ranking officials, including Gov. Pendleton Murrah. In
the First Frontier District the settlers knew they had no option; no
Indian raids had taken place for some months, but volunteers maintained patrols in case Throckmorton failed in his efforts to obtain peace
by treaty. The commander of the Northern Sub-District, Henry Mc-
Culloch, instructed the men of the Frontier Organization and volunteer militia groups to maintain patrols against Indian raids until re-

lieved by the U.S. Cavalry. Then, accompanied by twenty-seven men as an armed escort to protect him from retaliation by deserters who vowed to kill him, McCulloch left Bonham on May 28 to go home to Seguin.[16] The war against the Union was over; the war against the Plains Indians would be renewed in all its fury by summer's end.

Appendix 1.
Note on Sources

It is somewhat puzzling why there has been so much confusion by those who have written about the Frontier Organization to ascertain correctly just who commanded these districts, and the effective manpower enrolled in each. Quite a few secondary works, including a number of county histories, provide quotes from the law that created the Frontier Organization with an inaccurate listing of its commanders, but with little else. Scarcely more than three or four pages in any one account have ever been written about this organization, which formed the backbone, for good or bad, of frontier defense in Texas for the last one and one-half years of the Civil War.

Even the most reliable sources have not been completely accurate in relating what little information they presented about the origins of the Frontier Organization, including the most authoritative accounts published heretofore—by William C. Holden and Robert L. Kerby. Holden lists William Quayle, of the First District, with an initial troop strength of 1,517; George Erath of the Second with 1,413, and Gen. J. D. McAdoo of the Third with a force of 1,334. He cites two sources for these conclusions: Erath's memoirs, and a memorandum found in the Adjutant General's Records, Archives Division, Texas State Library.[1] Likewise, Robert L. Kerby gives the same troop strengths and the same commanders, also based on Erath's memoirs and the same memorandum, dated March, 1864.[2] He, at least, goes on to note that James W. Throckmorton replaced Quayle in "early 1865," while at the same time John Henry Brown took over the Third District. J. C. McConnell simply lists the chart given in *The Texas Almanac, 1865,* which contains commanders and company strengths for October, 1864. This chart gives Throckmorton as the First Frontier District commander, with Quayle as second in command; Erath as commander of the Second; and Gen. John D. McAdoo in charge of the Third, while McConnell adds Maj. James Hunter as second in command.[3]

Part of the problem in discovering just who commanded the districts, and when, lies with information found in *The Texas Almanac, 1865*. The organization and strength it gives for the Frontier Districts is for October, 1864, but the information it gives is often cited erroneously as the initial strength and command structure of the organization, effective as of March, 1864, when its commanders completed enrollment in the districts. The *Almanac* correctly gives George Erath as commander of the Second District, but it does not explain changes that took place in the other districts in 1864 and 1865.

Two theses which should contain a great deal about the Frontier Organization actually give few details. Caroline Ruckman quotes H. P. N. Gammel, ed., *Laws of the State of Texas*, to give the wording of the bill that created the organization but gives little else concerning leaders, strengths, or any other information.[4] Robert Overfelt gives the same leaders and strengths as McConnell, cites Erath's memoirs and McConnell's work, and then says little more of the organization.[5]

The page referred to in Erath's memoirs, as cited by the authors above, states that "I had some six or eight counties in my district, containing in all fourteen companies and about a thousand men."[6] The figure of 1,413 men for Erath's district comes from a memorandum cited by Holden and Kerby that was located in the Adjutant General's Records, Archives, Texas State Library, dated March, 1864.[7] As early as February 2 Erath estimated that he would have a total force of approximately 1,400; then three weeks later he declared that eighteen companies had reported, with six more expected. Finally, on April 1 he submitted his initial returns: 1,390 officers and men, representing twenty-one companies plus three squads, with two squads still expected to report, short of the total suggested by the March memorandum above.[8]

It is more difficult to reconcile the initial returns for the Third District with the total of 1,334 men as in the March memorandum cited by Holden and Kerby. On May 11, 1864, the Third District's commander, James Hunter, submitted a most detailed report in which he listed the strength, date of organization, and county of origin for each company. Earlier, on February 24, Hunter had complained that the enrolling officers of the southern counties in his district were exceedingly slow in filing their muster rolls with his office; only thirteen companies reported by that date. The May report gives the aggregate strength of his command as 1,211 (effective strength at only 1,061), with twenty-two companies reported and several still to do so.[9] It is difficult to see how 1,334 men could have been listed nearly two months earlier, particularly as slowly as the returns came in.

The First Frontier District returns also came in slowly, but with good reason; Major Quayle reported that several of his couriers, bearing muster rolls, turned back and hid when observers sighted hostile Indians in Wise, Parker, Jack, Cooke, and Montague counties.[10] By late February, however, he completed the organization and reported a total strength of 1,165, a force that would have been larger except that several men belonging to the Frontier Regiment joined the organization unlawfully and had to be removed from the rolls.[11] The next official district return that can be located for Quayle's district is that of June, 1864, when he reported a total strength of 1,353 officers and men in service.[12] Once more, it is doubtful that he could have reported a March strength of 1,517, as cited by Holden and Kerby.

Appendix 2.
Three Documents on Texas Rangers

The documents produced here represent a detailed look at regulations that governed Texas Ranger conduct in two organizations that defended the Texas frontier during the period 1861–65; namely, McCulloch's Texas Mounted Rifles and the Frontier Organization. For a third body, the Frontier Regiment, a list of regulations regarding camp discipline and procedure appears in James K. Greer, ed., *Buck Barry, Texas Ranger and Frontiersman* (1932; reprint, Lincoln: University of Nebraska, 1978), pp. 184–85. The three previously unpublished documents below allow a closer look at daily operations of the organizations charged with defense of the frontier in both the early and last days of the war. The documents are produced as found, except for minor corrections of spelling errors and punctuation. Sources follow each document.

Hd. Qrs. 1st T. M. R.
In the field near Camp Cooper
June 18, 1861

Special Orders
Number 40

Company "C," commanded by Capt. James B. Barry, will continue at Camp Cooper. Capt. Barry will command that Post until further orders.

This company will cover the country from its Post to the Willow Springs, on the road to the Camp on Red River, and will keep a detachment of 20 men under a Lieut. on a branch at or near the road, two or three miles beyond the Brazos, to be relieved by similar detachments every two weeks, if practicable, and will keep up weekly scouts, in small parties, from the Post to that detachment, by starting the scouts on each Friday morning, directing them to meet the detachment certainly on the next day. The detachment will send a scout on to the Willow Springs on Sunday, so as to meet and spend each Sunday night at that place, with the scouts from the Red river command.

This company will also send out such larger scouts above (from North West to North East) this Post as its commander may think proper, in order to keep the Indians out of the country, and chastise any that may be found in it. It will also furnish escorts to all wagons or trains passing to or from the Station on Red River and Camp Colorado, as far as the first Camp or detachment on each side of them, directing the troops stationed at these points to send escorts on to the next camp, so that every wagon or train passing with supplies for troops may be properly guarded against Indians. This company will cooperate with the companies at Camp Colorado, Phantom Hill and Red River in pursuing Indians, under a call from the commanding officer of any one of these Posts, and when thrown with any other troops the senior officer will command.

The Acting Assistant Commanding at this post will be authorized to contract, subject to the approval of Major Macklin, with any person to furnish the Company or Post with fresh beef, at a price not to exceed 8 cents per pound.

Commanding Officers of Posts being responsible for the condition of the Posts, the safe keeping of the property, and discipline of the troops at the same time, too much care cannot be taken in these matters, in order to promote the interest of the service, and sustain the reputation of the command, and let it be understood that good order, good conduct and gentlemanly deportment will be required of all men in this command, and in order to secure it, the officers are required to enforce the regulations of the Army.

The Sutlers at these posts will not be permitted to sell intoxicating liquors, nor should any of the Officers, Non-Commissioned Officers or men, be permitted to purchase it from others, except in the case of necessity, and not then without permission of the commanding Officer of the Post or Station.

Horse racing and gambling of every description is strictly forbidden, and if any gamblers come to the Posts, or about them, to filch the troops of their earnings, you will order them to stop their gambling or require them to leave at once.

Daily guard and Monthly Post returns must be regularly made.

The Commanding Officers cannot be too vigilant and careful respecting guard duty, and they must use great care and caution to prevent their horses and the Public mules from being stampeded or stolen.

It is especially enjoined upon all Officers that in following Indians, the pursuit must never be given up as long as men and horses are able to pursue. They should be caught at all hazards.

For further instructions, reference should be made to the Regimental Orders heretofore issued, and the Regulations of the Army.

By Order of Col. H. E. McCulloch
Wm. O. Yager
Adjutant

[SOURCE: Burleson Papers, Barker Texas History Center, University of Texas]

Hd. Quarters 1st Frontier Dist.
Decatur, Wise Co., March 9, 1864

General Orders Number 1

I. Commanders of Companies and Squads will see that their commands are divided in four Squads each and have them numbered. They will take charge of one themselves and each Lieut. one and the 1st Sergeant one. They will give orders to the Chief of each Squad to prevent the waste of ammunition when on Scout and notify their men that all ammunition wasted will be charged to them and all Officers will report every man who gets out of ammunition.

II. Officers of Squads or Scouts will call the roll of their Squads at Two O'Clock on the 1st day of each Scout and at Sunrise & Sundown on the remaining days except the last day when they will call at noon. They will report every man who fails or refuses to answer roll call and the reason of such failure. They will see that their men do not leave at night or at any other time during their term of duty. They will report to their Captains.

III. All Officers and men will use their best endeavors to arrest all persons who do not belong in the District who are of military age who are without leave of absence from a proper authority also all deserters from the Army. No certificates of disability of soldiers in the Confederate service will be respected except those given by doctors in the Confederate service.

IV. Scouts will take up their position in such parts of the counties as may be designated. They will report all fresh Indian signs to the nearest scouts and if numerous to these Head Quarters.

V. Captains will not permit men to move their families out of their counties without leave from these Hd. Quarters. They will not allow of any substitutes on Scout duty except of men who are regularly mustered into this service and sworn.

VI. Commanders of Companies & separate Squads will report monthly the number of men on each Scout, the number of days served by each, what men excused, what men failed or refused duty, and certify the same on honor. They will have Scouts serve ten days each until further orders. They will report to these Head Quarters by men detailed from their Companies who will be credited for the time on service rolls. In granting furloughs they will make them subject to approval by the District Commander if given for a term longer than five days, and will not give more than five from their Companies at a time. They will cause these orders to be read to their Companies by Officers of each Scout.

> By Order of Wm. Quayle
> Major Comdg. 1st Frontier District
> State Troops

[SOURCE: Adjutant General's Records, Archives Division, Texas State Library]

> Head Quarters 2nd & 3d Frontier
> Texas State Troops
> Fredericksburg, Dec. 15, 1864

General Orders Number 3

For the purpose of rendering the service of the Frontier Organization uniform throughout the different counties of this command; to increase the efficiency of the service and to facilitate concentrated and combined movements of the troops when necessary, it is ordered by the Brig. Genl. Commanding:

I. That within each county or company district, there shall be established a permanent camp or rendezvous; and that the different companies be divided into four squads of as nearly equal strength as possible, which said squads shall succeed each other in the scouting service regularly every ten days; that each squad be required to report promptly at the said company camp on the day the preceding scout is to be relieved.

II. When said camps are located the company commanders will forthwith notify the commander of the district of its location, and also the company commander in all the adjoining counties.

III.   It shall be the duty of the officers in command of said camp, to keep the forces thus collected constantly on scouting service, in those districts in which Indians, Bushwhackers, and Deserters are likely to found – detailing from said force a sufficient number of men only, to keep camp and act as couriers, should it be necessary to communicate with neighboring camps on the appearance of Indians or other contingency.

IV.   It shall be the duty of the officers in command of the camp detail, to dispatch immediately to the nearest county camp, by swift courier, any intelligence he may receive of Indians, or other danger threatening the Frontier, and such camp will communicate in like manner with the next, until the whole Frontier line is informed.

V.   When Indians are known to have penetrated the settlements, the different scouts will guard particularly the passes through which they usually go out with horses. All experience has shown that the most effective plan of operations against an Indian enemy is to head off the raiding parties as they leave the settlements with their plunder and booty. If they are able to get in through the scouting lines, see to it that they go out without spoils, and with severe punishment.

VI.   When camps are located they will not be changed without good reasons therefore, and when changed, the district commander and company commanders in the adjoining counties, will be notified of the location of the new camps. The commander of the district will be notified of the nearest Post Office to the different camps.

VII.   The companies of Captains [N.] Gussett and [James P.] King and Lieut. [John] Haynes and [C.] Herring will form one common camp to be selected by Captain King. The companies will cooperate in the scouting service, and senior officers present commanding the men on duty.

VIII.   When Indians have penetrated the settlements, the company commanders may call out a portion of their command not on their regular tour of duty, and if necessary the entire strength of their companies for the emergency. Let the Indians find themselves met by armed forces, not only on the outer line of the Frontier, but everywhere within those lines.

IX.   The greatest promptness and diligence are enjoined upon the officers and men of this command. The Brig. Genl. commanding has good reason to believe the Indians of the North-West are incited and perhaps led to depredate on the Frontier of Texas by White men, who are agents, if not officers and soldiers of the United States. Extra efforts and watchfulness should be at that period in each moon, when Indians usually visit our Frontier. The country expects her Frontier Organization to protect the Frontier, and the Brigadier General Commanding calls upon every officer and every man, to see to it that the public expectation is not disappointed.

By Command of Brig. Genl. J. D. McAdoo
Russell DeArmond
Maj. & A.A.A.G.

[SOURCE: Adjutant General's Records, Archives Division, Texas State Library]

Appendix 3.
Defense of the Indian Frontier

1861–65[1]

Organization	Date of Service	Commanders	Avg. Strength
Ranger Regiment [State]	Dec. 1860–Feb. 1861	Col. William Dalrymple	500
Texas State Troops (Secession Convention) [State]	Feb. 1861–Apr. 1861	Col. Henry E. McCulloch	400
First Regiment, Texas Mounted Riflemen [Confederate]	Apr. 1861–Apr. 1862	Col. Henry E. McCulloch Lt-Col. Thomas Frost Major Edward Burleson[2] Major James B. Barry	800–1,000
Frontier Regiment [State]	Apr. 1862–Feb. 1863	Col. James N. Norris Lt-Col. Alfred Obenchain[3] Major James E. McCord	1,200
Frontier Regiment (Mounted Regiment, Texas State Troops) [State]	Feb. 1863–Mar. 1864	Col. James E. McCord Lt-Col. James B. Barry Major W. J. Alexander	1,000
Frontier Regiment (Frontier Battalion)[4] [Confederate]	Apr. 1864–May 1865	Lt-Col. James B. Barry Capt. Henry Fossett	300
Border Regiment, Texas Cavalry [Confederate]	Aug. 1863–May 1865	Col. James Bourland Lt-Col. John R. Diamond Major C. L. Roff	500
First Frontier District[5] (Frontier Organization) [State]	Jan. 1864–June 1865	Maj. William Quayle Brg-Gen. J. W. Throckmorton	1,400
Second Frontier District (Frontier Organization) [State]	Jan. 1864–June 1865	Maj. George B. Erath	1,400
Third Frontier District (Frontier Organization) [State]	Jan. 1864–June 1865	Maj. James Hunter Maj. John Henry Brown Brg-Gen. J. D. McAdoo	1,200

Notes

INTRODUCTION

1. Walter Prescott Webb, *The Texas Rangers: A Century of Frontier Defense*, p. 219.

2. John D. McAdoo to D. B. Culberson, Sept. 15, 1864, Adjutant General's Record Group, Archives Division, Texas State Library, Austin.

CHAPTER 1. PRELUDE TO CIVIL WAR

1. Webb, *Texas Rangers*, pp. 20–22, 48–49, 67; H. P. N. Gammel, ed., *Laws of Texas, 1822–1897* 1:513, 526–27. Volumes 1 and 2 of the latter source contain the provisions of laws passed for protection of the frontier during the Republic.

2. Webb, *Texas Rangers*, p. 140.

3. Martin L. Crimmins, "The First Line of Army Posts Established in West Texas in 1849," *West Texas Historical Association Year Book* 19 (Oct., 1943): 121–27; Arrie Barrett, "Western Frontier Forts of Texas, 1845–1861," *West Texas Historical Association Year Book* 7 (June, 1931): 115–21; Walter Prescott Webb, et al., eds., *The Handbook of Texas*, 1:623–24, 626; Averam B. Bender, *The March of Empire: Frontier Defense in the Southwest, 1848–1860*, p. 132.

4. William Curry Holden, "Frontier Problems and Movements in West Texas, 1846–1900," Ph.D. diss., University of Texas, 1928, p. 43; Kenneth F. Neighbours, "Fort Belknap," *Frontier Forts of Texas*, ed. Harold B. Simpson, p. 5; Robert M. Utley, *Frontiersmen in Blue: The United States Army and the Indian, 1848–1865*, pp. 73–74.

5. Michael L. Tate, "Frontier Defense on the Comanche Ranges of Northwest Texas, 1846–1860," *Great Plains Journal* 11 (Fall, 1971): 45; Utley, *Frontiersmen in Blue*, p. 74.

6. Webb, *Texas Rangers*, p. 141, 143; Bender, *March of Empire*, pp. 139–40; Utley, *Frontiersmen in Blue*, p. 71.

7. *Texas State Gazette*, Nov. 24, Dec. 15, 1855; Webb, *Texas Rangers*, p. 146.

8. Gammel, *Laws of Texas* 3:1495; Rupert Norval Richardson, *The Comanche Barrier to South Plains Settlement*, pp. 211–12; Kenneth F. Neighbours, *Indian Exodus: Texas Indian Affairs, 1835–1859* p. 90.

9. Kenneth Franklin Neighbours, *Robert Simpson Neighbors and the Texas Frontier, 1836–1859*, p. 108; Neighbours, *Indian Exodus*, pp. 100–106; Bender, *March of Empire*, pp. 207–208; Robert S. Neighbors to George W. Manypenny, Commissioner of Indian Affairs, Sept. 16, 1854, *Annual Report of the Commissioner of Indian Affairs, 1854*, pp. 158–60; G. H. Hill, Special Agent Texas Indians, to R. S. Neighbors, Sept. 20, 1854, ibid., pp. 163–66; Robert S. Neighbors to George Manypenny, Commissioner of Indian Affairs, Sept. 18, 1856, *Report of the Commissioner of Indian Affairs, For the Year 1856*, pp. 173–76.

10. Harold B. Simpson, *Cry Comanche: The 2nd U.S. Cavalry in Texas, 1855–1861*, pp. 58–59.

11. Harold B. Simpson, "Fort Mason," *Frontier Forts of Texas*, p. 153; Barrett, "Frontier Forts," pp. 129–39.

12. Simpson, *Cry Comanche*, pp. 67–68; Neighbours, *Indian Exodus*, p. 110.

13. John Baylor to Elisha M. Pease, Dec. 11, 1856, Governor Elisha Marshall Pease Records, Archives Division, Texas State Library (all records and manuscript collections located in the Archives Division, Texas State Library, will be cited hereafter as TSL-A). The controversial John Robert Baylor was the first agent of the Comanche Reservation. The Indian superintendent, Robert S. Neighbors, later dismissed him after a disagreement over policies and he remained an implacable foe of the reservation system in Texas.

14. J. W. Wilbarger, *Indian Depredations in Texas*, p. 441; Neighbours, *Indian Exodus*, p. 118; Bender, *March of Empire*, p. 213.

15. E. M. Pease to Thomas C. Frost, Dec. 7, 1857, in Dorman Winfrey and James Day, eds., *Texas Indian Papers, 1846–1859*, 3:267.

16. E. M. Pease to Guy M. Bryan and John H. Reagan, Nov. 3, 1857, in Winfrey and Day, *Texas Indian Papers* 3:266; Lena Clara Koch, "The Federal Indian Policy in Texas, 1845–1860," *Southwestern Historical Quarterly* 28 (July, 1925): 21; George D. Harmon, "The United States Indian Policy in Texas, 1845–1860," *Mississippi Valley Historical Review* 17 (Dec., 1930): 397.

17. Llerna Friend, *Sam Houston: The Great Designer*, pp. 248–52, 322–25; Webb, *Texas Rangers*, pp. 148–51; Walter L. Buenger, *Secession and the Union in Texas*, pp. 110–12. In the 1857 campaign Runnels became the only person ever to defeat Houston in a political election. While the Texas Rangers achieved their most noteworthy victory over the Comanche Indians during Runnels's administration, the frontier counties expressed their dissatisfaction with the protection accorded them and voted heavily for Houston when he defeated Runnels in 1859.

18. Harmon, "United States Indian Policy in Texas," p. 397.

19. Ibid., p. 398. Of the five members of this committee, George Bernard Erath and James Webb Throckmorton served during the Civil War as commanders of the Frontier Organization, the last institution that evolved during the conflict to protect the frontier. Another, Henry Eustace McCulloch, would command the Northern Sub-District of Texas, created primarily to enhance the defense of the northwest frontier of Texas. A joint resolution of the state legislature the previous November likewise called for a mounted regiment of Rangers (Gammel, *Laws of Texas* 4:265).

20. Remarks Concerning the New Regiments Bill, Apr. 1, 1858, in Amelia W.

Williams and Eugene C. Barker, eds., *The Writings of Sam Houston, 1813–1863,* 7:55;
E. M. Pease to Maj. Gen. David Twiggs, Aug. 13, 1857, Governor Elisha M. Pease
Records, TSL-A.

21. Gammel, ed., *Laws of Texas* 4:77–78; Gov. H. R. Runnels to The President
of the Senate, Jan. 22, 1858, in Winfrey and Day, *Texas Indian Papers* 3:270–71.

22. Runnels to John S. Ford, Jan. 28, 1858, in Winfrey and Day, *Texas Indian
Papers* 3:272–73. The most complete sources for Rip Ford's life are W. J. Hughes,
Rebellious Ranger: Rip Ford and the Old Southwest, and Ford's story in his own words
in Stephen B. Oates, ed., *Rip Ford's Texas.*

23. Mark E. Nackman, "The Making of the Texan Citizen Soldier, 1835–1860,"
Southwestern Historical Quarterly 78 (Jan., 1975): 248–49.

24. An unusual riding contest held in 1843 demonstrated the ability of Rangers
to match their Indian counterparts in riding ability. This contest, between Texans
and a party of Comanche Indians, saw the Rangers equal the Indians in every
category of trick riding and marksmanship while on horseback (Wilbarger, *Indian
Depredations in Texas,* pp. 290–95; Webb, *Texas Rangers,* pp. 80, 131).

25. Gov. P. H. Bell to George M. Brooke, Nov. 8, 1850, in Winfrey and Day,
Texas Indian Papers 3:162–63. The only biography of Henry McCulloch is David
Paul Smith, "In Defense of Texas: The Life of Henry E. McCulloch," Master's the-
sis, Stephen F. Austin State University, 1975.

26. Henry McCulloch to Lt. John R. King, Dec. 2, 1850, John R. King Papers,
TSL-A; Henry McCulloch to Maj. George Deas, Jan. 4, 1851, Governor Peter Hansborough Bell Records, TSL-A.

27. Utley, *Frontier Regulars,* pp. 31–39, 42. For an excellent secondary account
of the hardships of outpost life for officers and men of the U.S. Army on the
Texas frontier see Robert Wooster, *Soldiers, Sutlers, and Settlers: Garrison Life on
the Texas Frontier.*

28. Frederick Law Olmsted, *A Journey through Texas; or, a Saddle-Trip on the
Southwestern Frontier,* p. 298.

29. For a brief analysis of the army's changing strategy in Texas see Robert
Wooster, "Military Strategy in the Southwest, 1848–1860," *Military History of Texas
and the Southwest* 15 (1979): 5–15. For the influence of Ranger methods on the army
in Texas see Henry W. Barton, "The United States Cavalry and the Texas Rangers," *Southwestern Historical Quarterly* 63 (Apr. 1960): 495–510.

30. John S. Ford to Gov. H. R. Runnels, Mar. 31, 1858, in Winfrey and Day,
Texas Indian Papers 3:279–80; Oates, *Rip Ford's Texas,* pp. 227–37; Ford to Runnels,
Apr. 26, 1858, Governor Hardin Richard Runnels Records, TSL-A. Detailed accounts of this famous battle may be found in Webb, *Texas Rangers,* pp. 155–58;
Richardson, *Comanche Barrier,* pp. 235–38; Wilbarger, *Indian Depredations in Texas,*
pp. 320–26; and Harold B. Simpson, "John Salmon (RIP) Ford," *Rangers of Texas,*
pp. 95–99.

31. The Second's colonel, Albert S. Johnston, took command of an expedition against the Mormons in Utah, and the Second Cavalry was to rendezvous
at Fort Leavenworth, Kansas, and prepare to reinforce him.

32. Runnels wrote Ford that "upon you and your command the duty must
still devolve for a time at least of protecting the lives and property of our Citi-

zens" (Runnels to Ford, May 28, 1858, in Winfrey and Day, *Texas Indian Papers*, 3:286).

33. Twiggs to Runnels, Sept. 9, 1858, Governor Hardin R. Runnels Records, TSL-A. Detailed accounts of the action may be found in Wilbarger, *Indian Depredations in Texas*, pp. 329–32, and Simpson, *Cry Comanche*, pp. 107–16. Rupert N. Richardson, *Comanche Barrier*, pp. 239–40, maintains that these Comanches were probably on their way to Fort Arbuckle to treat with the government but concludes that Van Dorn probably would not have changed his plan even had he known the facts.

34. Richardson, *Comanche Barrier*, pp. 237–38. See *Dallas Herald*, Sept. 28, 1858, Mar. 9, 1859, June 15, 1859; *Clarksville Northern Standard*, Nov. 6, 1858, Apr. 2, 1859, Oct. 22, 1859.

35. Neighbours, *Indian Exodus*, pp. 118–19; Neighbours, *Roebert Simpson Neighbors and the Texas Frontier*, pp. 201–202. Early in the Civil War Confederate officials removed Baylor from command in the Confederate Territory of Arizona when he advocated extermination of the Indians.

36. Oates, *Rip Ford's Texas*, p. 253; Edward J. Gurley to Gov. H. R. Runnels, Feb. 3, 1859, and Robert S. Neighbors to H. R. Runnels, Mar. 28, 1859, Governor Hardin R. Runnels Records, TSL-A; Neighbours, *Indian Exodus*, p. 131–33.

37. George Barnard to H. R. Runnels, May 4, 1859, Governor Hardin R. Runnels Records, TSL-A; Neighbours, *Robert Simpson Neighbors and the Texas Frontier*, pp. 237, 242–45.

38. John H. Brown to Runnels, July 22, 1859, Governor Hardin R. Runnels Records, TSL-A; Brown to Neighbors, July 14, 1859, and Neighbors to Brown, July 17, 1859, in Winfrey and Day, *Texas Indian Papers* 3:333–34, 335–36; Neighbours, *Indian Exodus*, p. 136.

39. Webb, *Texas Rangers*, p. 172, emphasis added. For a valuable collection of correspondence concerning the nuances of frontier defense in relation to the reservations in Texas, see volumes 3 and 4 of Winfrey and Day, *Texas Indian Papers*.

40. Gammel, *Laws of Texas* 4:1375–77. Governor Houston approved the bill on January 2, 1860.

41. Examples of these orders may be found in Sam Houston to John Connor, Jan. 9, 1860, Houston to White, Walker, and Salmon, Feb. 13, 1860, and Houston to J. M. W. Hall, Feb. 14, 1860, all in Williams and Barker, *Writings of Sam Houston* 7:402, 476, 478.

42. Houston to Dalrymple, Jan. 20, 1860, and Houston to Edward Burleson, Jr., Jan. 21, 1860, ibid. 7:424–27, 428–29.

43. Houston To The Legislature, Feb. 8, 1860, Houston to R. B. Wells, Feb. 20, 1860, Houston To The Chief Justices of Texas Counties, Mar. 9, 1860, and Houston to John B. Floyd, Mar. 12, 1860, all in ibid. 7:468–69, 485, 507–508, 512, 521–22. A number of these letters and petitions to Governor Houston in the spring of 1860 are found in Winfrey and Day, *Texas Indian Papers* 4:2–36. The counties in question, approximating the Frontier Organization of 1864–65, were Montague, Wise, Young, Palo Pinto, Eastland, Erath, Comanche, Bosque, Hamilton, Coryell, Llano, San Saba, Lampasas, Mason, Burnet, Gillespie, Bandera, Kerr, Uvalde, Blanco, Bexar, Medina, and Frio. An additional three hundred or more Rangers

were along the Rio Grande, along with elements of four companies of the U.S. Army, all involved in the Cortinas War of 1859-60 on the Mexican border.

44. Houston to James Buchanan, Feb. 17, 1860, Williams and Barker, *Writings of Sam Houston* 7:483; quotation found in Sam Houston to John B. Floyd, Mar. 12, 1860, ibid. 7:521-22.

45. Houston Message To The Legislature of Texas, in Extra Session, Jan. 21, 1861, ibid. 7:238-40. Historian of the Texas Rangers Walter Prescott Webb concludes that Houston actually magnified Indian depredations to the federal government but did not want or expect the Johnson expedition to succeed; in fact, he "cared little about either the Cortinas troubles or the Indian depredations." Webb goes on to say that Houston had in mind a daring filibustering expedition to "lead ten thousand Texas Rangers, supported by Indians and Mexicans, into Mexico, establish a protectorate, with himself in the leading role" (Webb, *Texas Rangers*, pp. 203, 197-216). Such a deduction, in the face of Houston's detailed attention to the suffering of the frontier citizens, is unconvincing.

46. Douglas Southall Freeman, *R. E. Lee: A Biography*, 1:405; Simpson, *Cry Comanche*, p. 140; Simpson, *Cry Comanche*, p. 154.

47. Utley, *Frontier Regulars*, pp. 140-41; quotation found in the *Weatherford Whiteman*, September 13, 1860.

48. Walter Louis Buenger, "Stilling the Voice of Reason: Texas and the Union, 1854-1861," Ph.D. diss., Rice University, 1979, pp. 195-96.

CHAPTER 2. FEDERALS, INDIANS, AND THE FRONTIER: 1861

1. Houston to E. W. Rogers, Dec. 26, 1860, in Williams and Barker, *Writings of Sam Houston*, 7:224-25.

2. Dalrymple to Capt. A. B. Burleson, Jan. 8, 1861, Dalrymple to Rogers, Feb. 5, 1861, and Dalrymple to Houston, Feb. 15, 1861, Adjutant General's Record Group (RG 401), TSL-A; Muster Roll of Capt. P. F. Ross, Indian Spy Company, July 1, 1860, Ross Family Papers, Texas Collection, Baylor University, Waco, Texas.

3. Stephen B. Oates, "Texas under the Secessionists," *Southwestern Historical Quarterly* 67 (Oct., 1963): 167-69; Larry Jay Gage, "The Texas Road to Secession and War: John Marshall and the Texas State Gazette, 1860-1861," *Southwestern Historical Quarterly* 62 (Oct., 1958): 209-11; Caroline Baldwin Darrow, "Recollections of the Twiggs Surrender," *Battles and Leaders of the Civil War*, ed. Clarence C. Buel and Robert U. Johnson 1:33.

4. Friend, *Sam Houston*, pp. 331-39; Ernest William Winkler, ed., *Journal of the Secession Convention of Texas, 1861*, pp. 9-12, 47-49. Houston's proclamations are found in Williams and Barker, *Writings of Sam Houston* 7:220-21, 257-58, 263.

Since the early days of the secession crisis, Houston, the old Unionist, had stated that in the event of secession he would prefer a separate Lone Star Republic. He believed that secession would bring ruin to Texas, but he would bear with the will of the people. In the end, Houston refused to take the oath of allegiance, required of all state officials, to support the Confederate States of America, and Lt. Gov. Edward Clark replaced him as governor on March 18.

5. Message To The Legislature of Texas, Feb. 6, 1861, in Williams and Barker,

Writings of Sam Houston 7:259–62; Gammel, *Laws of Texas* 5:346–47, 353–54; Winkler, *Journal of the Secession Convention*, p. 28.

6. Curiously, Indian raids during the first six months of 1861 were fewer and less damaging than at any time in the previous two years. William C. Holden, "Frontier Defense in Texas during the Civil War," *West Texas Historical Association Year Book* 4 (June, 1928): 16, simply calls their inactivity a mystery, while Webb, *Texas Rangers*, p. 219, concluded that the Indians, "overawed by the magnitude of the great war, drew back from the settlements, hoping perhaps that the white men would kill one another to the last man."

A more practical explanation may be that the constant warfare of the previous two years, where punitive expeditions severely punished the raiding tribes, along with earnest attempts by authorities at treaty negotiations, somewhat abated the Indian incursions.

7. Twiggs to Lt. Col. Winfield Scott, Jan. 15, 1861, in Robert N. Scott et al. eds., *The War of the Rebellion: A Compilation of the Official Records of the Union and Confederate Armies* 1:581. See also in ibid.: Twiggs to Scott, Dec. 13, 1860, 1:579; Twiggs to Lt. Col. Lorenzo Thomas, Dec. 27, 1860, 1:579; Twiggs to Thomas, Jan. 2, 1861, 1:580; Twiggs to Thomas, Jan. 7, 1861, 1:580; and George W. Lay to Twiggs, Dec. 28, 1860, 1:579.

8. Special Orders Number 22, Jan. 28, 1861, and Special Orders Number 16, Feb. 4, 1861, *Official Records* 1:584, 586. Of course, much speculation has been made of a possible scenario had Robert E. Lee remained in command of the department or replaced Twiggs before the crisis events of February. Lee received orders on February 4 to report to Washington, while Col. Carlos A. Waite received authority to replace Twiggs as department commander (Freeman, *R. E. Lee: A Biography*, 1:424–27).

9. Twiggs to Adjutant-General (Gen. Samuel Cooper), Feb. 4, 1861, *Official Records* 1:586; Oates, *Rip Ford's Texas*, p. 318; John C. Robertson to Col. Ben McCulloch, Feb. 5, 1861, and John C. Robertson to Col. Henry E. McCulloch, Feb. 5, 1861, in Winkler, *Journal of the Secession Convention*, pp. 305, 318, 366–67.

10. Twiggs to Thomas, A.A.G., Feb. 18, 1861, Report of Maj. Larkin Smith, Feb. 23, 1861, Report of Lt. Col. William Hoffman, Mar. 1, 1861, and Report of Capt. John H. King, Mar. 1, 1861, all in *Official Records* 1:502–16, 517–18, 519–20, 521–58, 590; Darrow, "Recollections of the Twiggs Surrender," pp. 34–36; O. M. Roberts, *Texas*, vol. 11 of *Confederate Military History*, ed. Clement Evans, pp. 15–26; Robert P. Felgar, "Texas in the War for Southern Independence," Ph.D. diss., University of Texas 1947, pp. 56–61.

11. General Orders Number 5, War Department, Mar. 1, 1861, *Official Records* 1:597.

12. Gammel, ed., *Laws of Texas* 5:396; Allen Johnson et. al., eds., *Dictionary of American Biography* 20:83; Patricia L. Faust, ed., *Historical Times Illustrated Encyclopedia of the Civil War*, p. 767.

13. H. E. McCulloch to John C. Robertson, Feb. 26, 1861, in Winkler, *Journal of the Secession Convention*, p. 370; Thomas Robert Havins, *Camp Colorado: A Decade of Frontier Defense*, p. 94; Simpson, *Cry Comanche*, p. 161. Just over two years later Kirby Smith would command the entire Confederate Trans-Mississippi De-

partment, holding that position until the last days of the war. Henry McCulloch would hold a sub-military district command in Texas, part of "Kirby Smithdom."

14. McCulloch to Robertson, Feb. 26, 1861, in Winkler, *Journal of the Secession Convention*, p. 370; Report of Capt. E. Kirby Smith, Mar. 1, 1861, *Official Records* 1:559.

15. McCulloch to Robertson, Feb. 26, 1861, *Official Records* 1:370–72; Havins, *Camp Colorado*, pp. 96–97. The Secession Convention reconvened on March 2 to count the votes, resulting in Texas's approval of the Ordinance of Secession by a vote of 46,166 to 14,747 (Joe T. Timmons, "The Referendum in Texas on the Ordinance of Secession, February 23, 1861: The Vote," *East Texas Historical Journal* 11, no. 2 «1973»: 16).

16. A. B. Burleson to Richard W. Johnson, Feb. 24, 1861 (quotation); General Orders Number 5, Feb. 18, 1861; Circular, Commissioners on Behalf of Committee of Public Safety; and Report of Capt. E. Kirby Smith, Mar. 1, 1861, all in *Official Records* 1:515–16, 559, 595.

17. McCulloch to Barry, Feb. 25, 1861, James Buckner Barry Papers, Eugene C. Barker Texas History Center, Austin, Texas (cited hereafter as BTHC); Henry C. McCulloch to Frost, Feb. 26, 1861, Adjutant General's Records, TSL-A; McCulloch to Robertson, Feb. 26, 1861, and McCulloch to Robertson, Mar. 1, 1861, both in Winkler, *Journal of the Secession Convention*, pp. 373–74, 376.

18. McCulloch to Robertson, Mar. 1, 1861, in Winkler, *Journal of the Secession Convention*, p. 377; Rupert N. Richardson, "The Saga of Camp Cooper," *West Texas Historical Association Year Book* 56 (Oct., 1980): 33. Dalrymple's correspondence in the matter is found in *Official Records* 1:541–43.

19. Morris to Waite, Feb. 28, 1861, and McCulloch to Carpenter, Feb. 28, 1861, both in *Official Records* 1:558, 543–44; McCulloch to Robertson, Mar. 1, 1861, in Winkler, *Journal of the Secession Convention*, pp. 374–75.

20. James K. Greer, ed., *Buck Barry, Texas Ranger and Frontiersman*, p. 127; McCulloch to Robertson, Mar. 9, 1861, *Official Records* 53:643–44; *Dallas Herald*, Mar. 20, 1861; McCulloch to Barry, Mar. 7, 1861, Barry Papers, BTHC.

21. McCulloch to Robertson, Mar. 9, 1861, *Official Records* 53:643–44; Greer, *Buck Barry*, pp. 127–28; Gammel, *Laws of Texas* 4:1530–32; Michael Reagan Thomasson, "James E. McCord and the Texas Frontier Regiment," Master's thesis, Stephen F. Austin State University, 1965, p. 19.

22. Walker to Ben McCulloch, Mar. 4, 1861, *Official Records* 1:610.

23. Hemphill and Oldham to Walker, Mar. 30, 1861, *Official Records* 1:618–19.

24. Greer, *Buck Barry*, pp. 127–28; Henry McCulloch to Walker, Mar. 30, 1861, *Official Records* 1:617–18.

25. Walker to Hemphill, Apr. 11, 1861 (quotation), and Clark to Davis, Apr. 4, 1861, *Official Records* 1:621–22.

26. Dudley G. Wooten, ed., *A Comprehensive History of Texas*, 2:131; C. W. Raines, ed., *Six Decades in Texas: The Memoirs of Francis R. Lubbock, Confederate Governor of Texas*, p. 357; Oates, *Rip Ford's Texas*, p. 324; P. N. Luckett to Col. Earl Van Dorn, May 2, 1861, *Official Records* 1:630–31. Rip Ford's regiment entered originally into state service when called by the legislature, because Secretary of War Walker believed that one cavalry regiment in Texas, McCulloch's, was ample protection.

At Texan urging and insistence, the government relented, and by late spring Ford's men entered Confederate service as the Second Regiment, Texas Mounted Rifles. Robert L. Kerby, *Kirby Smith's Confederacy: The Trans-Mississippi South, 1863–1865,* p. 14, inaccurately describes McCulloch's regiment as the one called up by the legislature.

27. McCulloch to Barry, Mar. 27, 1861, Barry Papers, BTHC; Regimental Returns, Personal Service Records, Henry E. McCulloch, Confederate Record Group 109, National Archives, Washington, D.C.; Regimental Order Number 2, Mar. 19, 1861, Adjutant General's Records, TSL-A.

28. Circular, First Texas Mounted Riflemen Reunion, Apr. 6, 1894, Garnett A. Dibrell Collection, TSL-A; Regimental Orders Number 10, June 16, 1861, James M. Holmsley Papers, BTHC. Webb's company replaced that of William Drake, who failed to report a company for duty.

29. Circular, First Texas Mounted Riflemen Reunion, Apr. 6, 1894, Garnett A. Dibrell Collection, TSL-A; Wooten, *Comprehensive History of Texas* 2:131; Raines, *Six Decades in Texas,* p. 357.

30. General Orders Number 1, Apr. 21, 1861, and Kirby Smith to Walker, Apr. 20, 1861, *Official Records* 1:627–28. Smith also proposed that fifteen companies of infantry be posted along "the El Paso road" and at forts guarding the Trans-Pecos region.

31. General Orders Number 8, May 24, 1861, ibid. 1:574–75.

32. Samuel Cooper to Van Dorn, Apr. 11, 1861, McCulloch to Walker, Apr. 17, 1861, and General Orders Number 4, May 3, 1861, all in *Official Records* 1:623, 627, 632; William H. Bell, "Ante Bellum: The Old Army in Texas in '61," *Magazine of History* 3 (Jan., 1906): 80–86; J. J. Bowden, *The Exodus of Federal Forces From Texas, 1861,* pp. 97–104.

33. Van Dorn to Cooper, May 10, 1861, and Col. Isaac V. D. Reeve to Thomas, May 12, 1861, *Official Records* 1:568–70, 572; Felgar, "Texas in the War for Southern Independence," p. 61.

34. Van Dorn to Cooper, June 3, 1861, Van Dorn to McCulloch, May 25, 1861, and Van Dorn to McCulloch, May 28, 1861, all in *Official Records* 1:573, 575–76; Lary C. Rampp and Donald L. Rampp, *The Civil War in the Indian Territory,* pp. 3–5; Webb et. al., *Handbook of Texas* 2:947–48.

35. The exact date is established by statement in a letter written by a young trooper in McCulloch's regiment (John Thomas Duncan, ed., "Some Civil War Letters of D. Port Smythe," *West Texas Historical Association Year Book* 37 [Oct. 1961]: 155).

36. J. Evetts Haley, *Charles Goodnight: Cowman and Plainsman,* p. 64; Albert Pike to the Governor of Texas, Aug. 9, 1861, Frontier Protection Papers, BTHC; McCulloch's survey on the Comanche tribes in the region may be found in "Different Bands of Comanches," June 8, 1861, Adjutant General's Records, TSL-A. In reference to the work of Henry McCulloch, Ed Burleson, and Albert Pike, Confederate Indian Commissioner, one historian noted that "the frontier would probably have fared worse had it not been for the efforts of conciliation on the part of these men" (Felgar, "Texas in the War for Southern Independence," p. 149).

37. Special Orders Number 56, July 12, 1861, and Special Orders Number 57, July 13, 1861, Burleson Papers, BTHC. Camp Jackson, northernmost outpost of the First Texas Mounted Rifles, was named in honor of James T. Jackson, a southern sympathizer who killed Col. Elmer Ellsworth, of the New York Fire Zouaves, at Alexandria, Virginia, on May 24, 1861.

38. McCulloch to Burleson, July 22, 1861, ibid.

39. McCulloch added these posts and ensured that Fort Belknap would remain occupied before he left San Antonio for the frontier (Special Orders Number 4, Apr. 20, 1861, Adjutant General's Records, TSL-A).

40. Special Orders Number 57, July 13, 1861, Burleson Papers, BTHC; Special Orders Number 46, June 17, 1861, Adjutant General's Records, TSL-A; Circular, Aug. 2, 1861, and McCulloch to Burleson, July 22, 1861, Burleson Papers, BTHC; McCulloch to King, Dec. 21, 1861, King Papers, TSL-A.

41. Circular, Aug. 2, 1861, Burleson Papers, BTHC. For a general discussion of the regiment's supply problems in 1861 see Havins, *Camp Colorado*, pp. 99-103. For a broader view of supply difficulties in the Trans-Mississippi Confederacy during the first year of the war, the best account is James L. Nichols, *The Confederate Quartermaster in the Trans-Mississippi*.

42. Special Orders Number 40, June 18, 1861, Burleson Papers, BTHC.

43. McCulloch to Burleson, Sept. 20, 1861, Burleson Papers, BTHC; McCulloch to Hebert, Sept. 20, 1861, *Official Records* 4:108.

44. Circular, Aug. 2, 1861, Special Orders Number 57, July 13, 1861, and McCulloch to Burleson, July 22, 1861, all in Burleson Papers, BTHC.

45. Circular, Aug. 2, 1861, ibid.

46. Duncan, "Some Civil War Letters of D. Port Smythe," p. 160.

47. Regimental Orders Number 19, Nov. 30, 1861, Barry Papers, BTHC; Thomas R. Havins, "The Texas Mounted Regiment at Camp Colorado," *Texas Military History* 4 (Summer, 1964): 76-77. The site of the battle is misspelled in the *Official Records* as the "Peosi" River (McCulloch to Hebert, Nov. 30, 1861, 4:35).

48. General Orders Number 17, Sept. 4, 1861, *Official Records* 4:100-101; Personal Service Record, Henry McCulloch, Confederate Record Group 109, National Archives, Washington, D.C.

49. Greer, ed., *Buck Barry*, p. 143; Yager to Burleson, Oct. 17, 1861, Burleson Papers, BTHC; Special Orders Number 206, Dec. 3, 1861, *Official Records* 4:151-52.

50. Clark to Hebert, Oct. 22, 1861, and Lubbock to John H. Reagan, Dec. 27, 1861, both in *Official Records* 4:126, 161; Raines, *Six Decades in Texas*, p. 357.

CHAPTER 3. THE FRONTIER REGIMENT: 1862-63

1. James M. Day, ed., *House Journal of the Ninth Legislature, Regular Session, November 4, 1861-January 14, 1862*, pp. 49-50; Raines, *Six Decades in Texas*, pp. 337-38, 357.

2. Day, *House Journal of the Ninth Legislature, Regular Session*, pp. 79-80.

3. McCulloch to Lubbock, Dec. 21, 1861, Governor Francis Richard Lubbock Records, TSL-A. About ten months earlier McCulloch reported seeing a large number of buffalo as far south as the road from Fort Chadbourne to Camp Cooper (McCulloch to Robertson, Mar. 9, 1861, *Official Records* 1:644).

4. McCulloch to Lubbock, Dec. 21, 1861, Governor Francis Richard Lubbock Records, TSL-A.

5. McCulloch to Commanding Officer at Camp Colorado, Dec. 20, 1861, James M. Holmsley Papers, BTHC; Gammel, *Laws of Texas* 5:452-54.

6. Lubbock to McCulloch, Dec. 24, 1861, Governor Francis Richard Lubbock Records, TSL-A.

7. Gammel, *Laws of Texas* 5:453-54.

8. Kerby, *Kirby Smith's Confederacy*, p. 15; Lubbock to John H. Reagan, Dec. 27, 1861, "[Act of] January 17, 1862," and Jefferson Davis to the Congress of the Confederate States, Jan. 22, 1862, all in *Official Records* 4:161-62, 53:770-71.

9. Greer, *Buck Barry*, p. 142; Regimental Orders Number 20, Dec. 5, 1861, Burleson Papers, BTHC; Simpson, *Cry Comanche*, p. 76.

10. Greer, *Buck Barry*, pp. 143-44; Harry McCorry Henderson, *Texas in the Confederacy*, p. 141; Wooten, *Comprehensive History of Texas*, p. 574; Wilfred Buck Yearns, *The Confederate Congress*, pp. 65-66.

11. Lubbock to Col. Jeremiah Yellott Dashiell, Jan. 29, 1862, Governor Francis Richard Lubbock Records, TSL-A; Lubbock to Dashiell, Jan. 3, 1862, Frontier Protection Papers, BTHC; Special Orders Number 11, Jan. 27, 1862, *Official Records* 53:775; William M. Walton to D. H. Farr, Feb. 4, 1861, Governor Francis Richard Lubbock Records, TSL-A.

12. Gammel, *Laws of Texas* 5:463; Raines, *Six Decades in Texas*, pp. 358-59.

13. Norris to Lubbock, Apr. 19, 1862, [posting of the Frontier Regiment] Apr. 21, 1862, and Norris to Dashiell, Apr. 23, 1862, all in Adjutant General's Records, TSL-A; Special Orders Number 12, Jan. 29, 1862, *Official Records* 53:776; Holden, "Frontier Defense," pp. 19-20.

14. Norris to Dashiell, Apr. 28, 1862, Adjutant General's Records, TSL-A; Holden, "Frontier Defense," pp. 20-21; Greer, ed., *Buck Barry*, pp. 146-47.

15. Lubbock to D. W. Taylor, Apr. 23, 1861, and D. W. Taylor to Lubbock, Apr. 12, 1862, both in Governor Francis Richard Lubbock Records, TSL-A; Greer, *Buck Barry*, p. 146; Holden, "Frontier Defense," pp. 22-23.

16. Norris to Dashiell, June 20, 1862, Adjutant General's Records, TSL-A; Dashiell to State Military Board, Apr. 25, 1863, Texas State Military Board Papers, TSL-A; Greer, *Buck Barry*, pp. 147-48.

17. Dashiell to Hebert, Oct. 1, 1862, *Official Records* 53:855; Greer, *Buck Barry*, p. 146; Estimate of Funds Needed by Texas Frontier Regiment, July-December, 1862, Dorman H. Winfrey and James M. Day, eds., *The Indian Papers of Texas and the Southwest, 1825-1916* 4:66; Holden, "Frontier Problems and Movements," p. 92.

18. Dashiell to Hebert, Oct. 1, 1862, and Davis to Dashiell, Nov. 8, 1862, both in *Official Records* 53:855-56.

19. Special Orders Number 237, Oct. 10, 1862; General Orders Number 1, Nov. 29, 1862; A. G. Dickinson to Bee, Dec. 31, 1862; General Orders Number 3, Jan. 17, 1863; and Dashiell to Bee, Jan. 12, 1863, all in ibid. 15:826, 880-81, 951, 53:841, 857-58; Raines, *Six Decades in Texas*, p. 469.

20. James M. Day, ed., *House Journal of the Ninth Legislature, First Called Session, February 2, 1863-March 7, 1863*, p. 9; Raines, *Six Decades in Texas*, p. 469.

21. Raines, *Six Decades in Texas*, pp. 470–71. Lubbock's plan was the genesis of the Frontier Organization of 1864–65, the last step in the evolution of frontier defense by the State of Texas.

22. Ibid., p. 475; Thomasson, "James McCord and the Texas Frontier Regiment," pp. 49–50.

23. Gammel, *Laws of Texas* 5:607–608.

24. Lubbock to Davis, Mar. 27, 1863, *Official Records* 53:852–53.

25. E. P. Turner to W. R. Scurry, Mar. 28, 1863, Bee to Dashiell, Jan. 17, 1863, and Turner to Scurry, Mar. 28, 1863, all in ibid. 15:1027–28, 53:858–59.

26. Turner to Scurry, Mar. 28, 1863, *Official Records* 15:1027; Raines, *Six Decades in Texas*, p. 483.

27. Thomasson, "James E. McCord and the Texas Frontier Regiment," pp. 5–6, 9–10, 16, 21.

28. McCord to Dashiell, Mar. 20, 1863, General Orders Number 3, Apr. 8, 1863, General Orders Number 5, Apr. 13, 1863, and General Orders Number 9, May 5, 1863, all in Adjutant General's Records, TSL-A; Greer, *Buck Barry*, pp. 146–47. Red River Station was located where Salt Creek emptied into the Red River; it would later be the jumping-off point of the Chisholm Trail. The site is nine miles northwest of present Nocona, Texas.

29. General Orders Number 12, May 26, 1863, Adjutant General's Records, TSL-A; John T. Rowland to Barry, June 18, 1863, Barry Papers, BTHC; Greer, *Buck Barry*, pp. 150–51.

30. General Orders Number 12, May 26, 1863, Adjutant General's Records, TSL-A; Greer, *Buck Barry*, pp. 152–55.

31. McCord to Barry, May 20, 1863, Rowland to Barry, Sept. 3, 1863, and Dashiell to McCord, Oct. 1, 1863, Barry Papers, BTHC; Turner to Lubbock, Oct. 6, 1863, *Official Records* 26(2):290; Greer, *Buck Barry*, pp. 149–50.

32. General Orders Number 16, Sept. 11, 1863, Adjutant General's Records, TSL-A.

CHAPTER 4. CREATION OF THE NORTHERN SUB-DISTRICT

1. Greer, *Buck Barry*, p. 147.

2. Gammel, *Laws of Texas* 5:346–47; Cliff Donahue Cates, *Pioneer History of Wise County: From Red Men to Railroads, Twenty Years of Intrepid History*, pp. 116–17; T. R. Fehrenbach, *Comanches: The Destruction of a People*, pp. 135–36; Ida Lasater Huckabay, *Ninety-Four Years in Jack County*, p. 78; A. Morton Smith, *The First 100 Years in Cooke County*, p. 32.

3. The term Jayhawker, coined in 1856, referred to free-state men in southeast Kansas who joined together to oppose the border ruffians of Missouri. During the Civil War a Jayhawker was a Unionist or abolitionist who made war on any southern sympathizers. Its southern counterpart was a "bushwhacker," a guerrilla who preyed upon the lives and property of Union citizens (Hildegarde Rose Herklotz, "Jayhawkers in Missouri, 1858–1863," *Missouri Historical Review* 18 [Oct., 1923], Part 2:267–68). Soldiers on the Texas frontier frequently referred to Jayhawkers in their dispatches and reports, always as those who rode with Indians on their raids, or who came through Indian Territory in small groups to raid North

Texas. In North Texas the term bushwhacker usually referred to a Texas citizen of Unionist sentiment who resisted conscription and stole from his neighbors.

4. John Henry Brown, *History of Texas: From 1685 to 1892* 2:406; Marcus J. Wright, *Texas in the War, 1861–1865*, ed. Harold B. Simpson, p. 115; Rampp and Rampp, *The Civil War in the Indian Territory*, pp. 3–5.

5. Graham Landrum and Allan Smith, *Grayson County: An Illustrated History of Grayson County, Texas*, pp. 45–47, 61–62; Clark to Hebert, Sept. 24, 1861, *Official Records* 4:110; Edward Clark to James J. Diamond, Sept. 19, 1861, James Bourland Papers, Manuscript Division, Library of Congress, Washington, D.C. This collection is also located on microfilm in the Charles Ramsdell Collection of the Barker Texas History Center, University of Texas. All citations herein refer to the photocopied collection of the Bourland Papers in the Library of Congress, copy in possession of the author.

6. Gammel, *Laws of Texas* 5:455; Hudson to Dashiell, Mar. 22, 1863, Adjutant General's Records, TSL-A; Holden, "Frontier Problems and Movements," pp. 349–53; J. P. Earle, *History of Clay County and Northwest Texas*, preface.

7. J. Y. Dashiell to Bourland, Dec. 30, 1861, Bourland Papers, Library of Congress; William S. Speer and John Henry Brown, eds., *The Encyclopedia of the New West*, pp. 355, 573; Williams and Barker, *Writings of Sam Houston* 4:472; Gammel, *Laws of Texas* 5:456–57; Michael Collins, *Cooke County, Texas: Where the South and the West Meet*, p. 11; Cates, *Pioneer History of Wise County*, pp. 117–18.

8. Loving to Bourland, Apr. 12, 1862, Bourland Papers, Library of Congress; Collins, *Cooke County, Texas*, p. 18.

9. General Orders Number 5, June 12, 1862, and Hudson to Dashiell, Sept. 15, 1862, both in *Official Records* 9:718, 53:827–28; Cates, *Pioneer History of Wise County*, p. 124.

10. Lubbock to Hebert, Sept. 25, 1862, and Special Orders Number 132, Sept. 30, 1862, *Official Records* 15:818, 53:827.

11. These counties, and their voting record on secession, included: Collin, 948 against, 405 for; Cooke, 221 against, 137 for; Fannin, 656 against, 471 for; Grayson, 901 against, 463 for; Jack, 76 against, 14 for; Lamar, 663 against, 553 for; Montague, 86 against, 50 for. Wise County's narrow vote was 76 against, 78 for (Ernest Wallace, *Texas in Turmoil*, p. 70; Winkler, *Journal of the Secession Convention*, pp. 89–90; Timmons, "The Referendum In Texas," pp. 12–28).

12. Claude Elliott, "Union Sentiment in Texas, 1861–1865," *Southwestern Historical Quarterly* 50 (Apr., 1947): 453; Ella Lonn, *Desertion during the Civil War*, pp. 4–7, 14–16. The most thorough source for the background and detail for the conspiracy and subsequent mass hangings at Gainesville is Richard Bryan McCaslin, "Tainted Breeze: The Great Hanging at Gainesville, Texas, October 1862," Ph.D. diss., University of Texas, 1988. The principal primary sources are: Sam Acheson and Julie Ann Hudson O'Connell, eds., *George Washington Diamond's Account of the Great Hanging at Gainesville, 1862*; Thomas Barrett, *The Great Hanging at Gainesville, Cooke County, Texas A.D. 1862*; and L. D. Clark, ed., *Civil War Recollections of James Lemuel Clark*.

13. McCaslin, "Tainted Breeze," pp. 10–15, 115–27, 168–73, 178; James Alan Marten, "Drawing the Line: Dissent and Disloyalty in Texas, 1856–1874," Ph.D.

dissertation, University of Texas, 1986, pp. 230–31. See also, James M. McPherson, *Battle Cry of Freedom: The Civil War Era*, pp. 611–17, and James Oakes, *Slavery and Freedom: An Interpretation of the Old South*, pp. 128–36.

14. John W. Hale to Lubbock, Mar. 23, 1863, Texas State Military Board Papers, TSL-A.

15. Joseph and Laura to C. M. Milam, Mar. 12, 1863, McKinney Family Papers, Special Collections, University of Texas at Arlington Library, Arlington, Texas (references to sources in the archives of this library will be referred to hereafter as UTA); Lubbock to Citizens of Wise, Parker, and Jack Counties, Texas, Apr. 11, 1863, Governor Francis Richard Lubbock Records, TSL-A.

16. Twitty to Steele, Mar. 3, 1863, *Official Records* 22(2):799. Accounts of the Indian attacks at this time are found in Marvin F. London, *Indian Raids in Montague County*, pp. 36–37, and W. R. Potter, *History of Montague County, Texas*, pp. 22–23.

17. Hudson to Dashiell, Nov. 29, 1862, Dec. 13, 1862, and Mar. 8, 1863, Adjutant General's Records, TSL-A.

18. Diamond to Steele, Mar. 3, 1863, Twitty to Steele, Mar. 3, 1863, and J. F. Crosby to Charles De Morse, Mar. 12, 1863, all in *Official Records* 22(2):799, 800, 802; Lubbock to Bourland, Mar. 11, 1863, and Lubbock to Citizens of Wise, Parker, and Jack Counties, Apr. 11, 1863, Governor Francis Richard Lubbock Records, TSL-A; Raines, *Six Decades in Texas*, pp. 483–84.

19. Regimental Returns, Bourland's Regiment Texas Cavalry, "Border Regiment," Confederate Record Group 109, National Archives; "Bourland's Texas Cavalry," typescript, Confederate Research Center, Hill Junior College, Hillsboro, Texas; Special Orders Number 23, Aug. 18, 1863, Special Orders Number [?], Oct. 8, 1863, and Special Orders Number 64, Oct. 9, 1863, Bourland Papers, Library of Congress; Samuel Bell Maxey to Henry E. McCulloch, Jan. 19, 1864, Maxey Papers, TSL-A.

20. "Hangman" quotation found in Speer and Brown, eds., *Encyclopedia of the New West*, p. 573; "good hater" quotation found in "Notes on the Great Hanging in Cooke Co., Texas, October, 1862," typescript, p. 298, Lillian Gunter Papers, Morton Museum, Gainesville, Texas.

21. Robert L. Kerby, *Kirby Smith's Confederacy: The Trans-Mississippi South, 1863–1865*, pp. 52–53.

22. General Orders Number 76, May 30, 1863, *Official Records*, ser. 1, vol. 26, pt. 2, p. 25; General Orders Number 82, June 5, 1863, ibid., ser. 1, vol. 26, pt. 2, p. 38; Raines, ed., *Six Decades in Texas*, p. 503.

23. General Orders Number 76, May 30, 1863, *Official Records*, ser. 1, vol. 26, pt. 2, p. 25; General Orders Number 97, June 23, 1863, ibid., ser. 1, vol. 26, pt. 2, p. 80; General Orders Number 1, July 9, 1863, Orders and Circulars, Department of Texas, 1861–1864, Confederate Record Group 109, National Archives.

24. Special Orders Number 8, July 22, 1863, Orders and Circulars, 1861–1864, Department of Texas, Confederate Record Group 109, National Archives; Lary C. Rampp and Donald L. Rampp, *The Civil War in the Indian Territory*, pp. 21–29; Robert L. Kerby, *Kirby Smith's Confederacy: The Trans-Mississippi South, 1863–1865*, p. 224. The Union activities of August and September unhinged the entire upper

Arkansas River line from the grasp of the Confederates and forced Gen. Kirby Smith to establish Indian Territory as a separate military district on October 11, 1863.

25. Bankhead to Turner, Aug. 20, 1863, Bankhead to Turner, Aug. 27, 1863, Roberts to Turner, Aug. 29, 1863, Roberts to Turner, Aug. 29, 1863, and Roberts to Turner, Sept. 13, 1863, all in *Official Records* 22(2):972–73, 981, 26(2):187–88, 225–26; Wright, *Texas in the War*, p. 13.

26. John C. Rushing to F. R. Lubbock, Aug. 12, 1863, Barry Papers, BTHC; H. Smythe, *Historical Sketch of Parker County and Weatherford, Texas*, p. 167; Wilbarger, *Indian Depredations in Texas*, p. 524; Joseph Carroll McConnell, *The West Texas Frontier, or a Descriptive History of Early Times in Western Texas* 2:82–83. McConnell spent four years in research that consisted largely of interviews with approximately five hundred Texas pioneers who lived during the period he portrayed. Most of the interviews are reliable; unfortunately, while many of those old settlers he interviewed could pinpoint the year an event took place, an exact day or month could not be determined. Such accounts have been used here only if the exact dates could be confirmed by other sources.

27. Rushing to Lubbock, Aug. 12, 1863, Barry Papers, BTHC; McConnell, *The West Texas Frontier* 2:83–84, 98; Wilbarger, *Indian Depredations in Texas*, p. 524.

28. Richard Montgomery Gano and Nathaniel Terry to Magruder, Aug. 12, 1863, *Official Records* 26(2): 159–60.

29. Rushing to Lubbock, Aug. 12, 1863, Barry Papers, BTHC.

30. James D. Wortham to Travis G. Wright, Aug. 10, 1863, George T. Wright Family Papers, BTHC.

31. Bankhead to Magruder, Aug. 9, 1863, and Bankhead to Turner, Aug. 16, 1863, both in *Official Records* 53:888–89, 890.

32. W. T. Carrington to Bankhead, Aug. 22, 1863, ibid. 22(2):975.

33. Bourland to F. M. Totty, Aug. 26, 1863, Bourland Papers, Library of Congress. Bourland established his headquarters at this time near Delaware Bend on the Red River at the Cooke-Grayson county line. Bourland directed the fourth squad to be stationed "near Bourland's." This may refer to his old trading post at Horseshoe Bend, on the Red River in Cooke County.

34. Bankhead to Magruder, Aug. 16, 1863, *Official Records* 53:890; McConnell, *The West Texas Frontier* 2:87–88.

35. Greer, *Buck Barry*, p. 166; Rowland to Barry, Sept. 3, 1863, Barry Papers, BTHC. Barry maintained that jealousy on the part of those under Bourland's command, and their criticism of its performance in August, led to much of the talk at this time about disbanding the Frontier Regiment.

36. William T. Hagan, *United States–Comanche Relations: The Reservation Years*, p. 19; Ernest Wallace and E. Adamson Hoebel, *The Comanches: Lords of the South Plains*, pp. 305–306; Fehrenbach, *Comanches*, p. 452; Mildred P. Mayhall, *The Kiowas*, pp. 195–96.

37. Guy M. Bryan to Magruder, Sept. 2, 1863, Special Orders Number 220, Aug. 16, 1863, Bryan to Magruder, Aug. 20, 1863, and E. P. Turner to Bankhead, Sept. 4, 1863, all in *Official Records* 26(2):171, 174, 200, 205.

38. Raines, ed., *Six Decades in Texas*, p. 503.

39. O. M. Roberts, *Texas*, p. 105.
40. *Dallas Herald*, Sept. 30, 1863.
41. Lubbock to Ford, Sept. 18, 1863, in Winfrey and Day, *The Indian Papers of Texas and the Southwest, 1825–1916* 4:77.
42. James M. Day, ed., *Senate Journal of the Tenth Legislature, Regular Session, November 3, 1863–December 16, 1863*, p. 16.

CHAPTER 5. THE NORTHERN SUB-DISTRICT AND FRONTIER DEFENSE: AUGUST, 1863–JANUARY, 1864.

1. McConnell, *The West Texas Frontier* 2:89–92. This raid struck on October 10. McConnell cites at least four additional attacks in Montague County that appear to have occurred at this time, but the pioneers he interviewed did not specify that they took place in the month of October.
2. Wilbarger, *Indian Depredations in Texas*, pp. 523–24; McConnell, *The West Texas Frontier* 2:93–94. McConnell's date given for the attack on the Tackett ranch, October 26, 1863, is preferred over Wilbarger, *Indian Depredations in Texas*, pp. 522–23, who gives a date of October, 1862. McConnell interviewed Tackett's nephews and used a manuscript of the episode based on Tackett's son's account.
3. McCulloch to Bourland, Oct. 29, 1863, Bourland Papers, Library of Congress; Lubbock to E. P. Turner, Oct. 12, 1863, Governor Francis Richard Lubbock Records, TSL-A.
4. McCord to Barry, Oct. 26, 1863, Barry Papers, BTHC; Bourland to McCord, Oct. 30, 1863, ibid.
5. Magruder to W. R. Boggs, Chief of Staff, Oct. 9, 1863, *Official Records* 26(2):297. During the first three weeks of October, McCulloch received two regiments from General Steele, who could ill afford to part with them. They included most of Bankhead's brigade, one four-gun battery, and three unattached companies.
6. They were often called brush men or bush men by contemporaries. The author leans with the majority and will use "brush." For brief but informative accounts of threats to the internal security of Texas by disruptive gangs of deserters and those resisting conscription, see Kerby, *Kirby Smith's Confederacy*, pp. 89–94; Ella Lonn, *Desertion during the Civil War*, pp. 3–7, 13–27; and Floyd F. Ewing, Jr., "Unionist Sentiment on the Northwest Texas Frontier," pp. 58–70. A more thorough treatment is found in McCaslin, "Tainted Breeze," pp. 309–75.
7. General Orders Number 38, Aug. 26, 1863, *General Orders, Headquarters, Trans-Mississippi, from 6 March 1863 to 1 January 1865*, p. 23. This order designated Bonham as one of two locations in Texas to receive those returning to duty, in addition to Houston (Magruder to Lubbock, June 4, 1863, Proclamation to the People of Texas, July 16, 1863, and Magruder to Lubbock, July 30, 1863, all in *Official Records* 26(2):34–35, 114–15, 126–27).
8. McCulloch to Magruder, Sept. 18, 1863, and Magruder to Kirby Smith, Oct. 20, 1863, both in *Official Records* 26(2):236, 369.
9. McCulloch to Epperson, Sept. 29, 1863, B. H. Epperson Papers, BTHC.
10. *Clarksville Northern Standard*, Oct. 10, 1863; Claude Elliott, *Leathercoat: The Life History of a Texas Patriot*, pp. 30–31.

11. E. S. C. Robertson to Mary Robertson, Oct. 11, 1863, Robertson Colony Collection, UTA; Roberts to Epperson, Oct. 7, 1863, Epperson Papers, BTHC; John H. Brown to Wife, Sept. 14, 1863, and John S. Ford to John H. Brown, Oct. 6, 1863, both in John H. Brown Papers, BTHC.

12. McCulloch to Epperson, Sept. 29, 1863, Epperson Papers, BTHC.

13. Smith to McCulloch, Oct. 2, 1863, *Official Records* 26(2):285.

14. E. S. C. Robertson to Mary Robertson, Oct. 13, 1863, Robertson Colony Collection, UTA; McCulloch to Magruder, Oct. 11, 1863, McCulloch to Magruder, Oct. 21, 1863, and McCulloch to Magruder, Oct. 21, 1863, all in *Official Records* 26(2):303, 344-45.

15. Thomas Lanagin to McCulloch, Nov. 28, 1863, Bourland Papers, Library of Congress; McCulloch to Boren, Oct. 24, 1863, *Official Records* 26(2):352.

16. Bryan to McCulloch, Oct. 29, 1863, Magruder to McCulloch, Oct. 6, 1863, Magruder to Kirby Smith, Oct. 27, 1863, and McCulloch to E. P. Turner, Nov. 1, 1863, all in *Official Records* 26(2):290, 359, 370, 378-79.

17. William Elsey Connelley, *Quantrill and the Border Wars*, p. 436.

18. Lary C. Rampp, "Incident at Baxter Springs on October 6, 1863," *Kansas Historical Quarterly* 36 (Summer, 1970): 183-97; Report of Col. W. C. Quantrill, Oct. 13, 1863, General Orders Number 187, Oct. 19, 1863, McCulloch to E. P. Turner, Oct. 22, 1863, all in *Official Records* 22(2):700-701, 26(2):339-40, 348.

19. E. S. C. Robertson to Mary Robertson, Oct. 24, 1863, Robertson Colony Collection, UTA. At the meeting with McCulloch one of the general's staff described the twenty-six-year-old guerrilla leader: "Have just seen him—Well he is nothing but a man—about five feet ten inches high—spare made—weighs about 150—has fair hair, blue eyes—red complexion. No mark of greatness about him that may not be found [in] many another Man of no worth at all" (E. S. C. Robertson to Mary Robertson, Oct. 26, 1863, Robertson Colony Collection, UTA). These two letters by Robertson provide us with the only evidence of Quantrill's visit to McCulloch at this time.

20. McCulloch to E. P. Turner, Oct. 22, 1863, *Official Records* 26(2):348.

21. Smith to McCulloch, Nov. 1, 1863, ibid. 26(2):383; W. R. Boggs to McCulloch, Nov. 12, 1863, Letters Sent, Trans-Mississippi Department, Confederate Record Group 109, National Archives. Kirby Smith's biographer, Joseph Howard Parks, *General Edmund Kirby Smith, C.S.A.*, is notably silent concerning the general's strong support of Quantrill's men in the Northern Sub-District; in fact, little mention is made of Kirby Smith's harsh policy toward deserters.

22. E. Cunningham to McCulloch, Nov. 19, 1863, *Official Records* 22(2):1073; O. M. Roberts, *Texas*, p. 105; E. Cunningham to Magruder, Nov. 20, 1863, *Official Records* 26(2):429-30; Albert Castel, *William Clarke Quantrill: His Life and Times*, pp. 159-60. One unsubstantiated contemporary source notes that during this time Quantrill's force "often stopped raids of Jay hawkers and Indians" ("Notes On Quantrill," Gunter Family Collection, University of North Texas Archives, Denton, Texas).

23. E. S. C. Robertson to Mary Robertson, Nov. 4, 1863, Robertson Colony Collection, UTA; McCulloch to Bourland, Oct. 29, 1863, Bourland Papers, Library of Congress.

24. McCulloch to Bourland, Oct. 29, 1863, Bourland Papers, Library of Congress.

25. Bourland to J. B. Anderson, [?], 1863, ibid.

26. Stephen D. Yancey to McCulloch, Nov. 6, 1863, *Official Records* 26(2):393–94.

27. Circular, Nov. 5, 1863, Orders and Circulars, Department of Texas, 1861–1864, Confederate Record Group 109, National Archives.

28. McCulloch to E. P. Turner, Nov. 9, 1863, *Official Records* 26(2):401; *Clarksville Northern Standard*, Nov. 7, 1863.

29. Historians of the period have been able to discover little about this unit, which served against Indians and gangs of deserters from November, 1863, to March, 1864. The most detailed published treatment of the subject, Kerby, *Kirby Smith's Confederacy*, p. 218, consists of three sentences, while McCaslin, "Tainted Breeze," pp. 323–26, concentrates on Baylor's brief sojourn with the battalion. It was not officially called the Brush Battalion, but for lack of a better descriptive term contemporaries often referred to it as such.

30. J. R. Diamond, Personal Service Record, Confederate Record Group 109, National Archives; *Houston Telegraph*, Nov. 25, 1863, Jan. 15, 1864; Kerby, *Kirby Smith's Confederacy*, p. 218; E. P. Turner to McCulloch, Nov. 21, 1863, and E. P. Turner to McCulloch, Nov. 18, 1863, *Official Records* 26(2):427, 433. The date that Diamond assumed command is unknown, but he served until relieved of command in March, 1864, when the force was broken up; two months later he became lieutenant colonel of Bourland's Border Regiment.

31. McCulloch to E. P. Turner, Nov. 9, 1863, *Official Records* 26(2):401; McCulloch to Bourland, Nov. 22, 1863, Bourland Papers, Library of Congress. During the day McCulloch reported that two additional companies showed up, giving him a total of over five companies with approximately five hundred men available for frontier service.

32. B. G. Duval to R. M. Gano, Nov. 29, 1863, *Official Records* 26(2):1080–81; McCulloch to Bourland, Nov. 22, 1863, Bourland Papers, Library of Congress; Bourland to Barry, Dec. 7, 1863, Barry Papers, BTHC.

33. Special Orders Number [?], Dec. 11, 1863, Bourland Papers, Library of Congress. These orders do not mention Archer County by name. I have concluded, however, that Bourland was referring to the North Fork of the Little Wichita, rather than to the East Fork, in eastern Clay County. Only troops placed on the North Fork would be consistent with the advanced screen of the four other companies of the battalion and would likewise cover the northern flank of the Frontier Regiment.

34. A. Cameron Petree to Ellen Galbraith, Mar. 30, 1864, Galbraith Family Papers; Genreal Orders Number [?], Dec. 11, 1863, Bourland Papers, Library of Congress.

35. Rowland to Barry, Dec. 5, 1863, and Bourland to Barry, Dec. 7, 1863, Barry Papers, BTHC.

36. John Henry Brown, *Indian Wars and Pioneers of Texas*, p. 115; McConnell, *The West Texas Frontier* 2:99–100; Smith, *The First 100 Years in Cooke County*, p. 40; Collins, *Cooke County, Texas: Where the South and the West Meet*, p. 19; Lillian Gunter Papers, typed mss, p. 400, Morton Museum, Gainesville, Texas.

37. Brown, *Indian Wars and Pioneers*, p. 116. Earlier that month, General Mc-
Culloch had requested that Patton's men be stationed at Gainesville to watch
for rumored raids by Jayhawkers (McCulloch to Bourland, Dec. 1, 1863, Bourland
Papers, Library of Congress).

38. Brown, *Indian Wars and Pioneers*, pp. 116–17; Collins, *Cooke County, Texas*,
p. 19; Smith, *Cooke County*, pp. 40–41.

39. Brown, *Indian Wars and Pioneers*, pp. 117–18.

40. Bourland to McCulloch, Dec. 22, 1863, Bourland Papers, Library of Congress; Lillian Gunter Papers, typed mss, p. 400, Morton Museum, Gainesville, Texas;
Bourland to McCulloch, Dec. 24, 1863, *Official Records* 26(2):531–32. Bourland
reported that the Comanches were tracked far to the west but had too great a
lead for the Texans to overcome. He concluded that their destination was the
headwaters of the Pease River, or the Prairie Dog Town Fork of the Red River
(Bourland to Barry, Jan. 1, 1864, Barry Papers, BTHC).

41. Bourland to John R. Diamond, Dec. 14, 1863, Bourland Papers, Library
of Congress; Brown, *Indian Wars and Pioneers*, p. 118. Barry insistently pointed out
that the raid occurred in "Colonel Bourland's section." Even Colonel McCord
could not resist a retort: "I wonder what the immortal Colonel Bourland thinks
now of keeping the Indians out?" (Greer, *Buck Barry*, p. 171).

42. Bourland to Barry, Dec. 7, 1863, Barry Papers, BTHC; Bourland to John R.
Diamond, Dec. 13, 1863, Bourland Papers, Library of Congress; Greer, *Buck Barry*,
pp. 168–69.

43. Maxey to McCulloch, Jan. 19, 1864, Maxey Papers, TSL-A. This letter
confirms that Bourland was by now under McCulloch's command, but no order
exists to document the exact date of transfer.

44. McCulloch to Bourland, Jan. 7, 1864, Bourland Papers, Library of Congress.

45. McCulloch to Bourland, Jan. 9, 1863, ibid.

CHAPTER 6. CREATION OF THE FRONTIER ORGANIZATION

1. Day, *Senate Journal of the Tenth Legislature, Regular Session*, pp. 95–96.

2. Stephen D. Yancey to McCulloch, Nov. 6, 1863, Magruder to Murrah,
Nov. 23, 1863, and Kirby Smith to Murrah, Jan. 18, 1864, all in *Official Records*
26(2):393–94, 441, 34(2):886.

3. Gammel, *Laws of Texas* 5:677, 689.

4. Ibid. 5:670, 677–78, 688.

5. McCord to Barry, Dec. 16, 1863, Barry Papers, BTHC.

6. Rowland to McCord, Jan. 9, 1864, Adjutant General's Records, TSL-A;
John Hunter to Kirby Smith, Jan. 28, 1864, Edmund Kirby Smith Papers, Ramsdell Microfilm Collection, BTHC.

7. McCord to D. B. Culberson, Jan. 13, 1864, Adjutant General's Records,
TSL-A; A. H. Lee to Barry, Jan. 14, 1864, Barry Papers, BTHC. The best secondary account of the Frontier Regiment on the Central Texas frontier, from its
transfer to the end of the war, is Havins, *Camp Colorado*, pp. 127–69, based almost
exclusively on the Barry Papers, and to a lesser extent, the Adjutant General's
Records.

8. Thomasson, "James E. McCord and the Texas Frontier Regiment," pp. 67–68; McCord to D. B. Culberson, Mar. 3, 1864, Adjutant General's Records, TSL-A.

9. Petition by Company E, Frontier Regiment, Jan. 21, 1864, Governor Pendleton Murrah Records, TSL-A.

10. Greer, *Buck Barry*, p. 172; A. H. Lee to Barry, Jan. 14, 1864, Barry Papers, BTHC; Havins, *Camp Colorado*, pp. 130–33.

11. Of the twenty counties in this Frontier District, only half had any population listed in the 1860 census; one, Shackelford, listed only four residents; Clay County's entire population of 109 abandoned the county during the war.

12. These nineteen counties included eight counties with no population listed for 1860.

13. Only five of these twenty counties were unpopulated in 1860. The breakdown of counties listed for the three Frontier Districts above is found in *The Texas Almanac, 1865,* pp. 42–43. In the Third Frontier District, the Dawson County listed, created in 1858, is now defunct. It included no part of present Dawson County, created in 1876. This same district also included present Real County, created in 1913 from parts of Bandera, Edwards, and Kerr counties.

14. James M. Day, ed., *Senate and House Journal of the Tenth Legislature, First Called Session, May 9, 1864–May 28, 1864,* p. 17.

15. Any generalizations made here about the Frontier Organization are based on a careful reading of several hundred pages of documents related directly to the Frontier Organization, found primarily in the Adjutant General's Records, Quayle Papers, and Bourland Papers.

16. Bell Irvin Wiley, *The Life of Johnny Reb: The Common Soldier of the Confederacy,* p. 331; Bell Irvin Wiley, *The Life of Billy Yank: The Common Soldier of the Union,* p. 303.

17. "Col. William Quayle," *Confederate Veteran* 10 (Oct., 1902): 372–73; Julia Kathryn Garrett, *Fort Worth: A Frontier Triumph,* pp. 197, 202–203, 361.

18. James M. Day, ed., *Senate Journal of the Ninth Legislature, First Called Session, February 2, 1863–March 7, 1863,* pp. 1, 160; James M. Day, ed., *House Journal of the Tenth Legislature, Regular Session, November 3, 1863–December 16, 1863,* pp. 73, 131–32.

19. Quayle to Culberson, Feb. 4, 1864, William Quayle Papers, Rare Book Room, University of Alabama Library, Tuscaloosa (all references to this collection will be cited hereafter as Quayle Papers, UAL). Only a short distance north of Decatur ran the old Butterfield Overland Express road that linked Gainesville to Fort Belknap, via Jacksboro.

20. Quayle to Culberson, Feb. 10, 1864, Adjutant General's Records, TSL-A.

21. Quayle to McCulloch, Feb. 20, 1864, and Bourland to Quayle, Mar. 9, 1864, Quayle Papers, UAL.

22. Elizabeth Lenoir Jennett, ed., *Biographical Directory of the Texan Conventions and Congresses,* pp. 80–81; George B. Erath, Personal Service Record, Confederate Record Group 109, National Archives.

23. "Memoirs of George B. Erath," typescript, p. 106, BTHC (cited hereafter as "Erath Memoirs"); List of Enrolling Officers, Jan., 1864, Erath to Culberson,

Jan. 18, 1864, Erath to Culberson, Feb. 2, 1864, Erath to Culberson, Feb. 8, 1864, Erath to Culberson, Feb. 15, 1864, and Erath to Culberson, Feb. 22, 1864, all in Adjutant General's Records, TSL-A.

24. Confederate Index File, James M. Hunter, TSL-A; A. J. Sowell, *Early Settlers and Indian Fighters of Southwest Texas*, pp. 561–66; "Major James M. Hunter," *Frontier Times* 6 (Oct., 1928): 1–2.

25. Gammel, *Laws of Texas* 5:698–99; Albert Burton Moore, *Conscription and Conflict in the Confederacy*, p. 247.

26. Magruder to Murrah, Dec. 18, 1863, Governor Pendleton Murrah Records, TSL-A.

27. Murrah to Magruder, Jan. 12, 1864, *Official Records* 53:926–30.

28. Kirby Smith to Murrah, Jan. 18, 1864, ibid. 34(2):886.

29. Magruder to W. R. Boggs, Chief of Staff, Feb. 16, 1864, ibid. 34(2):973–75.

30. Yearns, *The Confederate Congress*, p. 88; E. Merton Coulter, *The Confederate States of America, 1861–1865*, p. 322.

31. The correspondence between Murrah and Magruder concerning this matter in February and March, 1864, is found in *Official Records* 34(2):1087–95.

32. Magruder to E. B. Nichols, Apr. 2, 1864, and Magruder to Murrah, Apr. 5, 1864, both in ibid. 34(3):726–27, 735. There was also a small federal force in South Texas, the remnants of Banks's invasion at Brazos Santiago the previous November.

33. Murrah to Magruder, Apr. 7, 1864, ibid. 34(3):747. The best secondary account of the militia controversy is found in Kerby, *Kirby Smith's Confederacy*, pp. 276–79. Allan Coleman Ashcraft, "Texas, 1860–1866: The Lone Star State in the Civil War," Ph.D. diss., Columbia University, pp. 200–202, concludes that it was well that the Confederate Army took control of raising the troops, because the state conscription law and militia organization had been a failure.

34. Magruder to Col. H. B. Andrews, Aug. 16, 1864, Texas State Military Board Records; TSL-A; Gammel, *Laws of Texas* 5:773–75; Kerby, *Kirby Smith's Confederacy*, p. 279.

35. Erath to Culberson, Jan. 18, 1864, and Erath to Culberson, Feb. 22, 1864, both in Adjutant General's Records, TSL-A; Quayle to Culberson, Feb. 4, 1864, and Quayle to Culberson, Feb. 25, 1864, both in Quayle Papers, UAL.

36. Special Orders Number 40, Mar. 12, 1864, *Official Records*, ser. I, vol. 48, pt. 1, 1376; McCulloch to Quayle, Mar. 16, 1864, Quayle Papers, UAL.

37. Quayle to John W. Hale, Enrolling Officer, Wise County, Apr. 24, 1864, Quayle Papers, UAL.

38. Quayle to Greer, Apr. 24, 1864, Quayle Papers, UAL; W. H. Holland, Enrolling Officer, Burnet County, to James M. Hunter, May 13, 1864, Adjutant General's Records, TSL-A.

39. Jefferson Davis to Govr. P. Murray [sic], Apr. 26, 1864, in Dunbar Rowland, ed., *Jefferson Davis, Constitutionalist: His Letters, Papers and Speeches* 6:235–36; Day, *Senate and House Journal of the Tenth Legislature, First Called Session, May 9, 1864–May 28, 1864*, p. 19; Gammel, *Laws of Texas* 5:773.

40. Quayle to Murrah, Aug. 22, 1864, Quayle Papers, UAL.

41. Murrah to Quayle, Sept. 1, 1864, ibid.

42. West to Murrah, Oct. 19, 1864, *Official Records* 48(1):1376–77.

NOTES TO PAGES 104–110
43. James M. Day, ed., *Senate and House Journal of the Tenth Legislature, Second Called Session, October 15, 1864–November 15, 1864*, pp. 14, 17, 124–25; Murrah to Kirby Smith, Nov. 23, 1864, Governor Pendleton Murrah Records, TSL-A.

44. Murrah to Smith, Nov. 29, 1864, Governor Pendleton Murrah Records, TSL-A.

45. Throckmorton to Murrah, Dec. 9, 1864, ibid.

46. Throckmorton to Murrah, Jan. 13, 1865, ibid.

47. Kirby Smith to Jefferson Davis, Feb. 10, 1865, *Official Records* 48(1):1373–74. Historians have virtually ignored the debate over the fate of the Frontier Organization in the fall and winter of 1864–65, or they have included only brief passages taken from the *Official Records* or from the senate and house journals of the Tenth Legislature, Second Called Session. In a typical example, James Farber, *Texas, C.S.A.*, pp. 180–84, deals with the militia debate in the spring of 1864, but makes only one observation on the issue of the Frontier Organization and conscription: "[Murrah] short sightedly failed to see that by nullifying the Confederate draft laws by exempting all border residents from service in the Confederate Army, he was hamstringing victory."

CHAPTER 7. DISAFFECTION AND TURMOIL ON THE NORTHWEST FRONTIER

1. W. A. Pitts to E. S. C. Robertson, Jan. 8, 1864, Robertson Colony Collection, UTA. Pitts also stated that "our scouts are bringing them [deserters] in every day, and occasionally shooting one."

2. Maxey to McCulloch, Jan. 2, 1864, Samuel Bell Maxey Papers, TSL-A; Maxey to McCulloch, Jan. 20, 1864, Samuel Bell Maxey Papers, Thomas Gilcrease Museum Library, Tulsa, Okla.

3. Magruder to McCulloch, Jan. 29, 1864, and McCulloch to Kirby Smith, Feb. 5, 1864, both in *Official Records* 34(2):925–26, 945.

4. McCulloch to Bourland, Feb. 3, 1864, Bourland Papers, Library of Congress; Maxey to McCulloch, Feb. 4, 1864, and Maxey to Col. Charles DeMorse, Feb. 13, 1864, both in Maxey Papers, TSL-A; McCulloch to E. P. Turner, Feb. 14, 1864, *Official Records* 34(2):967.

5. McCulloch to E. P. Turner, Jan. 6, 1864, *Official Records* 53:923–25; McCulloch to Magruder, Dec. 18, 1863, Henry E. McCulloch, Personal Service Record, Confederate Record Group 109, National Archives; Kirby Smith to McCulloch, Jan. 4, 1864, McCulloch Papers, BTHC.

6. McCulloch to E. P. Turner, Jan. 6, 1864, *Official Records* 53:924; McCulloch to Bourland, Jan. 7, 1863, Bourland Papers, Library of Congress.

7. McCulloch to Magruder, Jan. 23, 1864, *Official Records* 34(2):909. Kerby, *Kirby Smith's Confederacy*, p. 218, concludes that the Brush Battalion, which he calls a "regiment of bushmen," relieved steadier troops for active duty in the field. This may have been the intent, but the converse came to be true in 1864. Additional troops were needed just to control the Brush Battalion.

8. McCulloch to Magruder, Jan. 23, 1864, and Bourland to McCulloch, Jan. 21, 1864, and McCulloch to Magruder, Feb. 3, 1864, all in *Official Records* 34(2):909–10, 942.

9. D. J. [Dr. Jefferson Mears] to McCulloch, n.d., Maxey Papers, Gilcrease

Museum, Tulsa; Maxey to McCulloch, Mar. 18, 1864, and Maxey to McCulloch, Mar. 21, 1864, both in Maxey Papers, TSL-A.

10. McCulloch to Murrah, Mar. 20, 1864, Governor Pendleton Murrah Records, TSL-A.

11. Lt. E. Cunningham to McCulloch, Mar. 25, 1864, Letters Sent, Trans-Mississippi Department, Confederate Record Group 109, National Archives; Personal Service Record, John R. Diamond, Confederate Record Group 109, National Archives.

12. McCulloch to Magruder, Feb. 3, 1864, *Official Records* 34(2):942.

13. Maxey to Gen. D. H. Cooper, Jan. 28, 1864, Maxey Papers, TSL-A; McCulloch to Kirby Smith, Feb. 5, 1864, and McCulloch to Bee, Feb. 9, 1864, both in *Official Records* 34(2):945, 957-58.

14. Throckmorton to Murrah, Mar. 28, 1864, Governor Pendleton Murrah Records, TSL-A; A. Cameron Petree to Ellen Galbraith, Mar. 30, 1864, Galbraith Family Papers, in possession of Charles Eversole, Jr., Grapevine, Texas. The headquarters scene above differs in detail from the two best secondary accounts: Castel, *William Clarke Quantrill: His Life and Times*, pp. 165-66, and Lary C. Rampp, "William C. Quantrill's Civil War Activities in Texas, 1861-1863," *Texas Military History* 8 no. 4 (1970): 225-31. Castel and Rampp did not have access to the two eyewitness accounts cited above.

15. McCulloch to E. P. Turner, Apr. 6, 1864, *Official Records* 34(3):742.

16. Bourland to McCulloch, Apr. 13, 1864, Quayle Papers, UAL. The copy sent to General Smith in Shreveport may be found in Bourland to McCulloch, Apr. 13, 1864, Letters and Telegrams Received, Trans-Mississippi Department, Confederate Record Group 109, National Archives, photocopy in possession of the author. It appears in a slightly altered version with minor rewording in Bourland to McCulloch, Apr. 13, 1864, *Official Records* 34(3):772-74.

17. McCulloch to Quayle, Apr. 14, 1864, Quayle Papers, UAL; McCulloch to Bourland, Apr. 14, 1864, Bourland Papers, Library of Congress.

18. Bourland to Quayle, Apr. 14, 1864, Quayle Papers, UAL; J. W. Ferris to Governor Murrah, Aug. 18, 1864, Governor Pendleton Murrah Records, TSL-A.

19. Bourland to McCulloch, Apr. 13, 1864, Special Orders Number 99, Apr. 15, 1864, McCulloch to Bourland, Apr. 15, 1864, McCulloch to Quayle, Apr. 15, and McCulloch to Quayle, Apr. 16, 1864, all in Quayle Papers, UAL; McCulloch to E. P. Turner, Apr. 16, 1864, and McCulloch to E. P. Turner, Apr. 16, 1864, *Official Records* 34(3):771-72.

20. Bourland to Quayle, Apr. 16, 1864, Quayle Papers, UAL.

21. Quayle to Culberson, Apr. 27, 1864, ibid.; Statements of J. Charles Adair and T. L. Stanfield to D. Howell, Chief Justice of Wise County, Dec. 19, 1864, Governor Pendleton Murrah Records, TSL-A.

22. J. W. Ferris to Murrah, Aug. 18, 1864, Governor Pendleton Murrah Records, TSL-A; Bourland to Quayle, Apr. 22, 1864, Quayle Papers, UAL; Smythe, *Historical Sketch of Parker County and Weatherford, Texas*, pp. 177-78. Smythe gives a detailed account of the aftermath of the arrests, including the fate of those arrested, noting that the affair took place sometime in April. He provides no information,

however, on the origins of the conspiracy or the preparations made by the military to break it up.

23. Quayle to Culberson, Apr. 27, 1864, Quayle Papers, UAL; J. W. Ferris to Murrah, Aug. 18, 1864, Governor Pendleton Murrah Records, TSL-A; Smythe, *Historical Sketch of Parker County and Weatherford*, pp. 179–83.

CHAPTER 8. FIRST FRONTIER DISTRICT: APRIL–SEPTEMBER, 1864

1. Thomasson, "James E. McCord and the Texas Frontier Regiment," p. 73; McCord to Barry, June 3, 1864, Barry Papers, BTHC.

2. Greer, *Buck Barry*, p. 174; McCulloch to E. P. Turner, Apr. 26, 1864, Magruder to W. R. Boggs, May 25, 1864, Special Orders Number 178, June 26, 1864, all in *Official Records* 34(3):795, 34(4):630, 695; McCord to Barry, June 3, 1864, Barry Papers, BTHC.

3. Barry to McCord, Apr. 1, 1864, Personal Service Record, James E. McCord, Confederate Record Group 109, National Archives; McCulloch to Bourland, May 14, 1864, Bourland Papers, Library of Congress.

4. *Gainesville Daily Register*, Aug. 30, 1948, Cooke County Centennial Edition, Cooke County College Library, Gainesville, Texas; Bourland to Quayle, Apr. 26, 1864, Quayle Papers, UAL. It is not clear whether the four companies returned from the coast, or whether Bourland created new ones to take their places. The latter action probably took place, based on correspondence in which Bourland indicated that he already had volunteers to form two companies; General McCulloch authorized him to recruit two more companies of about fifty men each from the First Frontier District, with Major Quayle's permission.

5. Regimental Return, Bourland's Texas Cavalry, "Border Regiment," Aug., 1864, Confederate Record Group 109, National Archives; Morning Report, Capt. W. C. McKaney, Company K, Border Regiment, Aug., 1864, Bourland Papers, Library of Congress; Personal Service Record, John R. Diamond, Confederate Record Group 109, National Archives; Bourland to Quayle, Aug. 17, 1864, Quayle Papers, UAL.

6. Special Orders Number 39, Feb. 21, 1865, Bourland Papers, Library of Congress. A proposal for a regular trice weekly courier between Decatur and Gainesville is found in Throckmorton to Quayle, Apr. 4, 1864, Quayle Papers, UAL.

7. Bourland to Quayle, Apr. 10, 1864, and Bourland to Quayle, July 21, 1864, Quayle Papers, UAL.

8. Bourland to Quayle, July 11, 1864, Quayle Papers, UAL; "Danvin Reminiscences," typescript, p. 131, Lillian Gunter Papers, Morton Museum, Gainesville, Texas.

9. General Orders Number 1, First Frontier District, Mar. 9, 1864, Adjutant General's Records, TSL-A.

10. McCord to Barry, Nov. 10, 1864, Barry Papers, BTHC; Greer, *Buck Barry*, pp. 174–75, 182.

11. McCulloch to Leroy P. Walker, Mar. 30, 1861, *Official Records* 1:618; Haley, *Charles Goodnight*, p. 64; Wilbur S. Nye, *Carbine and Lance: The Story of Old Fort Sill*, pp. 29–31; Webb et al., *Handbook of Texas* 2:789.

12. Baylor to Barry, Nov. 20, 1863, Barry Papers, BTHC; Haley, *Charles Goodnight*, p. 95; Gammel, *Laws of Texas*, 4:738–739; Day, *House Journal of the Tenth Legislature, Regular Session, November 3, 1863–December 16, 1863*, pp. 268–69.

13. Barry to Murrah, May 13, 1864, Governor Pendleton Murrah Records, TSL-A; Erath to Culberson, Feb. 8, 1864, Adjutant General's Records, TSL-A; Quayle to McCulloch, Feb. 20, 1864, Quayle Papers, UAL.

14. Muster roll, District Return of the 1st Frontier District for the Month of August 1864, Adjutant General's Records, TSL-A.

15. Culberson to Quayle, Sept. 26, 1864, Quayle Papers, UAL; Quayle to Murrah, Sept. 8, 1864, Governor Pendleton Murrah Records, TSL-A.

16. Quayle to Culberson, Oct. 7, 1864, and Throckmorton to Quayle, Nov. 28, 1864, both in Quayle Papers, UAL.

17. Throckmorton to Col. John Burke, Jan. 29, 1865, Adjutant General's Records, TSL-A; S. G. Thompson to Quayle, June 1, 1864, Barry Papers, BTHC.

18. Quayle to Culberson, Mar. 31, 1864, Adjutant General's Records, TSL-A; McCulloch to E. P. Turner, Mar. 15, 1864, *Official Records* 34(2):1045.

19. McCulloch to Murrah, Mar. 20, 1864, Governor Pendleton Murrah Records, TSL-A; McCulloch to Quayle, Mar. 28, 1864, Quayle Papers, UAL; Greer, *Buck Barry*, p. 173.

20. Bourland to McCulloch, Apr. 25, 1864, Abstract from Return of C. S. Troops, Northern Sub-District of Texas, for the Month of March, 1864, and McCulloch to E. P. Turner, Apr. 26, 1864, all in *Official Records* 34(2):1107, 34(3):792, 795; Bourland to Quayle, Apr. 18, 1864, and Bourland to Quayle, Apr. 26, 1864, both in Quayle Papers, UAL.

21. Bourland to Quayle, Apr. 29, 1864, and Bourland to George Isbell, May 1, 1864, both in Quayle Papers, UAL; "Danvin Reminiscences," p. 132, typescript, Lillian Gunter Papers, Morton Museum, Gainesville, Texas. This large hill, with an elevation of 1,189 feet, located about four miles north of the town of Bowie, is today called Queen's Peak. It is not to be confused with the more famous Victoria Peak of Culberson County. As all the contemporary correspondence designated it as Victoria Peak, I will refer to it as such.

22. Bourland to Quayle, May 7, 1864, Quayle Papers, UAL.

23. Capt. J. P. Rowland to Bourland, May 9, 1864, Bourland to Capt. J. Ward, May 11, 1864, and George Isbell to Quayle, May 11, 1864, all in Quayle Papers, UAL; Regimental Return, Bourland's Regiment Texas Cavalry, "Border Regiment," July, 1864, Confederate Record Group 109, National Archives; Muster Roll, Capt. H. J. Thompson's Company, 1st Frontier District, February 1–June 1, 1864, Adjutant General's Records, TSL-A; Rowland to Barry, May 28, 1864, Barry Papers, BTHC.

24. Bourland to McCulloch, June 2, 1864, and Quayle to Culberson, June 23, 1864, both in Quayle Papers, UAL.

25. Muster Roll of Lt. Thomas Smith's Company, First Frontier District, February 1–June 1, 1864, Adjutant General's Records, TSL-A.

26. Rowland to Barry, May 28, 1864, Barry Papers, BTHC.

27. McCulloch to Bourland, July 14, 1864, Quayle Papers, UAL.

28. Bourland to Quayle, July 19, 1864, ibid.

29. "Charges and Specifications prepared against James Bourland, Col. Comdg. Border Reg.," Quayle Papers, UAL.

30. Bourland to Quayle, Sept. 12, 1864, ibid.

31. McCulloch to Bourland, Sept. 12, 1864, ibid.

32. McCulloch to Bourland, Oct. 8, 1864, ibid.

33. Kirby Smith to Maj. C. S. West, Oct. 7, 1864, *Official Records* 41(3):987; C. B. Breedlove to Murrah, Nov. 19, 1864, H. R. Latimer to Murrah, Nov. 24, 1864, and Murrah to Kirby Smith, Nov. 27, 1864, all in Governor Pendleton Murrah Records, TSL-A.

34. Army of the Trans-Mississippi, Sept. 30, 1864, and Abstract from Return of the Third Cavalry Division, for the Month of December, 1864, both in *Official Records* 41(3):969, 41(4):1138.

35. General Orders Number 33, Dec. 29, 1864, *Official Records* 48(1):1310–11.

CHAPTER 9. FIRST FRONTIER DISTRICT: OCTOBER, 1864–MAY, 1865

1. Culberson to Quayle, Sept. 26, 1864, and Quayle to Culberson, Oct. 7, 1864, Quayle Papers, UAL.

2. Day, *Senate Journal of the Tenth Legislature, Regular Session, November 3, 1863–December 16, 1863,* pp. 56, 63, 140.

3. Gammel, *Laws of Texas* 5:98–99; Adjutant and Inspector General's Office, Mar. 1, 1864, *Official Records* 34(2):1011; Quayle to Murrah, Mar. 7, 1863, Throckmorton to Murrah, Mar. 20, 1863, and Throckmorton to Murrah, Mar. 28, 1864, both in Governor Pendleton Murrah Records, TSL-A; Throckmorton to Quayle, Apr. 4, 1864, Quayle Papers, UAL.

4. Day, *Senate and House Journal of the Tenth Legislature, First Called Session, May 9, 1864 – May 28, 1864,* p. 17; Elliott, *Leathercoat,* pp. 82–83.

5. Gammel, *Laws of Texas* 5:772.

6. Quayle to Culberson, Oct. 7, 1864, Quayle Papers, UAL.

7. *Dallas Herald,* Oct. 15, 1864; Throckmorton to Murrah, Dec. 9, 1864, Governor Pendleton Murrah Records, TSL-A.

8. Utley, *Frontiersmen in Blue,* pp. 285–88; Barbara A. Neal Ledbetter, *Fort Belknap, Frontier Saga,* pp. 109–10.

9. McConnell, *The West Frontier* 2:119; Kenneth Neighbours, "Elm Creek Raid in Young County, 1864," *West Texas Historical Association Year Book* 40 (Oct., 1964): 89; T. R. Fehrenbach, *Lone Star: A History of Texas and Texans,* p. 524; Mayhall, *The Kiowas,* pp. 197–98. Estimates of the size of the attacking force range from three hundred up to one thousand warriors, and some accounts mention the presence of a few Apaches as well. The best view was obtained from the roof of Fort Murrah by soldiers who used a telescope to count the opposition. Long after the battle, Indians who participated claimed that anywhere from six hundred to one thousand were in the invading party.

10. Mildred P. Mayhall, *Indian Wars of Texas,* p. 125; Carrie J. Crouch, *A History of Young County, Texas,* p. 27; Earl Burk Braly, "Fort Belknap of the Texas Frontier," *West Texas Historical Association Year Book* 30 (Oct., 1954): 107–109; "Notes of Francis M. Peveler," typescript, p. 1, BTHC.

11. Ledbetter, *Fort Belknap, Frontier Saga,* pp. 117–18; Fehrenbach, *Comanches,*

p. 454; McConnell, *The West Texas Frontier* 2:119–20; Henry Williams, "The Indian Raid in Young County, Texas," typescript, BTHC. Ledbetter's account is based on the eyewitness testimony of Elizabeth Fitzpatrick, who survived captivity and returned to her home.

12. Report of Lt. N. Carson, Border Regiment Texas Cavalry, Oct. 16, 1864, *Official Records* 41(1):885–86. It is Carson's report that gives "Murray" for the spelling of Fort Murrah, an error repeated in a number of modern accounts of the raid.

13. "Notes of Francis M. Peveler," pp. 5–7; Neighbours, "Elm Creek Raid in Young County, 1864," pp. 85–86; McConnell, *The West Texas Frontier* 2:123–24.

14. "Notes of Francis M. Peveler," p. 7; Quayle to Culberson, Oct. 7, 1864, and Bourland to Quayle, Oct. 15, 1864, both in Quayle Papers, UAL; Reports of Col. James Bourland, Border Regiment Texas Cavalry, Oct. 20, 1864, *Official Records* 41(1):884–85.

15. "Notes of Francis M. Peveler," pp. 7–8; Mayhall, *Indian Wars of Texas*, pp. 142–43; Fehrenbach, *Comanches*, p. 456.

16. McConnell, *The West Texas Frontier*, 2:124–25; Neighbours, "Elm Creek Raid in Young County, 1864," p. 89; Ledbetter, *Fort Belknap, Frontier Saga*, pp. 113–21; Report of Lt. N. Carson, Border Regiment Texas Cavalry; *Official Records* 41(1): 886. Accounts of the Texas dead range from ten to eighteen, but eleven is accepted by most historians. Indians themselves admitted years later to twenty dead in the action on the thirteenth, an admission I believe may have been what the Indians thought their white listeners wanted to hear.

17. Marilynne Howsley, "Forting Up on the Texas Frontier during the Civil War," *West Texas Historical Association Year Book* 17 (Oct., 1941): 71–76; Greer, *Buck Barry*, p. 180; J. R. Webb, ed., "Chapters from the Frontier Life of Phin W. Reynolds," *West Texas Historical Association Year Book* 21 (Oct., 1945): 115–17; General Orders Number 1, First Frontier District, Dec. 13, 1864, Governor Pendleton Murrah Records, TSL-A.

18. Quayle to Culberson, July 21, 1864, Quayle to Culberson, Aug. 19, 1864, and Bourland to Quayle, Oct. 15, 1864, all in Quayle Papers, UAL; Greer, *Buck Barry*, p. 180; Regimental Return, Bourland's Regiment Texas Cavalry, "Border Regiment," Nov., 1864, Confederate Record Group 109, National Archives.

19. Throckmorton to Murrah, Dec. 9, 1864, Governor Pendleton Murrah Records, TSL-A; Throckmorton to Quayle, Dec. 14, 1864, Quayle Papers, UAL; General Orders Number 1, First Frontier District, Dec. 13, 1864, Governor Pendleton Murrah Records, TSL-A; Elliott, *Leathercoat*, p. 88.

20. Throckmorton to Murrah, Dec. 20, 1864, Governor Pendleton Murrah Records, TSL-A.

21. McCulloch to Quayle, Mar. 22, 1865, Quayle Papers, UAL; Throckmorton to Bourland, Mar. 31, 1865, Bourland Papers, Library of Congress.

22. Throckmorton to Murrah, Dec. 20, 1864, and Throckmorton to Murrah, Dec. 9, 1864, both in Governor Pendleton Murrah Records, TSL-A.

23. *The Texas Almanac, 1861–1865*, p. 43; Abstract from Return of the Northern Sub-District of Texas for the Month of December, 1864, *Official Records* 41(4): 1140; Regimental Return, Bourland's Regiment Texas Cavalry, "Border Regiment,"

November, 1864, Confederate Record Group 109, National Archives. It might be noted here that the returns of December, 1864, list more than six hundred men marked as "absent" from Bourland's and Barry's commands.

24. Throckmorton to Murrah, Jan. 13, 1865, Governor Pendleton Murrah Records, TSL-A. Throckmorton's biographer devotes a brief paragraph to the plans for the campaign and mentions the meeting of the officers at Decatur, but he fails to cite the appropriate source (Elliott, *Leathercoat*, pp. 90–91).

25. Thomas F. Horton, *History of Jack County*, pp. 73–75; Throckmorton to Col. John Burke, Feb. 22, 1865, Adjutant General's Records, TSL-A; Roff to Bourland, Feb. 7, 1865, Bourland Papers, Library of Congress.

26. H. A. Whaley to Capt. S. J. McKnight, Feb. 12, 1865, Bourland Papers, Library of Congress.

27. Throckmorton to Burke, Feb. 22, 1865, Adjutant General's Records, TSL-A.

28. Throckmorton to Murrah, Jan. 13, 1865, Governor Pendleton Murrah Records, TSL-A; Throckmorton to Burke, Jan. 29, 1865, Adjutant General's Records, TSL-A.

29. Throckmorton to Murrah, Jan. 13, 1865, Governor Pendleton Murrah Records, TSL-A; Throckmorton to Burke, Jan. 29, 1865, Adjutant General's Records, TSL-A. Throckmorton's biographer, Claude Elliott, provides the only secondary account to detail the changes proposed by Throckmorton. Elliott's excellent biography, however, is woefully lacking in describing the policy and process of the Frontier Organization that Throckmorton commanded.

30. John R. Diamond to Capt. L. H. Randolph, Jan. 25, 1865, and Throckmorton to Bourland, Mar. 31, 1865, Bourland Papers, Library of Congress; Greer, *Buck Barry*, pp. 197–98; Regimental Returns, Bourland's Regiment Texas Cavalry, "Border Regiment," Confederate Record Group 109, National Archives.

31. Barry to Bourland, Jan. 31, 1865, and Capt. William C. Twitty to Maj. William G. King, Chief Quarter-Master, Northern Sub-District, Feb. 2, 1865, Bourland Papers, Library of Congress; John P. Hill to W. C. Walsh, Apr. 5, 1865, Adjutant General's Records, TSL-A; Cates, *Pioneer History of Wise County*, p. 139.

32. Capt. F. M. Totty to Col. James Bourland, Apr. 20, 1865, Adjutant General's Records, TSL-A; Cates, *Pioneer History of Wise County*, pp. 140–41; Hill to Walsh, Apr. 5, 1865, Adjutant General's Records, TSL-A. The accounts of Cates and Hill seem more reliable than the report of Captain Totty. Totty disagrees with Cates and Hill about the number of volunteers who made the attack, stating that there were thirty Confederates and about twenty militia volunteers. In his report, Totty plays the dominant role of the day and concludes: "I like Col. Diamond as a man but regard him as entirely incompetent & unfit to command in any respect."

33. Cates, *Pioneer History of Wise County*, p. 142; McCulloch to Bourland, Apr. 5, 1865, Bourland Papers, Library of Congress. William Charles Taylor, *A History of Clay County* (Austin, 1972), p. 51, states that the deserters were taken to Buffalo Springs to await trial, but this went against standard procedure used in the disposition of deserters. Normally, all deserters went first to Bonham, but in this instance General McCulloch ordered them delivered under guard directly to Houston.

34. Throckmorton to Murrah, Dec. 20, 1864, Governor Pendleton Murrah Records, TSL-A.

35. McCulloch to Bourland, Apr. 10, 1865, Adjutant General's Records, TSL-A.

36. Cates, *Pioneer History of Wise County*, p. 142. McCaslin, "Tainted Breeze," p. 373, states that many of the prisoners were forwarded to Galveston where they were not set free until after the war was over.

37. Throckmorton to Bourland, Mar. 31, 1865, Bourland Papers, Library of Congress; Elliott, *Leathercoat*, p. 92; Utley, *Frontiersmen in Blue*, pp. 310–12.

38. Kirby Smith to Gov. P. Murrah, Apr. 13, 1865, Letters Sent, Trans-Mississippi Department, Confederate Record Group 109, National Archives.

39. Kirby Smith to D. H. Cooper, Apr. 8, 1865, D. H. Cooper to Col. S. S. Anderson, May 15, 1865, and D. H. Cooper to J. W. Throckmorton, May 16, 1865, all in *Official Records* 48(2):1270–71, 1306, 1307.

40. Kirby Smith to McCulloch, May 1, 1865, Letters Sent, Trans-Mississippi Department, Confederate Record Group 109, National Archives; Elliott, *Leathercoat*, pp. 94–96; *Kirby Smith's Confederacy*, pp. 426–27; Richardson, *Comanche Barrier*, p. 274; Ledbetter, *Fort Belknap, Frontier Saga*, pp. 135–36, 156.

CHAPTER 10. SECOND FRONTIER DISTRICT: 1864–65

1. Erath to Culberson, Jan. 18, 1864, Adjutant General's Records, TSL-A.

2. Monthly Report of the State Troops of the 2nd Frontier District, Apr. 1, 1864, and Erath to Culberson, Apr. 28, 1864, Adjutant General's Records, TSL-A; Erath to Burney, May 6, 1864, Quayle Papers, UAL; Gammel, *Laws of Texas* 5:771.

3. Erath to Culberson, June 30, 1864, Adjutant General's Records, TSL-A.

4. John A. Hart, et al., *Pioneer Days in the Southwest from 1850–1879*, pp. 264–65; McConnell, *The West Texas Frontier* 2:114; Erath to Colonel Hendricks, Sept. 2, 1864, Adjutant General's Records, TSL-A. Hart states that twelve soldiers were present. McConnell lists the names of fourteen men and then adds that perhaps one or two others were also present. Major Erath's brief report of the affair states that it was twelve soldiers against thirty warriors.

5. Erath to Colonel Hendricks, Sept. 2, 1864, Adjutant General's Records, TSL-A; Hart et al., *Pioneer Days in the Southwest*, pp. 265–66; Ed T. Cox, "Early Days in Eastland County," *West Texas Historical Association Year Book* 17 (Oct., 1941): 86; McConnell, *The West Texas Frontier* 2:115. All of the sources cited on the battle mention that the poor quality of caps and powder contributed to the lack of success in the fight.

6. Quayle to Culberson, Aug. 19, 1864, Quayle Papers, UAL; Quayle to Murrah, Sept. 8, 1864, Governor Pendleton Murrah Records, TSL-A; D. S. Howell, "Along the Texas Frontier during the Civil War," *West Texas Historical Association Year Book* 13 (Oct., 1937): 86.

7. The best manuscript collection for details of Indian fights in the Frontier Districts, 1864–65, is the Adjutant General's Records, Archives Division Texas State Library (Austin), particularly the dozens of files, separated by month and year, labeled "General Correspondence." This collection reinforces the conclusion that,

except for three major incidents from October, 1864, to February, 1865, the problems of deserters, conscription, disaffection, and lawlessness dominated frontier defense for the last eighteen months of the war.

8. Erath to Culberson, Jan. 18, 1864, and Erath to Culberson, Feb. 22, 1864, Adjutant General's Records, TSL-A.

9. McCord to Barry, Mar. 14, 1864, Barry Papers, BTHC; Monthly Report of the State Troops of the 2nd Frontier District, Apr. 1, 1864, Adjutant General's Records, TSL-A.

10. Capt. W. W. Reynolds to Culberson, May 5, 1864, Adjutant General's Records, TSL-A.

11. Fossett to Barry, June 1, 1864, Barry Papers, BTHC; Erath to Culberson, June 30, 1864, Adjutant General's Records, TSL-A; Proclamation by the Governor, May 26, 1864, Governor Pendleton Murrah Records, TSL-A.

12. Erath to Culberson, Apr. 28, 1864, Adjutant General's Records, TSL-A.

13. Erath to Culberson, June 30, 1864, Adjutant General's Records, TSL-A.

14. McCulloch to Quayle, Mar. 21, 1864, McCulloch to Quayle, Apr. 11, 1864, Erath to George E. Burney, May 6, 1864, and Erath to Burney, May 7, 1864, all in Quayle Papers, UAL.

15. General Orders Number 6, Headquarters District of Texas, Sept. 24, 1864, Adjutant General's Records, TSL-A.

16. J. H. Earle to Culberson, June 4, 1864, Adjutant General's Records, TSL-A; McCulloch to Quayle, Oct. 8, 1864, and McCulloch to Bourland, Oct. 8, 1864, Quayle Papers, UAL.

17. McCulloch to J. E. Slaughter, May 28, 1864, *Official Records* 34(4):635.

18. Bourland to Quayle, Aug. 26, 1864, Quayle Papers, UAL.

19. Howell, "Along the Texas Frontier during the Civil War," pp. 85–86; Bourland to Quayle, Sept. 8, 1864, Bourland to Quayle, Sept. 12, 1864, McCulloch to Bourland, Sept. 12, 1864, and Bourland to Quayle, Sept. 20, 1864, Quayle Papers, UAL. The Howell article represents the memoirs of a man in Moore's company who made the trek to Hubbard Creek and back. In Moore's version of the affair, he told Bourland that someone in the house opened fire first and wounded one of his men; this was corroborated in part by Howell's account. To an outraged Quayle it sounded like murder; his protests to Bourland and McCulloch led to the court-martial of those who fired on the house. All were acquitted.

20. Howell, "Along the Texas Frontier during the Civil War," p. 86; Regimental Returns, Bourland's Regiment Texas Cavalry, "Border Regiment," Aug., 1864, Confederate Record Group 109, National Archives.

21. Howell, "Along the Texas Frontier during the Civil War," pp. 86–87.

22. Regimental Returns, Bourland's Regiment Texas Cavalry, "Border Regiment," Nov., 1864, Confederate Record Group 109, National Archives; Howell, "Along the Texas Frontier during the Civil War," pp. 86, 89–90.

23. Erath to Culberson, Sept. 21, 1864, and Erath to Culberson, Oct. 4, 1864, both in Adjutant General's Records, TSL-A; "Erath Memoirs," p. 107. Totten's Bosque County company was the first to organize in Erath's district. Since that time, even with more than twenty captains available for service, Erath came more

and more to rely upon Totten to move to the scene of any major trouble in the district.

24. N. W. Gillintine to J. B. Barry, Dec. 9, 1864, Barry Papers, BTHC; Greer, *Buck Barry*, p. 186; William C. Pool, "The Battle of Dove Creek," *Southwestern Historical Quarterly* 53 (Apr., 1950): 367.

25. Pool, "Battle of Dove Creek," p. 370; Havins, *Camp Colorado*, p. 144; J. Marvin Hunter, "The Battle of Dove Creek," *West Texas Historical Association Year Book* 10 (Oct., 1934): 75-77. Hunter's account is basically the printed reminiscences of I. D. Ferguson, a member of the Frontier Regiment who participated in the Dove Creek campaign.

26. Pool, "Battle of Dove Creek," p. 371; Havins, *Camp Colorado*, p. 145; Greer, *Buck Barry*, pp. 188-89. This latter source contains the daily log of Fossett's command as kept by a Bosque County trooper in the Frontier Regiment.

27. J. Evetts Haley, *Fort Concho and the Texas Frontier*, pp. 112-13; Hunter, "Battle of Dove Creek," pp. 77-78; Greer, *Buck Barry*, pp. 189-90; Pool, "Battle of Dove Creek," 374-76. Estimates of the Indian force usually range from six hundred to one thousand.

28. Report of Brig. Gen. J. D. McAdoo, Feb. 20, 1865, *Official Records* 48(1):27; Hunter, "Battle of Dove Creek," pp. 78-79; Pool, "Battle of Dove Creek," pp. 376-77; Greer, *Buck Barry*, pp. 190-91. McAdoo's report later indicated that the Indians were surprised in their camp but recovered quickly. Conflicting testimony, however, seems to bear out the fact that the Indians were prepared and waiting for the attack.

29. Hunter, "Battle of Dove Creek," pp. 82-83; Greer, *Buck Barry*, pp. 191-92.

30. J. D. McAdoo to Col. John Burke, Feb. 28, 1865, *Official Records* 48(1):29; George F. Adams to Col. John Burke, Jan. 22, 1865, Adjutant General's Records, TSL-A. Pool, "Battle of Dove Creek," pp. 382-83, gives a list of the names of the Texans killed and wounded.

31. The details of the agonizing journey home for the wounded Texans are best described in Haley, *Fort Concho*, pp. 115-17, and Havins, *Camp Colorado*, pp. 151-54.

32. Report of Brig. Gen. J. D. McAdoo, Feb. 20, 1865, *Official Records* 48(1): 26-29; Havins, *Camp Colorado*, pp. 154-56; Pool, "Battle of Dove Creek," p. 379; Haley, *Fort Concho*, p. 118; Throckmorton to Bourland, Jan. 27, 1865, Bourland Papers, Library of Congress.

33. George F. Adams to J. D. McAdoo, Jan. 22, 1865, Adjutant General's Records, TSL-A. Major Erath stated that a flag of truce should have been sent to them to determine the circumstances of their presence on the frontier; he then added that "I should have allowed them to pass had I been there" ("Erath Memoirs," p. 108).

34. Report of Brig. Gen. J. D. McAdoo, Feb. 20, 1865, *Official Records* 48(1):127.

35. A member of the Frontier Regiment at the battle described the arrival of Totten's men on the morning of the battle: "The 'flop-eared militia,' as we called them, were armed with all kinds of firearms, shot-guns, squirrel rifles, some muskets and pistols" (Hunter, "Battle of Dove Creek," p. 78).

CHAPTER 11. THIRD FRONTIER DISTRICT: 1864-65

1. Hunter to Culberson, Feb. 24, 1864, Adjutant General's Records, TSL-A; Kerby, *Kirby Smith's Confederacy*, p. 92; Allan Robert Purcell, "The History of the Texas Militia, 1835-1903," Ph.D. diss., University of Texas, 1981, p. 152.

2. Excellent accounts of German opposition to the war are found in Rudolph L. Biesele, *The History of the German Settlements in Texas*; Robert W. Shook, "German Unionism in Texas during the Civil War and Reconstruction," Master's thesis, North Texas State University, 1957; *Official Records* 9:615, 15:887-982; and (ser. II) 4:785; and Robert W. Shook, "The Battle of the Nueces, August 10, 1862," *Southwestern Historical Quarterly* 66 (July, 1962): 31-42.

3. C. Dorbandt to Culberson, Jan. 23, 1864, Adjutant General's Records, TSL-A; John Hunter to Kirby Smith, Jan. 28, 1864, Edmund Kirby Smith Papers, Ramsdell Microfilm Collection, BTHC.

4. Oates, *Rip Ford's Texas*, pp. 348-49.

5. Petition of Citizens of Gillespie, Kerr, and Kimble Counties, Mar. 31, 1864, Adjutant General's Records, TSL-A.

6. Oates, *Rip Ford's Texas*, pp. 343, 352; E. P. Turner to J. S. Ford, Dec. 22, 1863, *Official Records* 26(2):525-26; Report of N. Gussett, Live Oak County, Mar. 1, 1864, Adjutant General's Records, TSL-A. Gussett's report is one of sixteen detailed accounts filed by Hunter's office in two separate parts: Consolidated Report of Scouts against Indians & Deserters, 3rd Frontier District, May 14, 1864; and Supplementary Report of Scouts after Indians and Deserters, 3rd Frontier District, May 23, 1864. These two documents contain the best sources available for day-to-day patrol operations in the Frontier Organization from the perspective of the company commanders. All future citations to these documents will refer to the individual company reports contained within them.

7. Report of Capt. R. H. Williams, Frio County, April 23, 1864, Report of Capt. N. Gussett, Mar. 1, 1864, Report of Capt. Theopilus Watkins, Uvalde County, Apr. 30, 1864, Report of Capt. James S. Bourland, Llano County, May 9, 1864, and Hunter to Culberson, May 25, 1864, all in Adjutant General's Records, TSL-A; Oates, *Rip Ford's Texas*, p. 347.

8. Details of the offenses in question are found in Justice Court Sworn Affidavits, Justice Court, Precinct No. II, Mar. 4, 1864; Petition of Citizens of Gillespie, Kerr, and Kendall Counties, Mar. 31, 1864; Hunter to Julius Schultze, Mar. 4, 1861; and Statement of Fritz Schleidier, Mar. 26, 1864, all in Adjutant General's Records, TSL-A.

9. Hunter to Murrah, May 1, 1864, Winfrey and Day, *The Indian Papers of Texas and the Southwest, 1825-1916* 4:83-84; Hunter to Culberson, May 13, 1864, and Hunter to Culberson, May 25, 1864, Adjutant General's Records, TSL-A; William Banta and J. W. Caldwell, Jr., *Twenty-Seven Years on the Texas Frontier*, 189-94.

10. S. B. Gray to Murrah, May 28, 1864, Governor Pendleton Murrah Records, TSL-A.

11. Day, *Senate and House Journal of the Tenth Legislature, First Called Session*,

May 9, 1864–May 28, 1864, p. 18; Hunter to Culberson, May 13, 1864, Adjutant General's Records, TSL-A.

12. H. T. Edgar to Dickinson, May 11, 1864, E. M. Downs to Dickinson, May 11, 1864, and W. A. Lockhart to Dickinson, May 11, 1864, all in *Official Records* 34(3):816–17, 817–18, 818–19.

13. Petition to Lieutenant Colonel Barry, Mar. 10, 1864, Bourland Papers, Library of Congress.

14. Report of Capt. William E. Jones, Kendall County, May 18, 1864, and Report of Capt. William Wahrmund, Gillespie County, May 19, 1864, Adjutant General's Records, TSL-A.

15. Two years later three Comanche Indians told agents at Fort Leavenworth that Alice Todd was killed the day after she was captured (Ledbetter, *Fort Belknap, Frontier Saga*, pp. 145–46, 158–59).

16. Report of Capt. George Robbins, Medina County, Apr. 21, 1864, and Report of Capt. J. F. Tom, Atascosa County, May 22, 1864, Adjutant General's Records; W. A. Lockhart to Lt. Col. A. G. Dickinson, May 11, 1864, *Official Records* 34(3):818.

17. T. C. Doss to Governor Murrah, July 25, 1864, Governor Pendleton Murrah Records, TSL-A; Special Orders Number 484, Executive Office, June 20, 1864, and Magruder to Kirby Smith, Dec. 24, 1863, both in *Official Records* 26(2):530–31, 34(2):1011, 53:1001; Wright, *Texas in the War, 1861–1865*, p. 156.

18. McAdoo to Culberson, Sept. 15, 1864, Adjutant General's Records, TSL-A.

19. Ibid.

20. McAdoo to Culberson, Oct. 20, 1864, ibid.

21. General Orders Number 3, 2nd and 3rd Frontier Districts, Dec. 15, 1864, ibid.

22. McAdoo to Culberson, Sept. 15, 1864, ibid.; Hunter to Murrah, Jan. 19, 1865, Governor Pendleton Murrah Records, TSL-A.

23. L. G. Aldrich to A. C. Jones, n.d., and Slaughter to Murrah, Nov. 24, 1864, Governor Pendleton Murrah Records, TSL-A.

24. Slaughter to Murrah, Nov. 30, 1864, and Slaughter to Murrah, Nov. 24, 1864, both in ibid.

25. Register of Appointments, Personal Service Record, John Henry Brown, Confederate Record Group 109, National Archives; Brown to Murrah, Jan. 19, 1865, Governor Pendleton Murrah Records, TSL-A.

26. Brown to McCulloch, Nov. 21, 1862, John H. Brown Papers, BTHC.

27. Victor M. Rose, *The Life and Services of Gen. Ben McCulloch*, pp. 249–50; John H. Brown to Wife, May 9, 1864, John H. Brown Papers, BTHC; Muster Roll, June, 1864, Adjutant General's Records, TSL-A.

28. Brown actually confused the issue of command when he wrote in his two-volume history of Texas: "In 1864 the frontier was divided into three districts, northern, central and southern, of the northern district . . . Major Wm. Quails [*sic*] of Tarrant. Of the central district . . . Major George B. Erath of McLennan. Of the southern . . . Major John Henry Brown" (Brown, *History of Texas* 2:443). He made no mention of Hunter or McAdoo and thus perpetuated the belief in several secondary works to follow that he was sole commander of the Third Frontier District.

29. The following account, taken from Brown's narrative, represents the last such campaign ever undertaken by the Frontier Organization.

30. J. H. Brown to J. D. McAdoo, May 10, 1865, John Henry Brown Papers, BTHC.

CHAPTER 12. FRONTIER DEFENSE IN RETROSPECT

1. Walker to John Hemphill, Apr. 11, 1861, *Official Records* 1:621-22.

2. Carl Coke Rister, "Fort Griffin," *West Texas Historical Association Year Book* 1 (June, 1925): 16.

3. It is difficult to find a better narrative on the clash of culture between Comanches and Texans, and the nature of the their warfare than Fehrenbach's *Comanches*.

4. Charles William Ramsdell, *Reconstruction in Texas*, pp. 21-22; Fehrenbach, *Lone Star*, p. 354; Ashcraft, "Texas, 1860-1866: The Lone Star State in the Civil War," p. 292, gives ninety thousand as the total number of Texans in the field in late 1863.

5. Statement of Indian Depredations on the Texas Frontier, 1865-July 19, 1867, Winfrey and Day, *The Indian Papers of Texas and the Southwest, 1825-1916* 4:232-33; Fehrenbach, *Comanches*, p. 494; Richardson, *Comanche Barrier*, pp. 292-93; Hagan, *United States-Comanche Relations*, pp. 23-24.

6. Carl Coke Rister, *The Southwestern Frontier—1865-1881*, pp. 98-100; Ramsdell, *Reconstruction in Texas*, pp. 66-70. For an excellent account of the political climate in Texas that led to an emphasis by the federal government on the populated areas of the state rather than on the frontier see Robert W. Shook, "Federal Occupation and Administration of Texas, 1865-1870," Ph.D. diss., North Texas State University, 1970.

7. Rister, "Fort Griffin," pp. 16-17; Fehrenbach, *Comanches*, p. 452.

8. Fehrenbach, *Comanches*, p. 452; Holden, "Frontier Problems and Movements in West Texas, 1846-1900," pp. 104-106; Rister, *The Southwestern Frontier*, pp. 97-99; Kerby, *Kirby Smith's Confederacy*, pp. 429-30.

9. Rupert Norval Richardson, *The Frontier of Northwest Texas, 1846 to 1876: Advance and Defense by the Pioneer Settlers of the Cross Timbers and Prairies*, pp. 251-53.

10. Kerby, *Kirby Smith's Confederacy*, pp. 432-34, observes that the history of the Trans-Mississippi war offers abundant evidence that the continuing demoralization dated from the earliest days of the conflict.

11. Kerby, *Kirby Smith's Confederacy*, p. 433. More recently the epitaph in regard to the entire Confederate effort has been challenged by Beringer, et. al., *Why the South Lost the Civil War*, pp. 203-35, 443-57. See also David Donald, ed., *Why the North Won the Civil War*, pp. 77-90.

12. Fehrenbach, *Lone Star*, p. 523.

13. Inscription on the Confederate Memorial, Arlington National Cemetery, Washington, D.C., as quoted in Harold B. Simpson, *Hood's Texas Brigade: Lee's Grenadier Guard*, p. 477.

14. The quotation is taken from the well-known introduction in Edward Gibbon, *The Decline and Fall of the Roman Empire* (reprint, 2 vols., Chicago: Encyclopaedia Britannica, Inc., 1952), I, 1.

15. Havins, *Camp Colorado*, pp. 156-58.

16. Victor M. Rose, *The Life and Services of Gen. Ben McCulloch*, p. 250; Speer and Brown, *The Encyclopedia of the New West*, pp. 133-34, 281-82, 343; "Erath Memoirs," p. 108, BTHC; Richardson, *The Frontier of Northwest Texas*, p. 250; James T. DeShields, *They Sat in High Place: The Presidents and Governors of Texas*, pp. 246-47.

APPENDIX I.

1. The "Erath Memoirs" consist of a typed manuscript found in the Barker Texas History Center, University of Texas. The memoirs also appear in Lucy A. Erath, "Memoirs of George Bernard Erath," *Southwestern Historical Quarterly* 27 (Oct., 1923): 27-51. Both Holden and I used the original typed manuscript.

2. Kerby, *Kirby Smith's Confederacy*, p. 220.

3. McConnell, *The West Texas Frontier* 2:104-105.

4. Caroline Silsby Ruckman, "The Frontier of Texas during the Civil War," Master's thesis, University of Texas, 1926.

5. Robert Chellis Overfelt, "Defense of the Texas Frontier: 1861-1865," Master's thesis, Baylor University, 1968, p. 64. Overfelt had access to Day, *Senate and House Journal of the Tenth Legislature, First Called Session*, yet he still referred to McAdoo as the initial commander of the Third District; then four pages later, p. 68, he belatedly notes that Murrah replaced Hunter with McAdoo. Overfelt, in his listing of the counties included in the Frontier Organization, lists only those which contributed companies to the strength of each district.

6. "Erath Memoirs," p. 106, BTHC.

7. I have been unable to locate this particular memorandum. An examination of the Adjutant General's Records, TSL-A, failed to unearth it. It could not be found in the folders labeled General Correspondence for 1864, nor in the Ranger Records files, nor in the files for State Troops, 1864, nor in General and Special Orders for the Frontier Districts, nor in any related files for 1864. It has probably been misplaced.

8. Erath to Culberson, Feb. 2, 1864, Erath to Culberson, Feb. 22, 1864, and Monthly Report of the State Troops of the 2nd Frontier Dist. of Texas from the Organization [?] 1864 to April 1, 1864, all in Adjutant General's Records, TSL-A. These documents are obviously more accurate than Erath's memoirs.

9. Hunter to Culberson, Feb. 24, 1864, Adjutant General's Records, TSL-A; Consolidated Report of the Strength of the 3rd Frontier District, Texas State Troops, May 11, 1864, Adjutant General's Records, TSL-A.

10. Quayle to Culberson, Feb. 4, 1864, Quayle Papers, UAL.

11. Quayle to Culberson, Feb. 20, 1864, ibid.

12. District Return, 1st Frontier District, June, 1864, Adjutant General's Records, TSL-A.

APPENDIX III.

1. This chart does not include the Texas State Militia, of which the twentieth brigade district under William Hudson offered service against Indians on the northwestern frontier. In the militia reorganization of December, 1863, James W.

Throckmorton commanded Brigade District Number Six, replacing Hudson's command. The regular militia was rarely used on the Indian frontier, save by Hudson and Throckmorton on the northwest line of organized counties.

2. Burleson resigned before his term of service was over; Buck Barry replaced him.

3. After Obenchain's death in 1862 McCord moved to lieutenant-colonel and Barry to major.

4. Colonel McCord continued to command the six companies of the regiment that transferred to the interior, while Barry commanded a four-company battalion at Fort Belknap, and Fossett commanded the small two-company battalion at Camp Colorado.

5. The average strength totals given for the Frontier Districts represent the total strength for each district. By the state law of Dec. 15, 1863, only one-fourth of the total strength of each Frontier District was to be in the field at any one time.

Bibliography

DOCUMENTS

Adjutant General's Record Group (RG 401). Archives Division, Texas State Library, Austin, Texas.

Barrett, Thomas. "The Great Hanging at Gainesville, Cooke County, Texas, October, 1862." Barker Texas History Center, University of Texas, Austin, Texas. Typescript.

Barry, James Buckner. Papers. Barker Texas History Center, University of Texas, Austin, Texas.

Bell, Governor Peter Hansborough. Records. Archives Division, Texas State Library, Austin, Texas.

Bourland, James A. Papers. Manuscript Division, Library of Congress, Washington, D.C.

"Bourland's Texas Cavalry." Typescript. Confederate Research Center. Hill Junior College, Hillsboro, Texas.

Brown, John Henry. Papers. Barker Texas History Center, University of Texas, Austin, Texas.

Brown, John Henry. Personal Service Record. Regimental Returns. Micro Copy No. 331, Confederate Record Group 109. National Archives, Washington, D.C.

Burleson, Edward, Jr. Papers. Barker Texas History Center, University of Texas, Austin, Texas.

Confederate Index File. James M. Hunter. Archives Division, Texas State Library, Austin, Texas.

Diamond, John R. Personal Service Record. Regimental Returns. Micro Copy No. 323. Confederate Record Group 109. National Archives, Washington, D.C.

Dibrell, Garnett A. Collection. Archives Division, Texas State Library, Austin, Texas.

Elliott, Katherine. "The Frontier Regiment." Typescript. Barker Texas History Center, University of Texas, Austin, Texas.

Epperson, Benjamin H. Papers. Barker Texas History Center, University of Texas, Austin, Texas.

Erath, George B. "Memoirs of George Bernard Erath." Typescript. Barker Texas History Center, University of Texas, Austin, Texas.

Erath, George Bernard. Personal Service Record. Regimental Returns. Micro Copy No. 331, Confederate Record Group 109. National Archives, Washington, D.C.

Frontier Protection Papers. Barker Texas History Center, University of Texas, Austin, Texas.

Galbraith Family Papers. In possession of Charles Eversole, Jr. Grapevine, Texas.

General and Special Orders and Circulars Issued, 1861–1864, Department of Texas, Confederate Record Group 109. National Archives, Washington, D.C.

Gunter, Lillian. Papers. Morton Museum, Gainesville, Texas.

Gunter Family Collection. North Texas State University Archives, Denton, Texas.

Holmsley, James M. Papers. Barker Texas History Center, University of Texas, Austin, Texas.

King, John R. Papers. Archives Division, Texas State Library, Austin, Texas.

Letters and Telegrams Received, 1861–1865, Trans-Mississippi Department, Confederate Record Group 109. National Archives, Washington, D.C.

Letters Sent, September 16, 1861–October, 1862, Department of Texas, Chapter II, Volumes 129, 134, 135, and 135 1/2, Confederate Record Group 109. National Archives, Washington, D.C.

Letters Sent, March 7, 1863–May 19, 1865, Trans-Mississippi Department, Chapter II, Volumes 70, 71, 72, and 73 1/2, Confederate Record Group 109. National Archives, Washington, D.C.

Lubbock, Governor Francis Richard. Records. Archives Division, Texas State Library, Austin, Texas.

McCord, James E. Personal Service Record. Regimental Returns. Micro Copy No. 331, Confederate Record Group 109. National Archives, Washington, D.C.

McCulloch, Ben and Henry Eustace. Papers. Barker Texas History Center, University of Texas, Austin, Texas.

McCulloch, Henry E. Personal Service Record. Regimental Returns. Micro Copy No. 323, Confederate Record Group 109. National Archives, Washington, D.C.

McKinney Family Papers. Department of Special Collections, University of Texas at Arlington, Arlington, Texas.

Maxey, Samuel Bell. Papers. Archives Division, Texas State Library, Austin, Texas.

Maxey, Samuel Bell. Papers. Thomas Gilcrease Museum Library, Tulsa, Oklahoma.

Murrah, Governor Pendleton. Records. Archives Division, Texas State Library, Austin, Texas.

Pease, Governor Elisha Marshall. Records. Archives Division, Texas State Library, Austin, Texas.

Peveler, William R. "Diary of William R. Peveler." Typescript. Barker Texas History Center, University of Texas, Austin, Texas.

———. "Notes of Francis M. Peveler." Typescript. Barker Texas History Center, University of Texas, Austin, Texas.

Quayle, William. Papers. Rare Book Room, University of Alabama, Tuscaloosa, Alabama.

Regimental Returns, Bourland's Regiment Texas Cavalry, "Border Regiment." Confederate Record Group 109. National Archives, Washington, D.C.

Ross Family Papers. Texas Collection, Baylor University, Waco, Texas.

Robertson, Elijah Sterling Clack. Papers. Robertson Colony Collection. Department of Special Collections, University of Texas at Arlington, Arlington, Texas.

Runnels, Governor Hardin Richard. Records. Archives Division, Texas State Library, Austin, Texas.

Smith, Edmund Kirby. Papers. Ramsdell Microfilm Collection. Barker Texas History Center, University of Texas, Austin, Texas.

Texas State Military Board Papers. Archives Division, Texas State Library, Austin, Texas.

Williams, Henry. "The Indian Raid in Young County, Texas." Typescript. Barker Texas History Center, University of Texas, Austin, Texas.

Wright, George T. Papers. Barker Texas History Center, University of Texas, Austin, Texas.

BOOKS

Acheson, Sam, and Julie Ann Hudson O'Connell, eds. *George Washington Diamond's Account of the Great Hanging at Gainesville, 1862.* Austin: Texas State Historical Association, 1963.

Annual Report of the Commissioner of Indian Affairs, 1854. Washington: A. O. P. Nicholson, 1855.

Banta, William, and J. W. Caldwell, Jr. *Twenty-Seven Years on the Texas Frontier.* 1893. Reprint. Council Hill, Okla.: L. G. Park, n.d.

Barrett, Thomas. *The Great Hanging at Gainesville, Cooke County, Texas A.D. 1862.* Reprint. Austin: Texas State Historical Association, 1961.

Bender, Averam B. *The March of Empire: Frontier Defense in the Southwest, 1848–1860.* Lawrence: University of Kansas Press, 1952.

Beringer, Richard E., Herman Hattaway, Archer Jones, and William N. Still, eds. *Why the South Lost the Civil War.* Athens: University of Georgia Press, 1986.

Biesele, Rudolph L. *The History of the German Settlements in Texas.* Austin: Von Boeckmann–Jones, 1930.

Biggers, Don H. *German Pioneers in Texas.* Fredericksburg, Tex.: Fredericksburg Publishing Company, 1925.

Boatner, Mark Mayo. *The Civil War Dictionary.* New York: David McKay Company, 1959.

Bowden, J. J. *The Exodus of Federal Forces from Texas, 1861.* Austin: Eakin Press, 1986.

Breihan, Carl W. *Quantrill and His Civil War Guerrillas.* Denver: Sage Books, 1959.

Brown, John Henry. *History of Texas, from 1685 to 1892.* 2 vols. St. Louis: L. E. Daniell, 1893.

————. *The Indian Wars and Pioneers of Texas.* Austin: L. E. Daniell, n.d.

Buenger, Walter L. *Secession and the Union in Texas.* Austin: University of Texas Press, 1984.

Castel, Albert. *William Clark Quantrill: His Life and Times.* New York: Frederick Fell, 1962.

Cates, Cliff Donahue. *Pioneer History of Wise County: From Red Men to Railroads, Twenty Years of Intrepid History.* Decatur, Tex.: Wise County Old Settler's Association, 1907.

Clark L. D., ed. *Civil War Recollections of James Lemuel Clark.* College Station: Texas A&M University Press, 1984.

Collins, Michael. *Cooke County, Texas: Where the South and the West Meet.* Gainesville, Tex.: Cooke County Heritage Society, 1981.

Connelley, William Elsey. *Quantrill and the Border Wars.* Reprint. New York: Pageant Book Co., 1956.

Coulter, E. Merton. *The Confederate States of America, 1861–1865.* Vol. 7, *A History of the South.* Baton Rouge: Louisiana State University Press, 1950.

Crouch, Carrie J. *A History of Young County, Texas.* Austin: Texas State Historical Association, 1956.

Day, James M., ed. *House Journal of the Ninth Legislature, Regular Session, November 4, 1861–January 14, 1862.* Austin: Texas State Library, 1964.

————, ed. *House Journal of the Ninth Legislature, First Called Session, February 2, 1863–March 7, 1863.* Austin: Texas State Library, 1963.

————, ed. *House Journal of the Tenth Legislature, Regular Session, November 3, 1863–December 16, 1863.* Austin: Texas State Library, 1964.

————, ed. *Senate Journal of the Ninth Legislature, First Called Session, February 2, 1863–March 7, 1863.* Austin: Texas State Library, 1963.

————, ed. *Senate Journal of the Tenth Legislature, Regular Session, November 3, 1863–December 16, 1863.* Austin: Texas State Library, 1964.

————, ed. *Senate and House Journal of the Tenth Legislature, First Called Session, May 9, 1864–May 28, 1864.* Austin: Texas State Library, 1965.

————, ed. *Senate and House Journal of the Tenth Legislature, Second Called Session, October 15, 1864–November 15, 1864.* Austin: Texas State Library, 1966.

————, ed. *The Texas Almanac, 1857–1873.* Waco: Texian Press, 1967.

DeShields, James. T. *They Sat in High Place: The Presidents and Governors of Texas.* San Antonio: Naylor Co., 1940.

Donald, David, ed. *Why the North Won the Civil War.* Baton Rouge: Louisiana State University Press, 1960.

Dunlay, Thomas W. *Wolves for the Blue Soldiers.* Lincoln: University of Nebraska Press, 1982.

Earle, J. P. *History of Clay County and Northwest Texas.* Reprint. Austin: Brick Row Book Shop, 1963.

Elliott, Claude. *Leathercoat: The Life History of a Texas Patriot.* San Antonio: Standard Printing Co., 1938.

Farber, James. *Texas, C.S.A.* New York: Jackson Co., 1947.

Faust, Patricia L., ed. *Historical Times Illustrated Encyclopedia of the Civil War.* New York: Harper and Row, 1986.

Fehrenbach, T. R. *Comanches: The Destruction of a People.* Reprint. New York: Alfred A. Knopf, 1983.

————. *Lone Star: A History of Texas and the Texans.* New York: Macmillan Company, 1968.

Freeman, Douglas Southall. *Lee's Lieutenants: A Study in Command.* 3 vols. New York: Charles Scribner's Sons, 1942–44.

————. *R. E. Lee: A Biography.* 4 vols. New York: Charles Scribner's Sons, 1934–35.

Friend, Llerena. *Sam Houston: The Great Designer.* Austin: University of Texas Press, 1954.

Gammel, H. P. N., ed. and comp., *Laws of Texas, 1822–1897.* 10 vols. Austin: Gammel Book Co., 1898.

Garrett, Julia Kathryn. *Fort Worth: A Frontier Triumph.* Austin: Encino Press, 1972.

General Orders, Headquarters, Trans-Mississippi, from 6 March 1863 to 1 January 1865. Houston: E. H. Cushing Co., 1865.

Greer, James K., ed. *Buck Barry, Texas Ranger and Frontiersman.* Reprint. Lincoln: University of Nebraska Press, 1978.

Hagan, William T. *United States–Comanche Relations: The Reservation Years.* New Haven: Yale University Press, 1976.

Haley, J. Evetts. *Charles Goodnight: Cowman and Plainsman*. New York: Houghton Mifflin Company, 1936.

———. *Fort Concho and the Texas Frontier*. San Angelo, Tex.: San Angelo Standard-Times, 1952.

Hart, John A., et al. *Pioneer Days in the Southwest from 1850 to 1879*. Guthrie, Okla.: State Capitol Co., 1909.

Havins, Thomas Robert. *Camp Colorado: A Decade of Frontier Defense*. Brownwood, Tex.: Brown Press, 1964.

Henderson, Harry McCorry. *Texas in the Confederacy*. San Antonio: Naylor Co., 1955.

Horton, Louise. *Samuel Bell Maxey*. Austin: University of Texas Press, 1974.

Horton, Thomas F. *History of Jack County: Being Accounts of Pioneer Times, Excerpts from County Court Records, Indian Stories, Biographical Sketches, and Interesting Events*. Centennial edition. Privately printed, 1975.

Huckabay, Ida Lasater. *Ninety-Four Years in Jack County*. Reprint. Waco, Tex.: Texian Press, 1979.

Hughes, W. J. *Rebellious Ranger: Rip Ford and the Old Southwest*. Norman: University of Oklahoma Press, 1964.

Jennett, Elizabeth LeNoir, ed. *Biographical Directory of the Texan Conventions and Congresses*. Austin: Book Exchange, 1941.

Johnson, Allen, et al., eds. *Dictionary of American Biography*. 16 vols. New York: Charles Scribner's Sons, 1927–81.

Jones, C. N., ed. *Early Days in Cooke County*. Reprint. Gainesville, Tex.: Cooke County Heritage Society, 1977.

Journal of the Congress of the Confederate States of America, 1861–1865. Reprint. New York: Kraus Reprint Company, 1968.

Kerby, Robert L. *Kirby Smith's Confederacy: The Trans-Mississippi South, 1863–1865*. New York: Columbia University Press, 1972.

Kittrell, Norman G. *Governors Who Have Been, and Other Public Men of Texas*. Houston: Dealy-Adey-Elgin Co., 1921.

Landrum, Graham, and Allan Smith. *Grayson County: An Illustrated History of Grayson County, Texas*. Fort Worth: Historical Publishers, 1967.

Ledbetter, Barbara Neal. *Civil War Days in Young County, Texas, 1861–1865*. Newcastle, Tex.: Privately printed, 1965.

———. *Fort Belknap, Frontier Saga: Indians, Negroes and Anglo-Americans On the Texas Frontier*. Burnet, Tex.: Eakin Press, 1982.

London, Marvin F. *Indian Raids in Montague County*. Saint Jo, Tex.: S. J. T. Printers, 1958.

Lonn, Ella. *Desertion during the Civil War*. Reprint. Gloucester, Mass.: Peter Smith, 1966.

McConnell, Joseph Carroll. *The West Texas Frontier, or a Descriptive History of Early Times in Western Texas.* 2 vols. Palo Pinto, Tex.: Texas Legal Bank & Book Co., 1933–39.

McPherson, James M. *Battle Cry of Freedom: The Civil War Era.* New York: Oxford University Press, 1988.

Marshall, S. L. A. *Crimsoned Prairie.* New York: Charles Scribner's Sons, 1972.

Mayhall, Mildred P. *Indian Wars of Texas.* Waco, Tex.: Texian Press, 1965.

———. *The Kiowas.* Norman: University of Oklahoma Press, 1962.

Moore, Albert Burton. *Conscription and Conflict in the Confederacy.* New York: Macmillan Company, 1924.

Neighbours, Kenneth Franklin. *Indian Exodus: Texas Indian Affairs, 1835–1859.* Nortex Offsett Publications, 1973.

———. *Robert Simpson Neighbors and the Texas Frontier, 1836–1859.* Waco: Texian Press, 1975.

Newcomb, W. W., Jr. *The Indians of Texas from Prehistoric to Modern Times.* Austin: University of Texas Press, 1961.

Nichols, James L. *The Confederate Quartermaster in the Trans-Mississippi.* Austin: University of Texas Press, 1964.

Nye, Wilbur S. *Carbine and Lance: The Story of Old Fort Sill.* Norman: University of Oklahoma Press, 1937.

Oakes, James. *Slavery and Freedom: An Interpretation of the Old South.* New York: Alfred K. Knopf, 1990.

Oates, Stephen B., ed. *Rip Ford's Texas.* Austin: University of Texas Press, 1963.

O'Donnell, Pearl Foster. *Trek to Texas: 1770–1870.* Fort Worth: Branch-Smith, 1965.

Parks, Joseph Howard. *General Edmund Kirby Smith, C.S.A.* Baton Rouge: Louisiana State University Press, 1954.

Potter, W. R. *History of Montague County, Texas.* Reprint. Saint Jo, Tex.: S. J. T. Printing, 1975.

Rampp, Lary C., and Donald L. Rampp. *The Civil War in the Indian Territory.* Austin: Presidial Press, 1975.

Ramsdell, Charles W. *Behind the Lines in the Southern Confederacy.* Baton Rouge: Louisiana State University Press, 1944.

———. *Reconstruction in Texas.* Reprint. Gloucester, Mass.: Peter Smith, 1964.

Richardson, Rupert Norval. *The Comanche Barrier to South Plains Settlement.* Glendale, Calif.: Arthur H. Clark Company, 1933.

———. *The Frontier of Northwest Texas, 1846 to 1876: Advance and Defense by the Pioneer Settlers of the Cross Timbers and Prairies.* Glendale, Calif.: Arthur H. Clark Company, 1963.

Olmsted, Frederick Law. *A Journey through Texas; or, a Saddle-Trip on the Southwestern Frontier.* Reprint. Austin: University of Texas Press, 1978.

Price, George F. *Across the Continent with the Fifth Cavalry.* Reprint. New York: Antiquarian Press, 1959.

Raines, C. W., ed. *Six Decades in Texas: The Memoirs of Francis R. Lubbock, Confederate Governor of Texas*. Reprint. Austin: Pemberton Press, 1968.

Report of the Commissioner of Indian Affairs, for the Year 1856. Washington: A. O. P. Nicholson, 1857.

Rister, Carl Coke. *The Southwestern Frontier—1865–1881*. Cleveland: Arthur H. Clark Company, 1928.

Roberts, O. M. *Texas*. Vol. 11, *Confederate Military History*, edited by Clement Evans. Reprint. New York: Thomas Yoseloff, 1962.

Rose, Victor M. *The Life and Services of Gen. Ben McCulloch*. Reprint. Austin: Steck Company, 1958.

Rowland, Dunbar, ed. *Jefferson Davis, Constitutionalist: His Letters, Papers and Speeches*. 10 vols. Jackson, Miss.: J. J. Little & Ives Company, 1923.

Scott, Robert N., et al., eds., *The War of the Rebellion: A Compilation of the Official Records of the Union and Confederate Armies*. 70 vols. in 128 books. 1880–1901. Reprint. Harrisburg, Pa.: National Historical Society, 1971.

Simpson, Harold B. *Cry Comanche: The 2nd U.S. Cavalry in Texas, 1855–1861*. Hillsboro, Tex.: Hill Jr. College Press, 1979.

————. *Hood's Texas Brigade: Lee's Grenadier Guard*. Waco: Texian Press, 1970.

Smith, A. Morton. *The First 100 Years in Cooke County*. San Antonio: Naylor Company, 1955.

Smythe, H. *Historical Sketch of Parker County and Weatherford, Texas*. Reprint. Waco: W. M. Morrison, 1973.

Sowell, A. J. *Early Settlers and Indian Fighters of Southwest Texas*. Austin: Ben C. Jones and Co., 1900.

————. *Rangers and Pioneers of Texas*. Reprint. New York: Argosy-Antiquarian Ltd., 1964.

Speer, William S., and John Henry Brown, eds. *The Encyclopedia of the New West*. Marshall, Tex.: United States Biographical Publishing Company, 1881.

Taylor, William Charles. *A History of Clay County*. Austin: Eakin Press, 1972.

Texas Almanac, 1861–1865. Galveston and Austin: 1865.

Turner, Frederick Jackson. *The Frontier in American History*. Reprint. New York: Henry Holt and Company, 1950.

Utley, Robert M. *Frontier Regulars: The United States Army and the Indian, 1866–1890*. New York: Macmillan Publishing Co., 1973.

————. *Frontiersmen in Blue: The United States Army and the Indian, 1848–1865*. New York: Macmillan Publishing Co., 1967.

Wallace, Ernest. *Texas in Turmoil*. Austin: Steck-Vaughn Company, 1965.

————, and E. Adamson Hoebel. *The Comanches: Lords of the South Plains*. Norman: University of Oklahoma Press, 1952.

Warner, Ezra J. *Generals in Gray: Lives of the Confederate Commanders*. Baton Rouge: Louisiana State University Press, 1959.

Webb, Walter Prescott. *The Great Plains*. Boston: Ginn and Company, 1931.

————. *The Texas Rangers: A Century of Frontier Defense*. Reprint. Austin: University of Texas Press, 1965.

————, et al., ed. *The Handbook of Texas*. 2 vols. Austin: Texas State Historical Association, 1952.

Wilbarger, J. W. *Indian Depredations in Texas*. Austin: Hutchings Printing House, 1889.

Wiley, Bell Irvin. *The Life of Billy Yank: The Common Soldier of the Union*. Reprint. Garden City, N.Y.: Doubleday & Company, 1971.

————. *The Life of Johnny Reb: The Common Soldier of the Confederacy*. Reprint. Garden City, N.Y.: Doubleday & Company, 1971.

Williams, Amelia W., and Eugene C. Barker, eds. *The Writings of Sam Houston, 1813–1863*. 8 vols. Austin: University of Texas Press, 1942.

Winfrey, Dorman H., and James M. Day, eds., *The Indian Papers of Texas and the Southwest, 1825–1916*. 5 vols. Austin: Pemberton Press, 1966.

————, and ————, eds. *Texas Indian Papers, 1846–1859*. 4 vols. Austin: Texas State Library, 1961.

Winkler, Ernest William. *Journal of the Secession Convention of Texas, 1861*. Austin: Texas Library and Historical Commission, 1912.

Wooster, Robert. *Soldiers, Sutlers, and Settlers: Garrison Life on the Texas Frontier*. College Station: Texas A&M University Press, 1987.

Wooten, Dudley G., ed. *A Comprehensive History of Texas*. 2 vols. Dallas: William G. Scarff, 1898.

Wright, Marcus J. *Texas in the War, 1861–1865*, edited by Harold B. Simpson. Hillsboro, Tex.: Hill Junior College Press, 1965.

Yearns, Wilfred Buck. *The Confederate Congress*. Athens: University of Georgia Press, 1960.

ARTICLES

Barrett, Arrie. "Western Frontier Forts of Texas, 1845–1861." *West Texas Historical Association Year Book* 7 (June, 1931): 115–21.

Barton, Henry W. "The United States Cavalry and the Texas Rangers." *Southwestern Historical Quarterly* 63 (April, 1960): 495–510.

Bell, William H. "Ante Bellum: The Old Army in Texas in '61." *Magazine of History* 3 (January, 1906): 80–86.

Braly, Earl Burk. "Fort Belknap of the Texas Frontier." *West Texas Historical Association Year Book* 30 (October, 1954): 83–114.

Britton, Wiley. "Resume of Military Operations in Missouri and Arkansas, 1864–1865." In *Battles and Leaders of the Civil War*, edited by Clarence C. Buel and Robert U. Johnson. Reprint. Vol. 4. New York: Thomas Yoseloff Co., 1956.

Castel, Albert. "The Guerrilla War, 1861–1865." *Civil War Times Illustrated*, special issue (October, 1974): 3–50.

"Col. William Quayle." *Confederate Veteran* 10 (August, 1902): 372–73.

Cox, Ed T. "Early Days in Eastland County." *West Texas Historical Association Year Book* 17 (October, 1941): 83–93.

Crimmins, Martin L. "The First Line of Army Posts Established in West Texas." *West Texas Historical Association Year Book* 19 (October, 1943): 121–27.

Darrow, Caroline Baldwin. "Recollections of the Twiggs Surrender." In *Battles and Leaders of the Civil War,* edited by Clarence C. Buel and Robert U. Johnson. Vol. 1. Reprint. New York: Thomas Yoseloff, 1956.

Duncan, John Thomas, ed. "Some Civil War Letters of D. Port Smythe." *West Texas Historical Association Year Book* 37 (October, 1961): 147–76.

Elliott, Claude. "Union Sentiment in Texas, 1861–1865." *Southwestern Historical Quarterly* 50 (April, 1947): 449–77.

Erath, Lucy A., ed. "Memoirs of George Bernard Erath." *Southwestern Historical Quarterly* 27 (October, 1923): 27–51.

Ewing, Floyd F., Jr. "Unionist Sentiment on the Northwest Texas Frontier." *West Texas Historical Association Year Book* 33 (October, 1957): 58–70.

Gage, Larry Jay. "The Texas Road to Secession and War: John Marshall and the Texas State Gazette, 1860–1861." *Southwestern Historical Quarterly* 62 (October, 1958): 191–226.

Geise, William Royston. "Kirby Smithdom, 1864: A Study of Organization and Command in the Trans-Mississippi West." *Military History of Texas and the Southwest* 15, no. 4 (1979): 17–35.

Harmon, George D. "The United States Indian Policy in Texas, 1845–1860." *The Mississippi Valley Historical Review* 17 (December, 1930): 377–403.

Havins, Thomas R. "The Texas Mounted Regiment at Camp Colorado." *Texas Military History* 4 (Summer, 1964): 67–79.

Herklotz, Hildegarde Rose. "Jayhawkers in Missouri, 1858–1863." *Missouri Historical Review* 18 (October, 1923): 64–101.

Holden, William C. "Frontier Defense in Texas during the Civil War." *West Texas Historical Association Year Book* 4 (June, 1928): 16–31.

Howell, D. S. "Along the Texas Frontier during the Civil War." *West Texas Historical Association Year Book* 13 (October, 1937): 82–95.

Howsley, Marilyne. "Forting Up on the Texas Frontier during the Civil War." *West Texas Historical Association Year Book* 17 (October, 1941): 71–76.

Hunter, J. Marvin. "The Battle of Dove Creek." *West Texas Historical Association Year Book* 10 (October, 1934): 74–87.

Kimbrough, W. C. "The Frontier Background of Clay County." *West Texas Historical Association Year Book* 18 (October, 1942): 116–31.

Koch, Lena Clara. "The Federal Indian Policy in Texas, 1845–1860." *Southwestern Historical Quarterly* 28 (July, 1925): 19–35.

"Major James M. Hunter." *Frontier Times* 6 (October, 1928): 1–3.

Nackman, Mark E. "The Making of the Texan Citizen Soldier, 1835–1860." *Southwestern Historical Quarterly* 78 (January, 1975): 231–53.

Neighbours, Kenneth F. "Elm Creek Raid in Young County, 1864." *West Texas Historical Association Year Book* 30 (October, 1964): 83–89.

———. "Fort Belknap." In *Frontier Forts of Texas*, edited by Harold B. Simpson. Waco: Texian Press, 1966.

Oates, Stephen B. "Texas under the Secessionists." *Southwestern Historical Quarterly* 67 (October, 1963): 167–212.

Pool, William C. "The Battle of Dove Creek." *Southwestern Historical Quarterly* 53 (April, 1950): 367–85.

Rampp, Lary C. "Incident at Baxter Springs, on October 6, 1863." *Kansas Historical Quarterly* 36 (Summer, 1970): 183–97.

———. "William C. Quantrill's Civil War Activities in Texas, 1861–1863." *Texas Military History* 8, no. 4 (1970): 221–31.

Richardson, Rupert N. "The Saga of Camp Cooper." *West Texas Historical Association Year Book* 56 (October, 1980): 14–34.

Rister, Carl C. "Fort Griffin." *West Texas Historical Association Year Book* 1 (June, 1925): 15–24.

Shook, Robert W. "The Battle of the Nueces, August 10, 1862." *Southwestern Historical Quarterly* 66 (July, 1962): 31–42.

Simpson, Harold B. "Fort Mason." *Frontier Forts of Texas*, edited by Harold B. Simpson. Waco, Tex.: Texian Press, 1966.

———. "John Salmon (RIP) Ford." In *Rangers of Texas*. Waco: Texian Press, 1969.

Smallwood, James. "Disaffection in Confederate Texas: The Great Hanging at Gainesville." *Civil War History* 22 (December, 1976): 349–60.

Tate, Michael L. "Frontier Defense on the Comanche Ranges of Northwest Texas, 1846–1860." *Great Plains Journal* 11 (Fall, 1971): 41–56.

Timmons, Joe T. "The Referendum in Texas on the Ordinance of Secession, February 23, 1861: The Vote." *East Texas Historical Journal* 11, no. 2 (1973): 12–28.

Webb, J. R., ed. "Chapters from the Frontier Life of Phin W. Reynolds." *West Texas Historical Association Year Book* 21 (October, 1945): 110–43.

Williams, J. W. "Military Roads of the 1850's in Central West Texas." *West Texas Historical Association Year Book* 18 (October, 1942): 77–91.

Wilson, Glen O. "Old Red River Station." *Southwestern Historical Quarterly* 61 (January, 1958): 350–58.

Wooster, Robert. "Military Strategy in the Southwest, 1848–1860." *Military History of Texas and the Southwest* 15, no. 2 (1979): 5–15.

THESES AND DISSERTATIONS

Ashcraft, Allan Coleman. "Texas, 1860–1866: The Lone Star State in the Civil War." Ph.D. diss., Columbia University, New York, 1960.

Buenger, Walter Louis, Jr. "Stilling the Voice of Reason: Texans and the Union, 1854–1861." Ph.D. diss., Rice University, Houston, Texas, 1979.

Donnell, Guy Renfro. "The History of Montague County, Texas." Master's thesis, University of Texas, Austin, Texas, 1940.

Felgar, Robert P. "Texas in the War for Southern Independence." Ph.D. diss., University of Texas, Austin, Texas, 1947.

Haynes, Billy Dwayne. "Unionism in Texas: 1860–1867." Master's thesis, North Texas State University, Denton, Texas, 1954.

Holden, William Curry. "Frontier Problems and Movements in West Texas, 1846–1900." Ph.D. diss., University of Texas, Austin, Texas, 1928.

McCaslin, Richard B. "Tainted Breeze: The Great Hanging at Gainesville, Texas, October, 1862." Ph.D. diss., University of Texas, Austin, Texas, 1988.

Marten, James Alan. "Drawing the Line: Dissent and Disloyalty in Texas, 1856 to 1874." Ph.D. diss., University of Texas, Austin, Texas, 1986.

Overfelt, Robert Chellis. "Defense of the Texas Frontier: 1861–1865." Master's thesis, Baylor University, Waco, Texas, 1968.

Purcell, Allan Robert. "The History of the Texas Militia, 1835–1903." Ph.D. diss., University of Texas, Austin, Texas, 1981.

Ruckman, Caroline Silsby. "The Frontier of Texas during the Civil War." Master's thesis, University of Texas, Austin, Texas, 1926.

Shook, Robert W. "Federal Occupation and Administration of Texas, 1865–1870." Ph.D. diss., North Texas State University, Denton, Texas, 1970.

———. "German Unionism in Texas during the Civil War and Reconstruction." Master's thesis, North Texas State University, Denton, Texas, 1957.

Smith, David Paul. "In Defense of Texas: The Life of Henry E. McCulloch." Master's thesis, Stephen F. Austin State University, Nacogdoches, Texas, 1975.

Thomasson, Michael Reagan. "James McCord and the Texas Frontier Regiment." Master's thesis, Stephen F. Austin State University, Nacogdoches, Texas, 1965.

Newspapers

Clarksville Northern Standard. Nov. 6, 1858, Apr. 2, 1859, Oct. 22, 1859, Oct. 10, 1863, Nov. 7, 1863.

Dallas Herald. Sept. 28, 1858, Mar. 9, 1859, June 15, 1859, Sept. 16, 1863, Sept. 30, 1863, Oct. 15, 1864.

Gainesville Daily Register, Aug. 30, 1948.

Houston Telegraph, Nov. 25, 1863.

Texas State Gazette, Nov. 29, 1853, Nov. 24, 1855, Dec. 15, 1855.

Weatherford Whiteman, Sept. 13, 1860.

Index

Alexander, W. J., 53
Anderson, J. B., 118, 133
Ashby, Travis H., 31

Bankhead, Smith P., 66–70
Banks, Nathaniel Prentiss, 75, 100, 113, 116
Banta, William, 158
Barry, James Buckner: and battle of Dove Creek, 152, 154; at Fort Belknap, 65, 69, 73–74, 82, 85, 92, 116–17, 119, 135–36; in Frontier Regiment, 48–49, 53–54, 57; mentioned, 91, 121, 123–24, 138, 149, 198n.35, 202n.41; and surrender of forts, 25–28; and Texas Mounted Rifles, 31–32, 37–39, 44
Baylor, John Robert: and Brush Battalion, 81; and Indian removal, 9, 16, 186n.13; mentioned, 74, 83, 85; Ranger service of, 28, 78; and secession, 22
Bee, Hamilton Prioleau, 50, 52, 111
Bell, Peter H., 12
Blunt, James Gillpatrick, 66, 72, 78
Bogges, Milton M., 31
Bonham, 66–67, 71–72, 74–75, 77–78, 110–11, 113–14, 118, 125–27, 130, 148, 164, 174, 199n.7
Border Battalion, 66
Border Regiment: and Brush Battalion, 82; and brush men, 107, 109–10; deserters in, 123; and Elm Creek Raid, 131–32; and "great western scout," 136–37; mentioned, 72, 116, 126, 169, 172; and Northern Sub-District, 117, 119–20, 124, 139; organization of, 64; and pur-

Border Regiment (*cont.*)
suit of deserters, 74, 141, 149. *See also* Bourland, James
Boren, Henry, 77, 79, 82, 109
Bourland, James: and Border Regiment, 64–65; and Brush Battalion, 82, 109; and Cooke County Raid, 84–86; and deserters, 74, 80, 109, 124–27, 149; in 1863, 69, 73, 198n.33; in 1864, 117–19, 133–36, 148, 202nn.40–41, 207n.4; and Frontier Conspiracy of 1864, 112–14; in Indian Territory, 66, 73; mentioned, 59, 68, 78, 83, 96, 123, 129, 148, 198n.35; and Twenty-first Brigade District, 59–60
Bradfute, William, 52
Brooke, George Mercer, 4–5, 12
Brown, John Henry, 76, 164–66, 173
Brunson, A., 45
Brush Battalion: break-up of, 110, 123; and Cooke County Raid, 83, 85; inefficiency of, 107, 108–10, 205n.7; mentioned, 112; origin of, 81, 201n.29
brush men, 74–77, 80–81, 106–109, 123, 128, 199n.6
Bryan, Guy Morrison, 77
Buffalo Springs, 124, 141
Buffalo Station, 139
Burke, John, 138
Burleson, Aaron, 26, 37
Burleson, Edward, Jr., 18, 21, 33–35, 53

Cabell, William L., 67
Callahan, James Hughes, 6
Camp Belknap, 45

232

Placido, 120
Plains Indians, 10, 19, 30, 37, 66–68, 72–73, 82, 131, 134, 142–43, 168–69, 174, 190n.6
Potter, C., 138

Quantrill, William Clarke, 78–79, 110–12, 200nn.19, 21–22
Quayle, William: commanding First Frontier District, 94–96; and conscription and desertion, 101–102, 125–27, 148; and Elm Creek Raid, 133–35; and Frontier Conspiracy of 1864, 112–15; and frontier defense, 104, 119, 121; and James W. Throckmorton, 129–30, 136; mentioned, 123–24, 131, 142, 146–47, 149, 158, 213n.19

Rangers: antebellum service, 3–9; description of, 11, 29, 31, 95, 187n.24; mentioned, 13, 15, 17, 19, 21–22, 30, 43, 49, 51, 53, 168–69, 171–72; tactics of, 12, 14, 17–18, 28, 163. See also Border Regiment; First Regiment, Texas Mounted Riflemen; Frontier Organization; Frontier Regiment
Reagan, W. P., 143
Red River Station, 45–46, 53, 69, 73, 82–83, 85, 91, 117–18, 124, 195n.28
Ringgold Barracks, 50
Rio Grande Station, 46
Robb, Thomas, 46
Robbins, George, 160
Roberts, Samuel A., 67, 76
Robertson, Elijah Sterling Clark, 76
Roff, Charles L., 82, 118, 124, 136–37
Rogers, E. W., 21, 27–28
Rowland, John T., 55, 69, 82–85, 91, 117, 124–25, 139
Runnels, Hardin Richard, 9–11, 15–17, 186n.17, 187n.32

Sadler Bend, 83
Salmon, John, 45
Salt Creek Station, 135, 139
San Antonio, 32–33, 35, 39, 87, 159
San Lucas Springs, 33
Sayles, John, 98
Scurry, William Read, 52, 70

Second Frontier District: conscription and desertion in, 101, 144, 146–47, 151, 155; frontier defense in, 136, 144, 146, 151–52, 155, 165, 173; organization of, 92–94, 97, 164
Second United States Cavalry, 8, 10, 13–15, 19, 25
Shannon, S., 141
Shoemaker, William H., 141
Sivells Bend, 60, 119
Slaughter, James Edwin, 87, 163–64
Smith, Edmund Kirby: and conscription and desertion, 75, 77, 79, 98–99, 102–105, 127; mentioned, 70, 74, 80, 88, 100–101, 128, 164, 169; and Plains Indians, 142–43; and Second U.S. Cavalry, 25, 31; and Trans-Mississippi command, 65–66
Smith, Henry, 165–66
Smith, Persifor F., 5, 7
Sons of the South, 113, 115
Spanish Fort, 118, 139
state militia: and conscription conflict, 98–100; and frontier defense, 59–61, 64, 68; mentioned, 75, 79–80, 129–30, 161, 172
state's rights, 30, 102–103, 171
Steele, Frederick, 100
Steele, William, 63–64, 67, 69, 72
Sublett, David L., 21
Sweet, George, 131

Tackett, Mann D., 73
Taylor, Richard, 116
Terry, Nathaniel, 68
Texas Legislature: and Frontier Organization, 88, 101–104, 130; and Frontier Regiment, 41–43, 50–51, 63, 87; mentioned, 96, 121, 134; organization of militia, 45, 57, 98–100, 129
Texas State Military Board, 48
Third Frontier District: and conscription and desertion, 102, 158; frontier defense in, 106, 158, 160, 163, 165, 173; organization of, 92–94, 97, 156, 161–62, 164
Thompson, H. J., 124
Throckmorton, James Webb: and deserters, 75–77; and Frontier Organization, 104, 129–31, 135–36, 138–39; men-

Throckmorton, James Webb (*cont.*)
  tioned, 111, 155, 158; and Plains Indians,
  142–43, 173
Tobin, William G., 31
Todd, Alice, 160
Todd, George, 160
Tom, John Files, 160, 165–66
Tomlinson, James M., 165
Tonkawa Indians, 7, 14, 21, 34, 94, 120–
  21, 152
Totten, Silas, 146, 148, 151–55, 213n.23
Totty, F. M., 118, 211n.32
Twiggs, David: mentioned, 9–10, 14–15,
  19; and U.S. Army posts, 23–25, 27, 32
Twitty, William C., 61, 63, 118

U.S. Army, 4–6, 9–11, 13–16, 18–19, 23–
  28, 30, 33, 168–71

Van Dorn, Earl, 15–16, 31–33, 39, 46,
  97
Victoria Peak, 118, 123–24, 139, 208n.21

Walker, John G., 120
Walker, Leroy Pope, 28–30, 168
Walthersdorff, Albert, 157
Ward, Joseph, 114–15, 124, 138
Watie, Stand, 110
Webb, Milton, 31
West, Charles S., 103
White, A. B., 83, 85, 118, 133–34
Wood, George, 5

Young, Hugh, 61
Young, William Cocke, 33, 58
Young County, 5

Frontier Defense in the Civil War was composed into type on a Compu-graphic digital phototypesetter in eleven point Goudy Old Style with two points of spacing between the lines. Goudy Old Style was also selected for display. The book was designed by Jim Billingsley, typeset by Metricomp, Inc., printed offset by Thomson-Shore, Inc., and bound by John H. Dekker & Sons, Inc. The paper on which this book is printed carries acid-free characteristics for an effective life of at least three hundred years.

TEXAS A&M UNIVERSITY PRESS : COLLEGE STATION